Aura Rosenberg
What Is Psychedelic

Aura Rosenberg

What Is Psychedelic

Mishkin Gallery
Pioneer Works Press

Contents

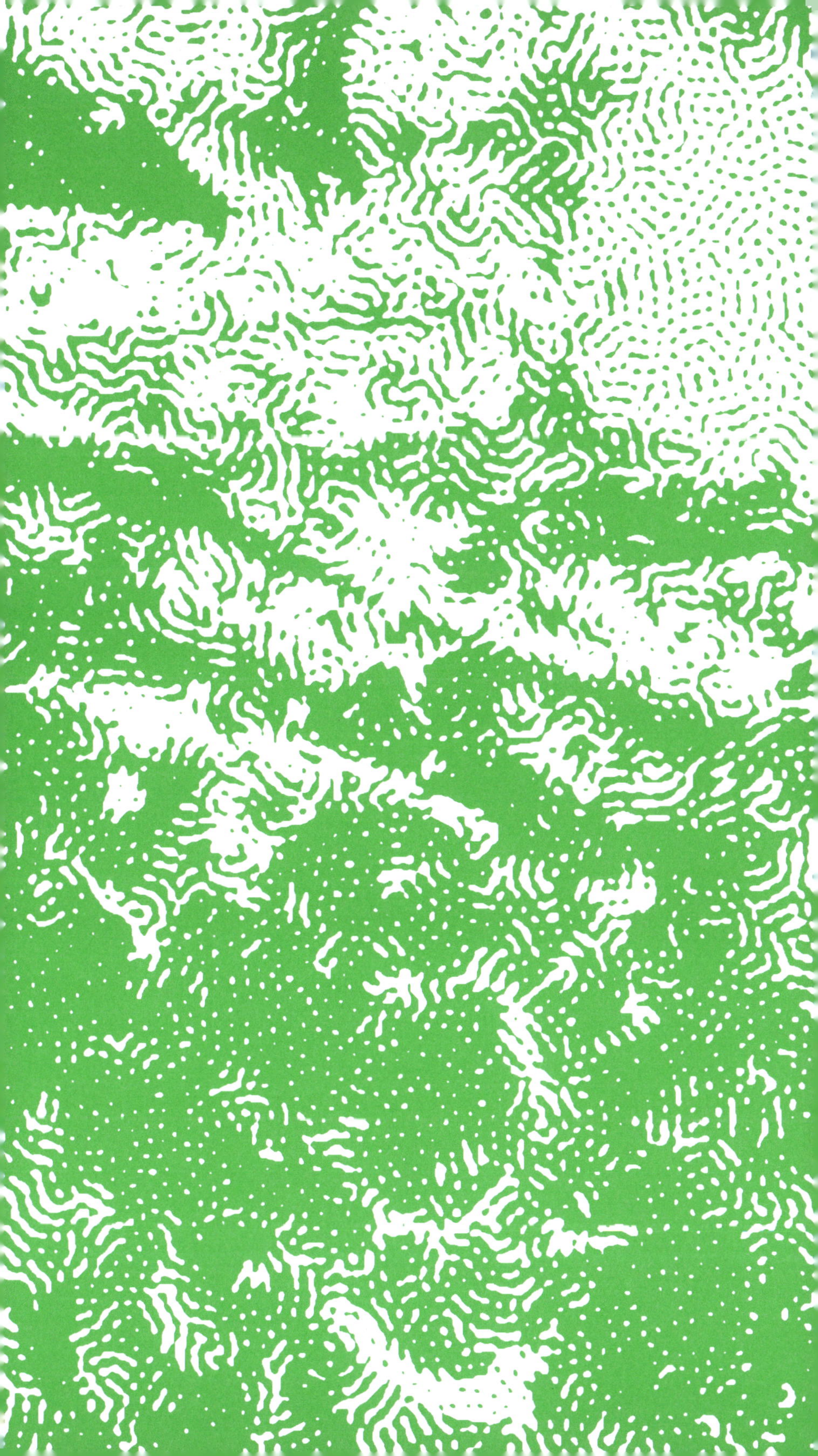

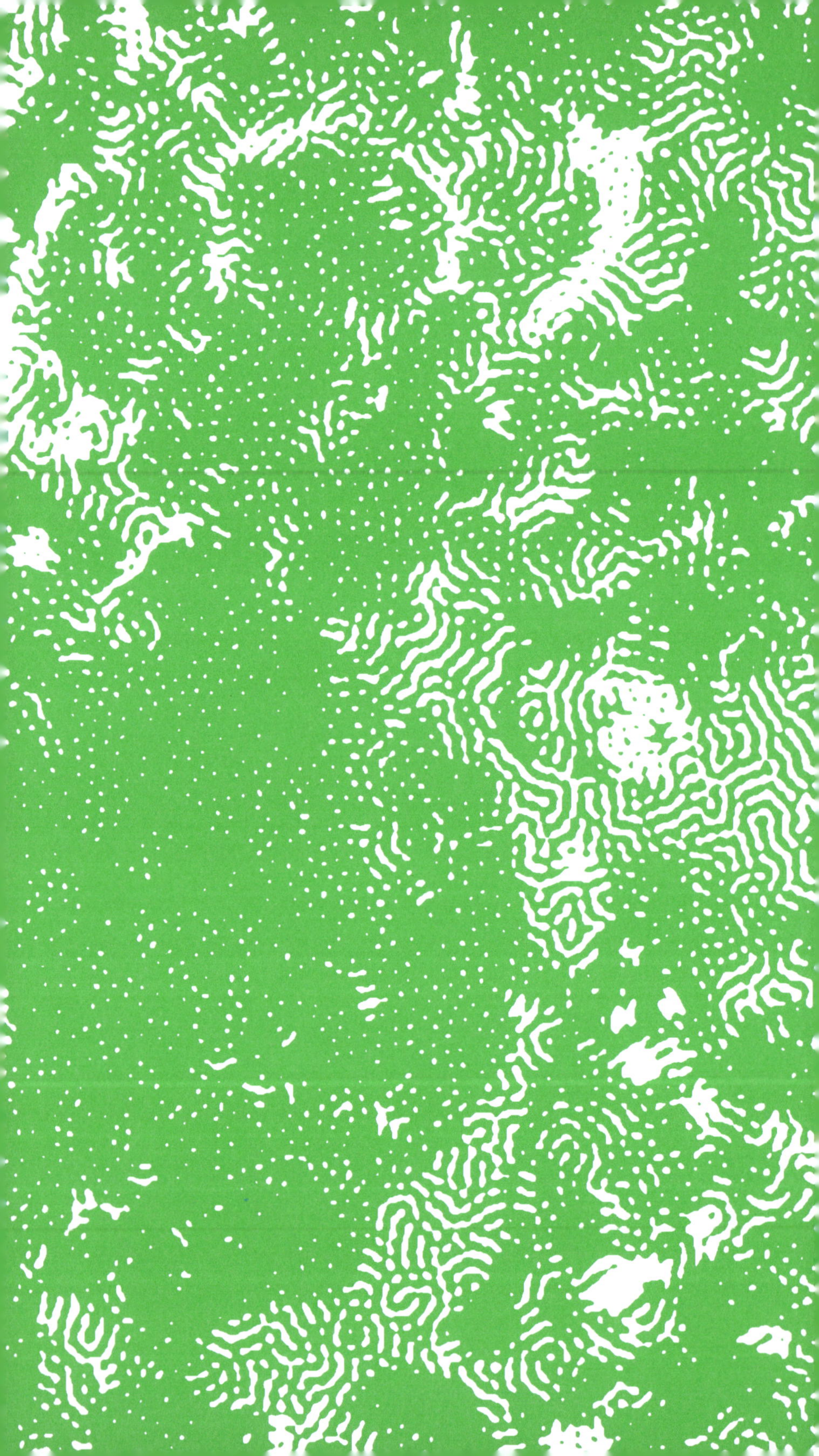

Tracing the Early Paintings of Aura Rosenberg, 1969–89

Alaina Claire Feldman

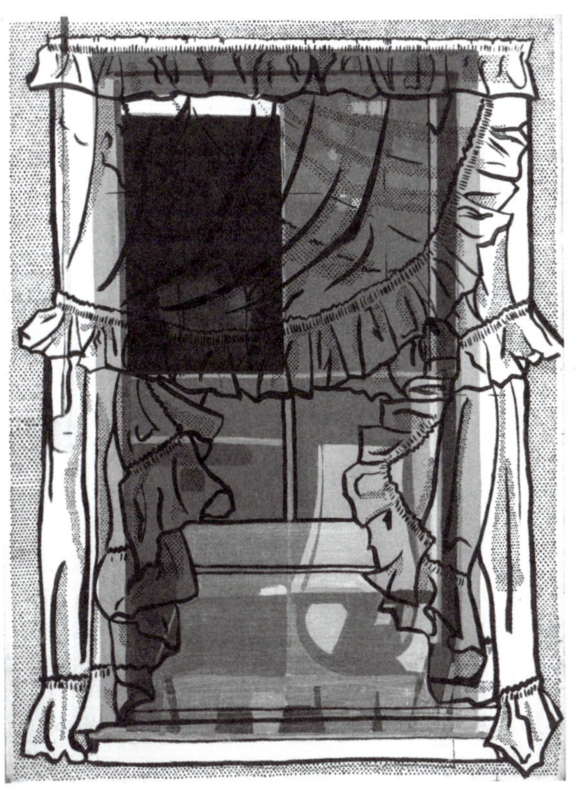

The Window, c. 1975. Acrylic on canvas, 77¼ × 57 in.

In 1969, Marcia Tucker was a PhD student at CUNY's Graduate Center and working on her dissertation with Leo Steinberg. As part of the curriculum, graduate students were encouraged to teach undergraduates. Her freshman survey class, which broadly covered everything from the Great Pyramids to Pollock, captivated the young artist Aura Rosenberg, who was a native New Yorker straight out of the High School of Music and Art. Rosenberg retained her relationship with Tucker while also establishing another with the art historian Barbara Rose, who was teaching Sarah Lawrence where Rosenberg had transferred to the following year. Both women recognized Rosenberg's curiosity and enthusiasm and encouraged her to apply to the newly established Whitney Independent Study Program, which was in Lower Manhattan on Cherry Street. Many artists who go through the program say the Whitney ISP's rigorous critical and theoretical debates encourage a rethinking of the conditions of artistic production, and such was the case for Rosenberg. During this period, 1969–70, Rosenberg was producing minimal stained canvas paintings, something akin to Helen Frankenthaler. One day, Richard Artschwager came to do a studio visit and asked, "Why is this artist doing this?" resulting in Rosenberg's first self-reflective crisis.[1] Why was she doing this? What is a painting and what even is a painter, anyway?

To be an experimental painter in Manhattan in the early 1970s was to be somewhat of an outcast. Painting discourse at the time was conservative and

1 This text relies heavily on a number of in-person interviews with Rosenberg which took place in the summer of 2022.

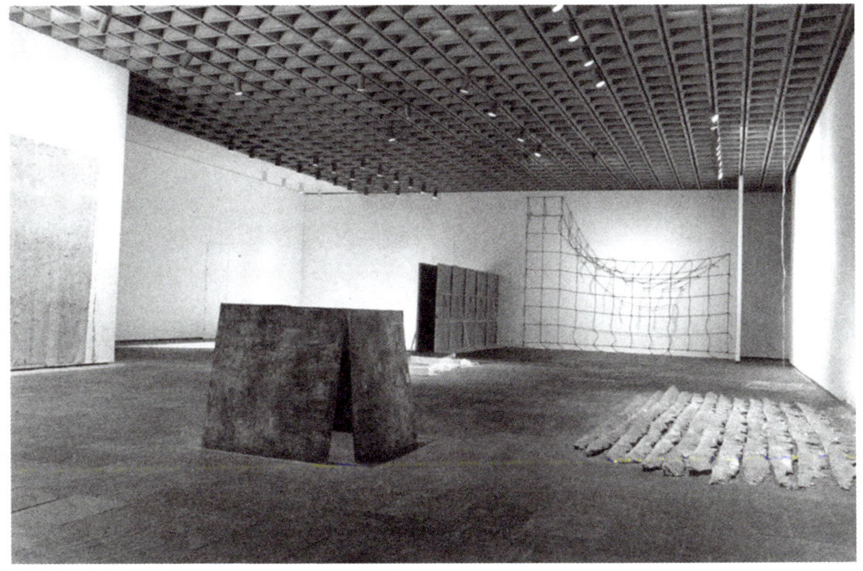

Installation view, *Anti-Illusion: Procedures/Materials,* Whitney Museum of American Art, New York, May 19–July 6, 1969. Photo: Peter Moore; © Northwestern University.

fueled by Greenbergian formalism. Michael Fried's "Three American Painters: Kenneth Noland, Jules Olitski, Frank Stella," which Rosenberg read and was intrigued by, added to debates around formalism and Minimalism. Yet, many had declared "the end of painting" while sculpture dominated the art scene. Luckily, her former professor Marcia Tucker was now a curator of painting and sculpture at the Whitney Museum and challenging such formalism through organizing Post-Minimalism exhibitions like *Anti-Illusion: Procedures/Materials* in 1969, exactly when this personal crisis reached Rosenberg. The two remained close, as Rosenberg had previously taken an independent study with Tucker, who in turn later invited her to come see the shows she was curating. *Anti-Illusion: Procedures/Materials* was the first substantial American exhibition to include artists such as Richard Serra, Chuck Close, Phillip

Glass, Bill Bollinger, and Eva Hesse (all whom Rosenberg remembers seeing) and included works that did not have the representational function of modern sculpture and painting.

Many artists at the time were rejecting Minimalism's cold and impersonal rhetoric, responding with sculptures of more expressive qualities, often evoking the body and the personal. Painting was opening up to the social world around it. Many experimental downtown artists at the time—like Lynda Benglis, Alan Shields, Carolee Schneemann, Jack Whitten, and so many more—did not see painting as a transcendent space separate from the world but rather understood painting as an object *in* the world. Importantly, this period collided with a wave of hallucinogenic, hippie, and consciousness-expanding culture as well. Rosenberg herself was interested in the relationship of such culture and the phenomenological substance of painting. She wanted to see if she could reintroduce a figure that defied illusionism, that was different than formalist painting, that created a picture plane without hierarchy, that allowed the painter and viewer to have a "higher" experience, and that expanded the definition of painting altogether.

Wanting to continue her education, Rosenberg enrolled in Hunter College (CUNY)'s MFA program where she studied under Robert Morris. What came next was a series of works where Rosenberg built up the canvas with modeling paste and dozens of layers of paint in geometric patterns with text. *Spaced*, a 75-by-77-inch work from the early 1970s, has two convergent diagonal fields of raised modeling paste painted in acrylic green and blue.

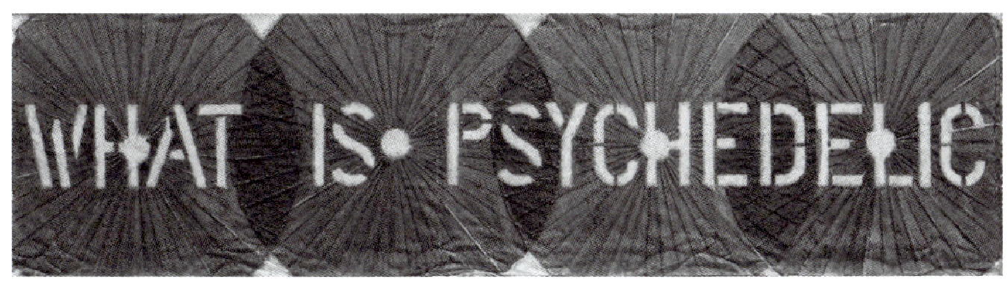

What Is Psychedelic, 1973. Acrylic and acrylic gel on canvas, 32 × 120 in.

Across both color planes in capital letters is the word "SPACED," as if looking at this work could make one really "space out." It also suggests a more formal meaning because the painting was made by applying countless layers of watery pigment, so that as the color built up, the lettering appeared sealed into the color planes. In another work from this period, the banner-like *What Is Psychedelic*, which is 32 inches wide and 120 inches long, Rosenberg painted four pinwheels over a light-green-stained canvas. Again, using hundreds of thin color layers, Rosenberg build up the pinwheels except where she had stenciled the letters "What is Psychedelic." The result was that the words, although they belonged to the canvas surface, appeared to float in front of the pinwheels. By adding in rhetorical phrases, Rosenberg collapsed the making and experiencing of painting. Other works from this period include raised canvases, and brightly saturated and metallic paints which added depth and shine and played with two- and three-dimensional spatial properties of her artwork. Rosenberg remembers when Tony Smith, a professor at Hunter at the time, came to her studio on Canal Street during a recurring critique course, saw these works and said, "Well, you don't need to come to class anymore."

Under Morris, who was also her thesis advisor, Rosenberg learned about deconstructing the art object, dabbled in performance, and moved farther away from the formalist painting championed by Greenberg. Morris challenged his students to think about making work in public space in new ways. She organized a performance in a quiet reading room of the New York Public Library wherein, once giving the signal, she and her classmates would whisper "Attica," as if to remind the public of the Attica prison rebellion which had just occurred in upstate New York. Rosenberg's work at the time did not come out of a vacuum. It was related to art historical and political factors in the early 1970s: the feminist movement, the war in Vietnam, the civil rights movement, Minimalism, conceptual art. While she was always painting, Morris also challenged her to think about making art that related to world around her.

After Hunter, Rosenberg continued to paint and supported herself with work in the art direction department at major magazines like *Rolling Stone* and *Esquire*. Newly accustomed to looking at staged photography all day, Rosenberg began to trace these images with her paintbrush back in her studio. After Modernism and the reign of Greenbergian formalism, how does a painter put an image back into a painting without falling into traditional tropes of illusionism/anti-illusionism? One way was to paint things that already existed as flat surfaces (Jasper Johns had his flags, Sturtevant had her Jasper Johns); reproducing magazine images by painting on top of them followed this logic. *Focus on Your Best Feature* is a long, horizontal painting (14 by 74 inches) from 1974. In this work, Rosenberg appropriated a cover story from a women's magazine by painting over the image and removing all the text except for the titular phrase. *Focus on Your Best Feature* critiques the idealized female body as well as the production and circulation of these images. Tracing these works with her own line allowed Rosenberg to take control of these images by inserting her unique mark onto the picture plane.

In the late 1970s, she began a series of large works in which she painted images of so-called masterpieces by well-known male artists. Simultaneously commenting on the de-subjective practice of copying master works to learn how to paint, as well as disrupting the idea of virtuosity and proficiency in the long legacy of painting, Rosenberg carefully reproduced "great" paintings of Matisse, Lichtenstein, and Van Gogh with acrylic on canvas. She then applied a secondary image over the works, just enough so that the initial image was still visible: large multicolored polka dots over Matisse's *The Red Studio* (1911), multicolored stripes over Van Gogh's *The Night Cafe* (1988), a flat image of the World Trade Center over Matisse's *Dance* (1910), and large monochrome polka dots over Lichtenstein's *Still Life with Goldfish* (1974) (inadvertently, an appropriation of Matisse to begin with). She considers these secondary layers to be dialectical images that were in dialogue with the original works. Ironically, the more she painted these images, the better skills she acquired as a painter.

In *The Window* from around 1975, Rosenberg paints a realistic but flat, green-tinted window with four panes. Sitting in the window frame is a black table lamp and five empty flowerpots. It was the window in her studio. Over this personal image is a meticulous remake of Lichtenstein's 1962 simple black-line painting *Curtains*. From Lichtenstein, to Matisse, to Bonnard to Vermeer—windows have been motifs, subjects and framing devices in Western art which confront a particular gaze. As such, *The Window* critically addresses the canon of painting as well as the limits of pictorial space and the literal conditions of painting itself. Now it is Lichtenstein who becomes the dialectical layer over Rosenberg's original projection of depth and space. It is an important breakthrough where Rosenberg maintains a central position and personal perspective within the larger field of painting. The work is less about emulating the pervasive pop artist and more about inserting oneself in the discourse.

In *Barn with Snow and Body Imprint* a work from around the same time (c. 1976), Rosenberg meticulously paints a wintery pastoral landscape. She then covers herself in white paint and presses her own body over left side of the rustic image, as if mimicking the form of the nearby birch tree. A nude in the landscape turns forcefully from the flattened space of the canvas to the kinetic body of the artist. The practice of registering a body to confront "the prohibition of illusionistic space which seemed to preclude a figure" is one that continues to inspire her and reappears in later works such as *The Dialectical Porn Rock* (1989–93) where the "natural" is confronted and collapsed, or in *The Astrological Ways* (2012) where members of Rosenberg's community become figures imprinted on black velvet.[2]

2 Email exchange with the artist, July 4, 2022.

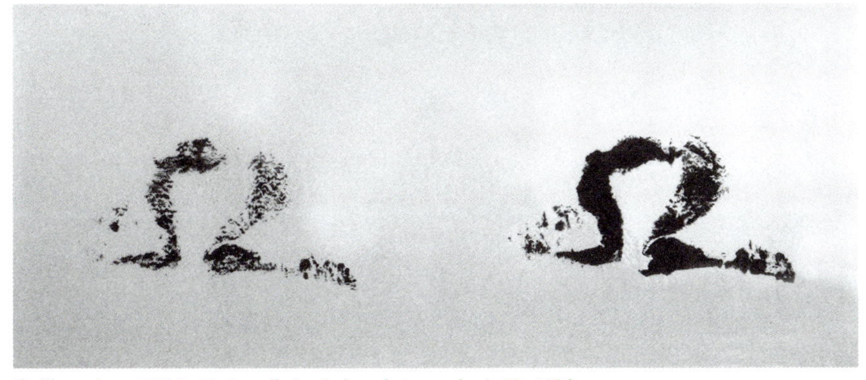

Calligraphs, c. 1984–85. Acrylic body imprints on vinyl, 48 × 118 in.

By the 1980s, Rosenberg abandoned all external images and turned entirely to her own body. Continuing the luminosity of her early-70s paintings, she continued to make these body imprints on bright neon vinyl and luxurious blue, green, and red velvets. The works are created by an extremely physical process of painting over her body and pressing herself onto the surface hard enough so a visible mark was made, thus producing an image that also registered the process. They vary from black to white to neon orange paint, and are not always full body impressions, some are of just legs, some just torsos, and even a vertical line of shoes (as if walking down the spine of a painting).[3] These paintings record an action and the process of making the painting, which Richard Shiff has referred to as "declarative" paintings, or paint applied "very matter-of-factly."[4] Of her body imprints, Rosenberg has said, "I was thinking about making a figure

3 David Hammons's body imprints might come to mind, as he produced these works which also address body politics around the same time as Rosenberg.

4 Richard Shiff, "Autonomy, Actuality, Mangold," *Robert Mangold* (London: Phaidon, 2000): 7–58.

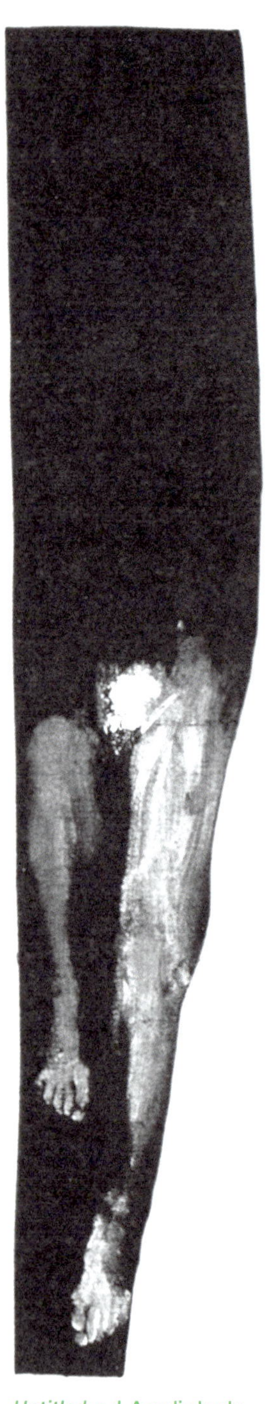

Untitled, n.d. Acrylic body imprint on gray felt, 80 × 15 in.

without depicting it, without having to will it into being. It's already there—you paint your body, you print it, and you have a figure."[5]

The body imprints defy the boundaries between an original and a copy and between abstraction and representation. This was a task Rosenberg was most interested in complicating. Her *Animal Skin* series, from around 1982–85, are also proto-body imprints of sorts. Rosenberg sought to literally turn a painting into skin, eventually also pressing her body over the animals as if to camouflage herself within them. The paintings are just that: flat, unstretched canvas with colorful realist paintings of zebra and cheetah skins. The canvas is cut to outline their anatomy, there is no background or foreground. Carol Ann Klonarides curated these body imprint and animal skin paintings into their first public presentations in the 1983 group exhibition *Borrowed Time* at Baskerville + Watson Gallery in New York. Artists in these exhibitions included Louise Lawler, Richard Prince, and others who would come to be known as the Pictures Generation. Douglas Crimp first noted, "For their pictures, these artists have turned to the available images in the culture around them. But they subvert the standard signifying function of those pictures, tied to their captions, their commentaries, their narrative sequences—tied, that is, to the illusion that they are directly transparent to a signified."[6]

Rosenberg brought painting supplies with her on holiday in 1988 when a group of friends decided to rent a house together in the countryside. She found the new bucolic environment incongruous

5 Interview with the artist, June 28, 2022.
6 Douglas Crimp, *Pictures* (New York: Artists Space, 1977); essay repr. in *X-tra* 8, no. 1 (fall 2005): 17–30.

with her painting, and instead played a practical joke on her friend Mike Ballou, an artist and avid trout fisherman. Ballou had been using pornographic magazines for his own sculptures at the time. Like she had meticulous traced over the models in *Focus on Your Best Feature* or imprinted her own figure straight onto the canvas, Rosenberg pasted onto stone some carefully torn porn silhouettes and then placed the sculptures in the river hoping he would stumble upon them. He never did. Intrigued by her own gesture, Rosenberg grabbed a camera and documented the shimmering bodies in their new pastoral landscape, initiating the *Dialectical Porn Rock* series. She wouldn't return to painting again for several decades.

Throughout history, men have projected women's bodies onto nature only to be recast as nature itself, a founding trope of the pastoral which allowed for nature's domination. Geographer Gillian Rose argues that "[t]his compelling figure of Woman both haunts a masculinist spectator of landscape and constitutes him."[7] Reflecting on Rosenberg's earlier painting *Barn with Snow and Body Imprint* in which the female figure asserts her presence in contrast within the snowy pasture, it becomes apparent that a female positionality in her work often contradicts the "master subject" position.[8] Tracing the body is not just a technique but an active message within itself.

In *The Dialectical Porn Rock* Rosenberg found a way to overcome the exteriority of painting that lets "being" and "doing" coexist in the same medium,

7 Gillian Rose, *Feminism and Geography: The Limits of Geographical Knowledge* (Cambridge: Polity Press, 1993).

8 Donna Haraway, "Situated Knowledges: The Science Question in Feminism and the Privilege of Partial Perspective," *Feminist Studies* 14, no. 3 (1988): 575–99.

just as she had earlier in the declarative body imprints. These early experiments of injecting performative reconfigurations onto two-dimensional work set in motion ideas that she would continue to return to throughout her career. Beyond the poetic and metaphorical readings her work can inspire, her practice can also be understood as attempting to revise the limits of a medium, whether photography, performance, sculpture, or painting.

A Conversation between
Matt Keegan and Aura Rosenberg

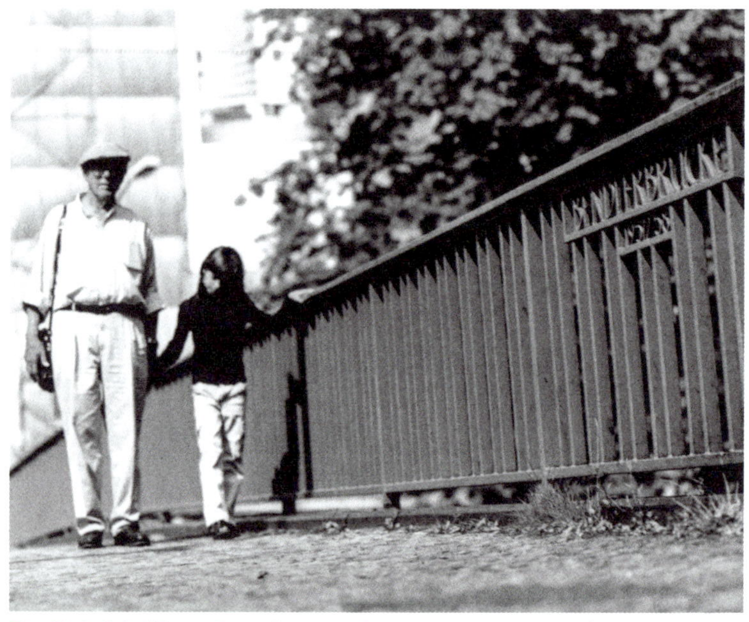

Bendlerbrücke (Ernest Rosenberg and Carmen Rosenberg-Miller), 1997, from *Berlin Childhood.*

MATT KEEGAN: In 2004, Chantal Benjamin, the granddaughter of Walter Benjamin, saw an exhibition featuring *Berlin Childhood*—your work inspired by her grandfather's writing of the same title—and contacted you. Please tell me more about how this friendship and ongoing collaboration with Chantal and her daughter Lais began.

AURA ROSENBERG: Chantal saw my work in a show at Haus am Waldsee titled *Schrift, Bilder, Denken: die Kunst der Gegenwart und Walter Benjamin* (Text, Image, Thought: Walter Benjamin and Contemporary Art). Shortly after, I was surprised to receive an email with a rose emoji next to her name. The war shattered Walter Benjamin's scholarly legacy to his granddaughters; Chantal moved to Berlin to learn about his work and life. I told her that making images from Benjamin's texts helped me understand some of his core ideas. Still, my approach is intuitive, and I take liberties that I'm not sure he would have liked. Turning his texts into pictures is another way of learning that I believe his imagistic writing fosters.

After publishing my book *Berlin Childhood* (Steidl/DAAD, 2002), I thought my work with Benjamin's memoir was over. Slowly, almost against my will, when Chantal's daughter, Lais, was born in 2006, I started filming them both, always with *Berlin Childhood* in mind. The prospect of making a short film for each of the 42 texts in Benjamin's memoir is daunting, so I asked the artist Frances Scholz to collaborate with me. It's become our joint project. Chantal is also crucial to the films—she has good intuitions and sometimes contributes footage. But the project was actually a joint family undertaking. Together with Chantal, Lais's father Marcelo de Souza Campos Granja prepared her for our adventures, coaching her to understand the locations and camera work. We were all involved in giving Lais a child-friendly context that enabled her to identify with Walter Benjamin's writing as she was growing up.

Most importantly, Chantal and Lais concretize Benjamin's childhood experiences and bring them into the present. The three of us took trips to many of the locations Benjamin mentions, enabling Lais to relive the events her great-grandfather describes. For example, we visited Peacock Island. In the 18th century, the Prussian king Wilhelm II turned this island into a proto-amusement park filled with fake ruins and peacocks that roam freely. Benjamin visited here during his summer holidays and fantasized that discovering a peacock feather would make him ruler of the island. Not finding one was a devastating disappointment for the young boy. His text "Peacock Island and Glienicke," written in exile, registers his fear that he might never again have a home. In stark contrast, Lais found a peacock feather on our first visit. We also often visited the zoo, where Benjamin sought the fish otter, an animal he found mysterious and elusive. While he particularly liked

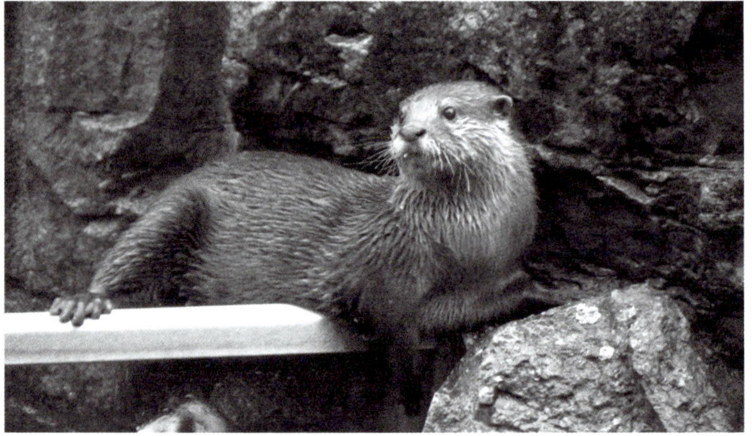

Still from *The Fish Otter*, 2022, from *Berlin Childhood*. Video, approx. 12 min.

to watch the otter in the rain, Lais sang about her love of the sun. And the fish otters we encountered were more like cartoon characters. These two instances illustrate the contrast between Lais's childhood and that of her great-grandfather, whose memories were overshadowed by the Third Reich.

MK: In your above reply, you write that "Chantal and Lais concretize Benjamin's childhood experiences and bring them into the present." Watching *Berlin Childhood*, I was struck by how we see Lais age as well as return to being younger within single chapters and over the course of the series. I wondered if your editing decisions were rooted in facilitating asynchronous time.

Can you say some more about how working with a young subject, as well as your commitment to this long-term collaboration generates an ever-shifting present and if/why this is relevant to your broader project?

AR: Because Benjamin wrote the *Berlin Childhood* texts as montages, I filmed them in sections. Recording segments over many years was also a practical decision required for working with a small child. With these fragments edited together, we see Lais growing up. One of the texts, "Two Riddles," is about deferring a child's understanding of death until adulthood. In this film, I dissolved clips of Lais at different ages into one another. Just as Chantal and Lais embody Benjamin's memoir, so the films encapsulate time. Also, shooting over many years meant working with changing technologies. I started recording on tape, then went to digital; recently, I switched from HD to 4K. These changes in image resolution also concretely capture time.

In "Theses on the Philosophy of History," Benjamin writes that the angel of history "would like to... awaken the dead and make whole what has been smashed." The angel recognizes how official history is the one the victors write for themselves—leaving many histories unwritten. I think there's a real awareness of this today. The effort to correct omissions of the past makes time asynchronous.

MK: In *A Christmas Angel*, part of the *Berlin Childhood* series, you film young Syrian refugees who had recently emigrated to Germany. Please say more about your decision to include these children.

AR: When I started the *Berlin Childhood* films, I planned to follow the narrative of Benjamin's texts closely. The texts are composed like montages, jumping from one scene to the next. Benjamin compared them to cinema using edits with shifting paces, closeups, panning, and wide-angle shots.

In December 2015, I went to Berlin to film *A Christmas Angel*. I generally spend the summer in Berlin, so I'd never had the opportunity to work on texts that take place in winter. I was staying with my friends, Dirk and Ise Kössendrup, who I first met at the playground when my daughter Carmen and their daughter Julie were babies. Ise helped me read the Benjamin texts in German, and the Kössendrup family figures importantly in my photo version of *Berlin Childhood*.

Dirk and Ise belong to a group called Flüchtlingspaten Syrien. *Flüchtlinge* means refugees in German, and *Paten* are godparents. Dirk and Ise had adopted two Syrian boys. They were organizing a Christmas party for the refugees and asked if I'd like to come with Chantal and Lais. This party was significant because *Berlin Childhood* is essentially a story about exile. I realized that the refugees mirrored Benjamin's experience 80 years earlier. After this, I decided to include material that wasn't directly part of Benjamin's narrative but would allow me to draw out the latent historical implications of his texts.

MK: I found certain aspects of the other chapters of *Berlin Childhood* to be quite dreamy and the inclusion of the Christmas party for Syrian refugees anchored this video in an ongoing refugee crisis. Additionally, this decision seemed rooted in more traditional documentary practices. I'm curious to hear your thoughts on this shift in style and why it opened up your ability to include material that was less directly related to Benjamin's writing.

AR: Again, to some extent, Benjamin's montage approach might suggest these shifts, but I also sought them out. For example, working on *Carousel*, I learned that in the Middle Ages, carousels were used to train Turkish and Arab cavalry for combat. Benjamin doesn't mention this in the text, but I thought it was essential to include. To illustrate this, I inserted a clip from an old Hollywood movie of battling Crusader soldiers on horseback. Frances and I made *Departures and Returns* from many diverse parts. Much of it is documentary footage of Chantal and Lais leaving on trips. But we also staged a shoot at Matt

Mullican's Berlin apartment, draping the furniture with white clothes to make it appear the family was away. We included footage of Lais interpreting the text and discussing her feelings about leaving home. There's also a very early conversation between Lais and Chantal about Benjamin's exile and subsequent suicide.

MK: I really enjoyed this conversation between Chantal and Lais, as well as Lais's insightful analysis of her great-grandfather's writing. I wonder if you want to discuss an autobiographical element to this project. You are a mother who has collaborated with your daughter on previous projects, perhaps most notably *Who am I? What am I? Where am I?* and your father fled Germany during WWII. You've traveled to Berlin since the 1990s and while working on *Berlin Childhood* over the past two decades, you became a dual German citizen. Is there a dimension to this project that is in dialogue with your father and interwoven with your own family's history?

AR: Carmen and I also worked together on *Berlin Childhood,* which made filming Lais and Chantal somewhat uncanny. I'm familiar with the mother-daughter tensions generated by working together. I understand Carmen and Lais's desire for autonomy—their resistance to being controlled by their mothers. Nevertheless, these collaborations offered something special. Carmen is now an art historian with first-hand experience of making art. In the acknowledgments of her dissertation, she wrote: "My mother taught me the immense pleasure and possibility of creativity." For Lais, the films offer a personal glimpse into her great-grandfather's life; they structured part of her growing-up experience.

My family's forced emigration from Germany in 1939 is a subtext to *Berlin Childhood.* Later, on his visits to back to Berlin, my father took part in the project. There is a photograph of him in the book we published walking with Carmen across the Bendlerbrücke. Nevertheless, though I've worked with my own family and now Benjamin's descendants, autobiography is subordinate to the allegories these texts represent. In his foreword to *Berlin Childhood,* which he started writing in 1932, Benjamin wrote: "[T]hese compositions thoroughly deemphasize biographical traits, which register themselves more in the continuity of experience than in any profundity. And so, too, have physiognomies been deemphasized—those of my family as well as my comrades'. Instead, I have sought to take possession of the images that are precipitated by urban experience in a child of the bourgeois class... images of my urban childhood may be capable of pre-forming within themselves subsequent historical experience." Today's migrant crisis around the world makes this memoir timelier than ever—it overlays Benjamin's exile and retrieves past experience for the present.

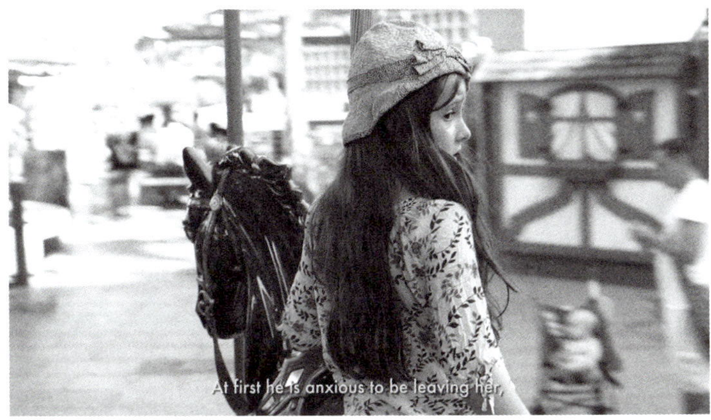

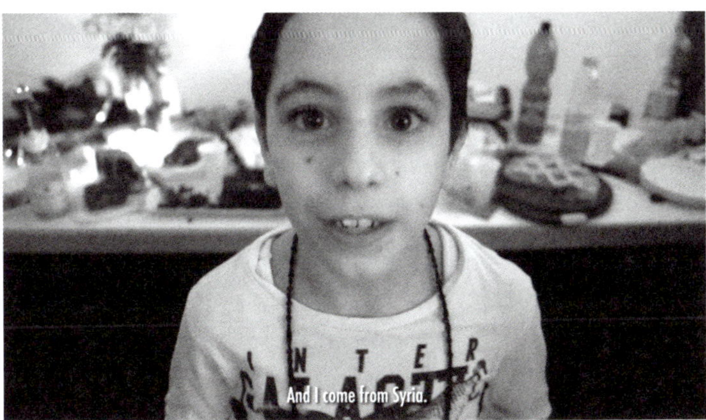

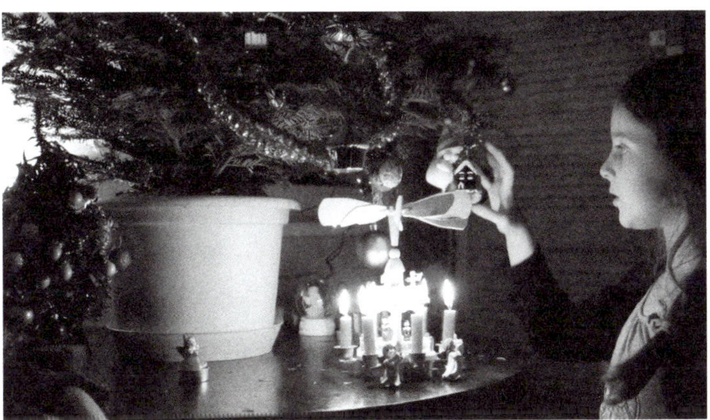

Top: still from *The Carousel*, 2015, 6 min, 15 sec.
Middle & bottom: stills from *A Christmas Angel*, 2015, 12 min, 8 sec.
Both from *Berlin Childhood*.

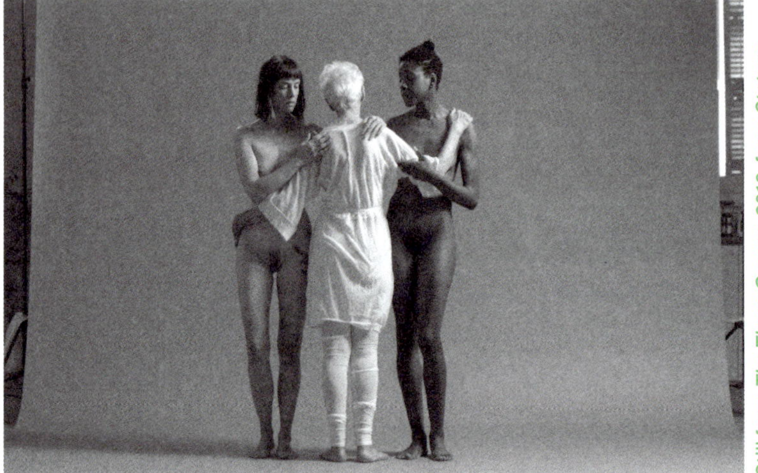

Still from *The Three Graces*, 2016, from *Statues Also Fall in Love*. Cinematography: Dan Walworth. Performers: Raquel Nave, Valda Setterfield and Sharon Steven. Video, 3 min.

MK: In our email correspondence you wrote, "An unexpected connection between the *Berlin Childhood* movies and *Statues Also Fall in Love*: I was filming Lais in the Tiergarten where the statues of Königin Luise and König Wilhelm face one another across an expanse of gardens. I was setting up the camera when I realized that Lais was playing and inventing a conversation between the statues. It made me think about the inner lives of statues." This anecdote provides a useful bridge to discussing *Statues Also Fall in Love*, as well as *Angel of History*. From the *Statues* series, I'm interested in *The Three Graces* and the related lenticular photographs you've been making in recent years, some of which I had the opportunity to see at your solo show at New York's Martos Gallery in 2019.

Unlike the ongoing, multi-chapter *Berlin Childhood* video series, these works employ a more graphic rendering in which the still image is at the root of their production. With the lenticulars, the viewer's moving body animates the photographs from one state to another. *The Three Graces* operates in a similar manner as creating an animated and embodied version of the referenced statue. In *Angel of History*, an animation makes use of clip art, art history and world history image plates, and audio/video clips to create a trash strewn collaged amalgam of the past.

How does your long-standing work in photography inform these videos and lenticulars to make use of the still image as its fulcrum? How does illustration (c/o Merriam Webster: "a picture or diagram that helps make something clear or attractive") operate in your work?

AR: You're right to point out that photography is at the core of *Statues Also Fall in Love*. I started this work in 2018 as a response to *The Dialectical Porn Rock*, a series from 1989–93 in which I decoupaged photos of bodies torn from porn magazines onto rocks. *Statues Also Fall in Love* revisits this work by decoupaging photos of classical marble statues onto marble fragments. The narratives that the marble figures suggested got me thinking about how we project life into them; this led to making short films in which statues morph into performers enacting fantasy scenarios. In this, two of Mike Kelley's projects, *Extracurricular Activity Projective Reconstruction* (2000) and *Day Is Done* (2005), also influenced me. He used still images from high school drama productions as a starting point for a series of videos, installations, and lenticular prints. Lenticular images flip back and forth between two or more images as you move side to side in front of them. In my lenticulars, classical marble statues convert seamlessly into contemporary porn actors in the same pose. My film *The Three Graces* starts with a photo of a second-century Greek relief that turns into three women in the same pose. *The Three Graces* is considered an allegory of gift giving. The three performers improvise a clichéd conversation about offering and receiving while passing a wrapped box back and forth.

Angel of History is a five-minute animated film based on Walter Benjamin's description of *Angelus Novus*, a Paul Klee watercolor. The angel is witnessing the catastrophe of history. To illustrate this, I used an assortment of images I found online, mostly photos. The artist and filmmaker Lisa Crafts did the actual animation. For the period before photography, we often turned to illustration, as in the case of the Tower of Babel. However, Moses receiving the Ten Commandments was represented by a still from the Hollywood movie with Charleston Heston. There are many historic photographs in the film, including Daguerre's photo of a Parisian street that captured a man having his shoes shined, believed to be the earliest photo of a person. There's also Robert Capa's image of a Spanish Civil War soldier being shot, Ernest Wither's 1968 photo of Black sanitation workers on strike in Memphis carrying signs saying "I Am A Man" and many more. Sometimes I think of the film as a history of photography.

The *Angel of History* animation is a pictorialization of Benjamin's *"Theses on the Philosophy of History."* Curiously, Benjamin was inspired by a picture, so there's a circularity to what I did. Similarly, in *Berlin Childhood,* one can consider my filming the places and things Benjamin writes about illustrative. Of course, the surplus of information in these images asserts an independence or autonomy that doesn't boil down to illustration alone.

The Dialectical Landscapes of Aura Rosenberg's Porn Rocks

Alexandra Tell

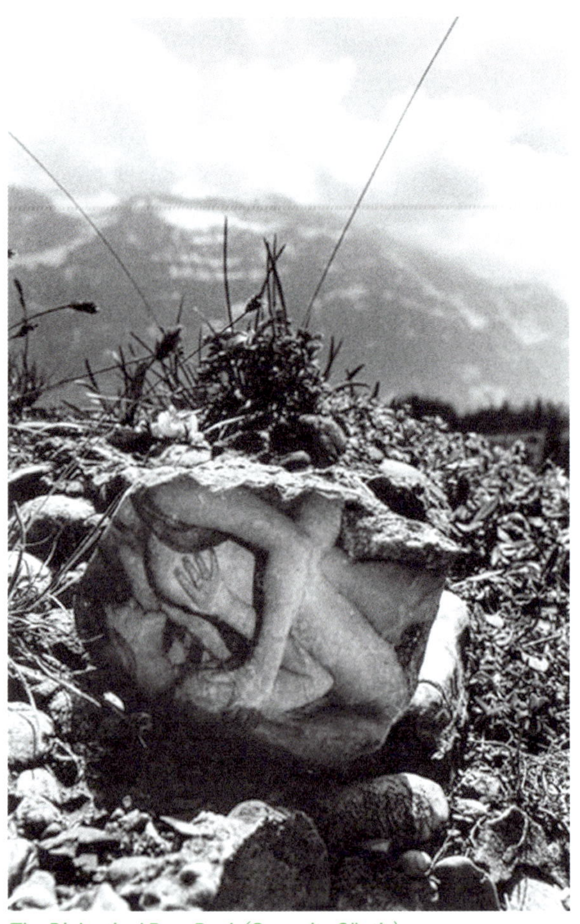

The Dialectical Porn Rock (Opposite Säntis), 1993. C-print, 20 × 16 in. and 40 × 30 in.

Aura Rosenberg's series *The Dialectical Porn Rock* (1989–93) started as a practical joke. While sharing a home with friends upstate, Rosenberg plastered bits of pornographic material cut from "dirty" magazines onto rocks sourced from the landscape. She had stolen these clippings from her friend, the artist Mike Ballou, who was using the magazines in his own sculptures. She arranged her "porn rocks" in a nearby stream, in hopes that they would surprise Ballou who, out fishing, would see these stray body parts, nude and lustful, as an amorous hallucination. Struck by the visual appeal of the rocks in the water, Rosenberg began arranging and photographing the porn rocks in different configurations in the landscape. If Medusa's gaze turned the animate into stone, the camera is not entirely dissimilar, freezing bodies in a moment in time. What is photography if not an act of petrifaction? The pornographic photographs that Rosenberg uses in *The Dialectical Porn Rock* series—taken from magazines published during a period of the 1970s and 1980s that is now, nostalgically, referred to as pornography's "Golden Age"—capture moments at the height of desire, release, and ecstasy to evoke the same feelings in the viewer. Placed onto stone, these erotic moments bear the trace of the photographic process. But these rocks do not contain full scenes or acts, often presenting only a disembodied part or an awkwardly cropped concatenation of bodies. Petrified into rocks, the pornographic photographs become fossil-like historical records of the performance of desire.

In 1968, American land artist Robert Smithson displayed the first in his series of "nonsite" works, an accumulation of rocks, gravel, and concrete contained within geometric steel containers. The geological fragments—which Smithson also called "indoor earthworks"—were accompanied by documentation, including photographs, maps, and sometimes text, of the landscapes from which Smithson gathered his rocks.[1] Smithson's sculptures were governed by what he described as the "site/nonsite dialectic," the conceptual gap between the sculpture's place of display (the gallery) and its place of origin (exurban industrial New Jersey), and ultimately their now inextricable link.[2] Like the multimedia display of Smithson's nonsites, Rosenberg's *The Dialectical Porn Rock* series (whose title is a nod to Smithson's 1973 *Artforum* essay "Frederick Law Olmsted and the Dialectical Landscape") comprises both photographs of porn rocks in various settings, rural and urban alike (beaches, national parks, sidewalks, a Berlin metro station), as well as the rocks themselves exhibited in the gallery as sculpture. Like Smithson's conceptually linked earthworks, Rosenberg's rocks bear a curious relationship to both their source material and the landscape, participating in what Smithson might call a "semiotic game."[3] A pornographic fragment reads differently when posed in a grassy field, or on a dramatic geological formation, or in front of a statue of Vladimir Lenin, or positioned on the gallery floor.

1 Robert Smithson, "A Provisional Theory of Nonsites" (1968), in *Robert Smithson: The Collected Writings*, ed. Jack Flam (Berkeley: University of California Press, 1996): 364.
2 Smithson, "Note on the Dialectic of Site and Nonsite" (c. 1960), Robert Smithson and Nancy Holt papers, 1905–87, Archives of American Art, Smithsonian Institution.https://www.aaa.si.edu/collections/items/detail/note-dialectic-site-and-nonsite-21375
3 Ibid.

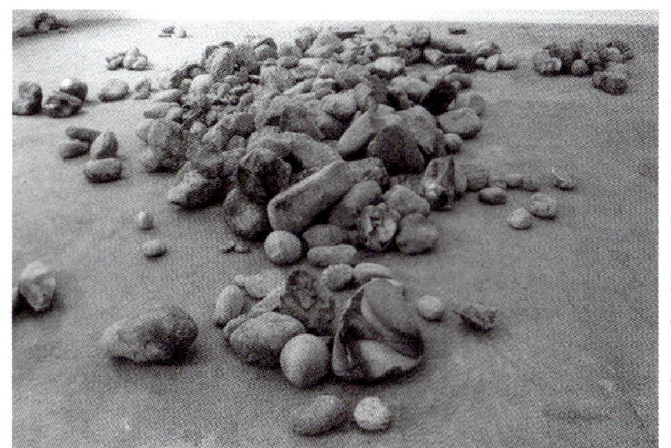

The Dialectical Porn Rock. Installation view, Kunst Halle Sankt Gallen, St. Gallen, Switzerland, 1993.

In one of Rosenberg's photographs, Säntis, the tallest peak in the Swiss Alps, appears beyond a canyon. In the foreground is a curious rock that bears its own image, torn at the edges to accommodate its craggy contours: a tangle of bodies—arms, legs, and breasts—that one can perceive as two women engaging in a sexual act. Nestled into its alpine setting, placed neatly with other stones atop mountain grasses and wildflowers and the snow-covered peaks appearing in soft focus in the background, this image-within-an-image of female bodies almost appears as a harmonious aspect of the landscape. Isn't sex natural after all? Through the repetition of *Dialectical Porn Rock* images one recognizes the visual language of pornography, the performance of sex for the camera. Seeing these natural-unnatural rocks depicting natural-unnatural acts conditions the viewer to reconsider the "naturalness" of the landscape around them, reminding us of the constructed-ness of sexualized imagery and landscape alike. As such, they perform what W. J. T. Mitchell describes as the "double role" of landscape as a medium: "it naturalizes a social and cultural construction, representing the artificial world as if it were simply given and inevitable, and it also makes that representation operational by interpellating its beholder in some more or less determinate relation to its givenness as a sight and site."[4]

The site most readily associated with the erotic is the domestic. In her series *Scene/Obscene* (2013)—consisting of painted-over film stills and photos from the Golden Age of porn, culled from porn websites and inkjet-printed—Rosenberg explored this notion of the site/sight of pornography. While some paintings include the full pornographic scene, in others she zeroes in on the scenography (furniture, props, decor), excising the pornographic acts entirely from the frame. *Scene/Obscene* plays on the ancient Greek theater term "ob skene," which refers to a curtain off-stage, behind which everything that was considered unsuitable for audiences to see took place. Curtains are an important motif in the series—in one painting all we see is brown-and-white patterned window drapes hanging in front of patterned wallpaper. Other paintings are brief tableaus of the domestic: a coat rack draped with a

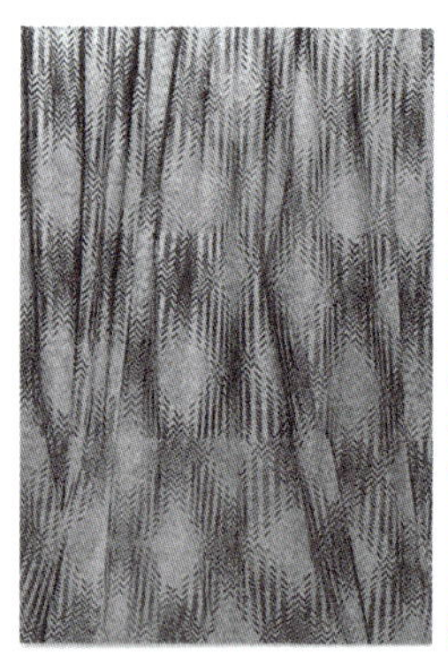

Obscene: Gold-Green Curtain, 2014, from *Scene/Obscene*. Acrylic and inkjet print on gold metallic photo paper mounted to dibond, 10 × 6 in.

4 W. J. T. Mitchell, "Introduction," in *Landscape and Power*, ed. Mitchell (Chicago: University of Chicago Press, 2002): 2.

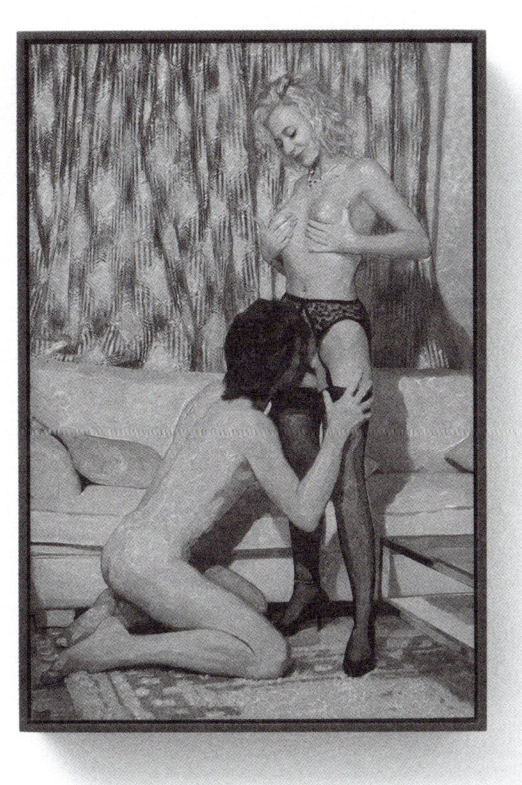

Scene: Naked Man, 2014, from *Scene/Obscene*. Acrylic and inkjet print on gold metallic photo paper mounted to dibond, 10 × 6 in.

fur-trimmed coat; a coffee table strewn with liquor bottles and used glasses; a vase of flowers.

In the 1964 case Jacobellis v. Ohio, the US Supreme Court ruled that Louis Malle's film *Les amants* was not obscene, and therefore protected under the First Amendment. In the decision, Justice Potter Stewart articulated a threshold test for what *could* be considered pornographic: "I know it when I see it" (a term Rosenberg borrowed as an exhibition title). Producers of pornography began to decorate their sets with elements associated more with high culture than hard-core porn—books, still lives, statues, wine—as if to throw potential censors off their scent. Rosenberg, in painting domestic

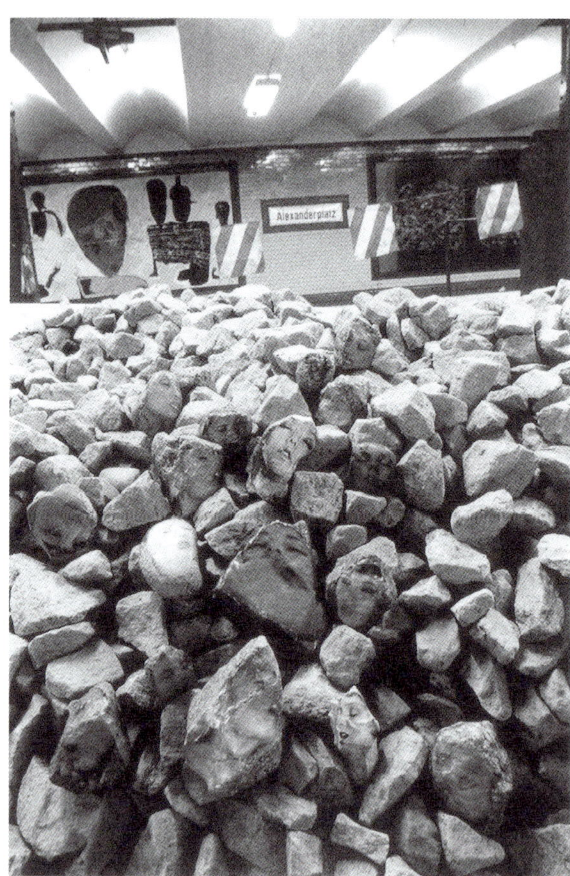

The Dialectical Porn Rock (Alexanderplatz U-Bahn Station), 1993. C-print, 20 × 16 in. and 40 × 30 in.

fragments from these pornographic films, draws our eyes away from the "action" and points to the work these decorative elements are doing for the scene. Though perhaps they were placed there to have the opposite effect, when Rosenberg decontextualizes them, the objects themselves become erotically charged. The dialectic emerges again: the trappings of the domestic are sexualized as the pornographic is domesticated.

Writing about the golden age of *Playboy,* Paul Preciado notes that what rendered the magazine pornographic "was not the use of certain photographs considered obscene by government authorities in charge of censorship and protecting public decorum; it was the fact that, through it, what had until then been considered private burst onto the public sphere."[5] *The Dialectical Porn Rock* series is decidedly non-domestic. The inverse from the *Scene/Obscene* paintings, *The Dialectical Porn Rock* contains none of the highly crafted scenography to contextualize the pornographic act—no stage-setting, no ambience, often not even a full body. Rather, the porn rocks are given new landscapes, ones that do not typically pulse with the erotic charge of the domestic. Rosenberg photographs the rocks in public settings—plazas, parks, sidewalks, beaches, some of which are legible as specific sites (a U-Bahn station at Berlin's Alexanderplatz, for example). Often, however, the landscapes are too cropped, or in soft-focus, or are nondescript enough to be any number of locations. If what makes erotic images pornographic is the act of making them public, Rosenberg pushes this logic further. Magazines and movies, which are often consumed in private, feel clandestine in comparison to the utter publicness in which these rocks are photographed. When they are displayed as sculptural objects, they bear their pornographic material in the (semi)public space of exhibition—performing their own form of exhibitionism. By unleashing these pornographic fragments into the wild, Rosenberg's porn rocks negotiate with their landscapes, and ask us to do the same.

5 Paul Preciado, *Pornotopia: An Essay on Playboy's Architecture and Biopolitics* (Brooklyn: Zone Books, 2019): 27.

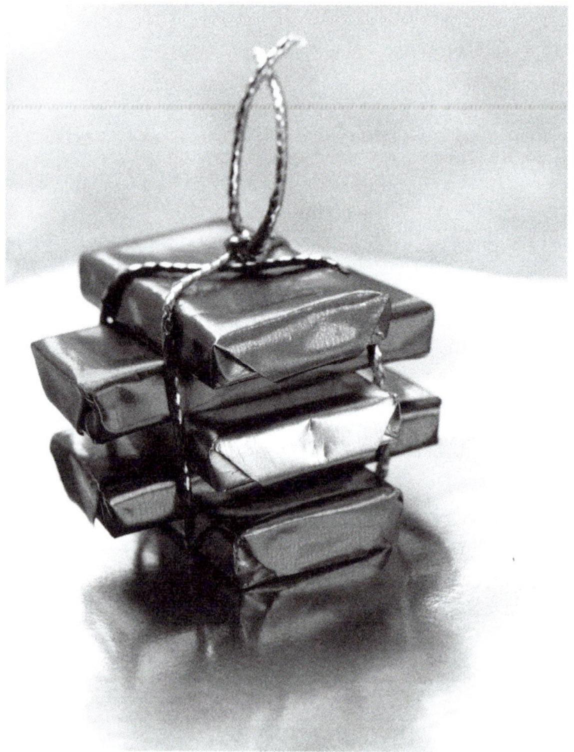

The Colors, 1999, from *Berlin Childhood*. C-print, 40 × 30 in.

Shiny colorful papers wrapping chocolate bars stacked crosswise, tied with a golden ribbon, not yet unpacked, and larger than life: *Die Farben/Schokolade* (1999). It was the first work of Aura Rosenberg's that I ever saw, and I will never forget it. This was also my first encounter with Walter Benjamin. The large chocolates were part of an installation in the 3rd Berlin Biennale (2004), *Complex Berlin*, curated by Ute Meta Bauer. This work appeared alongside 20 other photographs from Rosenberg's 1990s series *Berliner Kindheit* (*Berlin Childhood*), titled after Walter Benjamin's *Berliner Kindheit um neunzehnhundert* (*Berlin Childhood around 1900*). This selection included works I would present in Rosenberg's subsequent exhibitions many years later. They depicted experiences, objects, and places that directly referenced the 42 texts that comprise Benjamin's chronicle. They are, however, contemporary interpretations, personal redactions—the results of revisiting Berlin 100 years later: *Tiergarten* (Grolmanstraße), *Krumme Straße* (Städtisches Volksbad), *Der Lesekasten* (Museum Kindheit und Jugend), *Der Fischotter* (Zoologischer Garten), *Das Karussell* (Gedächtniskirche), *Knabenbücher* (Savignyplatz), *Der Nähkasten* (Auguststraße), or *Das Telefon* (Kantstraße).

An edition of miniature models of the Siegessäule (Victory Column), an emblematic Berlin monument accompanied these large photographs. Rosenberg produced the models as an edition of 1,000 for the Biennale and titled this work *The Missing Souvenir* after noticing there were no souvenirs of this monument in Berlin. Even though I was not yet well versed in Benjamin, I immediately understood the

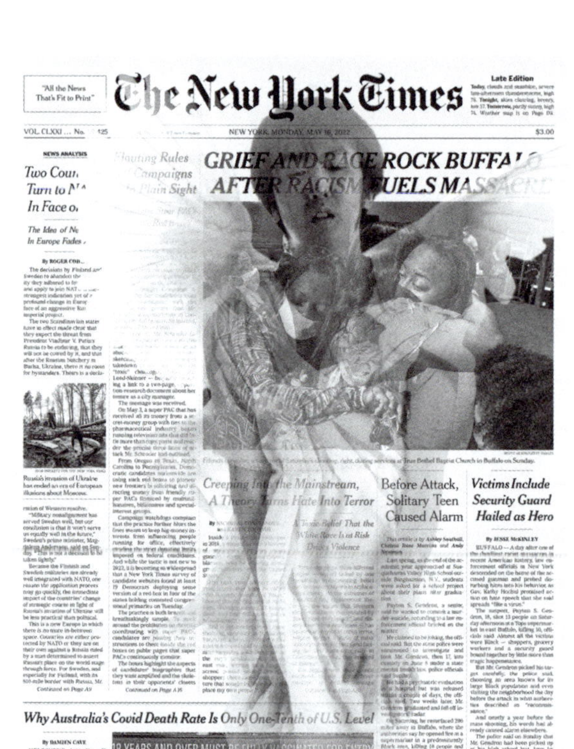

Angel of History (New York Times, May 16, 2022), 2022. Inkjet print, 24 × 13 in.

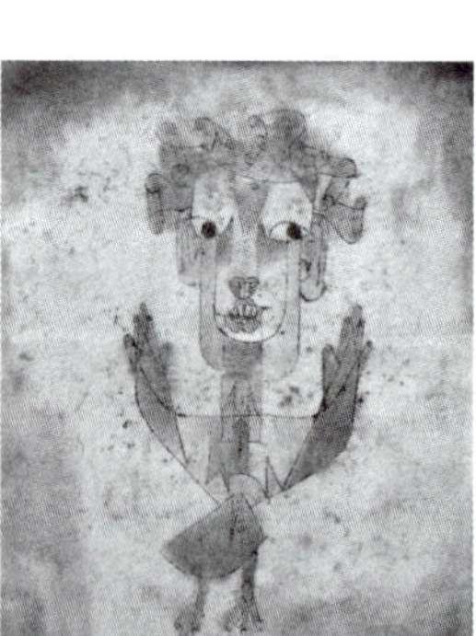

Paul Klee, *Angelus Novus*, 1920. Oil transfer and watercolor on Paper, 12½ × 9½ in.

artist's allegorical procedure: appropriation and transformation of the object. Soon after, I reviewed this Biennial in an article for *Sekcja*, the magazine of Warsaw University's art history department. I met Rosenberg and Meta Bauer one year later, through mutual friends running Orchard, a cooperative project space in New York with which I collaborated at that time. Two artists from this circle, both familiar with Benjamin, brought up Rosenberg's work. They were Rebecca (R. H.) Quaytman (who later discovered that Paul Klee's watercolor monotype *Angelus Novus* was glued to a 19th-century engraving portraying Martin Luther), and Dan Graham, whose work, such as his 1987 *Corporate Arcadias*, had been informed by Benjamin consistently. Later, at a reception, Rebecca introduced me to Aura. Dan, for his part, recommended I check out Aura's *Angel of History* series in which she superimposed images of angels onto front pages from *The New York Times* to create contemporary allegories.

In 2001, Rosenberg first presented her *Berlin Childhood* photographs at Berlin's daadgalerie. The series addressed the 42 texts that comprise *Berlin Childhood around 1900*. Benjamin began his memoir in 1932, when, fearing the growing repressiveness of the Third Reich, he fled Germany. Rosenberg began the series in 1992 while shooting black-and-white snapshots of her daughter's kindergarten class. Klaus Biesenbach, then a young curator, invited her to show these pictures at the Likor Fabrik on Auguststraße in Berlin. His assistant, Maria Kreuzer, suggested the title and told Rosenberg about Benjamin's book. Intrigued by the chronicle and the imagistic quality of Benjamin's writing, she began to look for contemporary equivalents to Benjamin's texts in post-Soviet Berlin, the country to which she "returned" in 1991 after her family's forced emigration. Her daadgalerie exhibition was accompanied by a comprehensive catalog of 150 photographs shot in Berlin between 1996–2001. The book combined passages from Benjamin with the artist's personal commentaries and included texts by Esther Leslie and Friedrich Meschede. As Benjamin noted in his introduction to *Berlin Childhood around 1900*:

> In 1932 it began to be clear to me that I would soon have to bid a long, perhaps lasting farewell to the city of my birth: I have made an effort to get hold of the images in which the experience of the big city is precipitated in a child of the middle class.... But, then, the images of my metropolitan childhood perhaps are capable, at their core, of preforming later historical experience. I hope they will at least suggest how thoroughly the person spoken of here would later dispense with the security allotted his childhood.

Aura's daughter, Carmen, who spent much of her childhood in Berlin, became the series's new protagonist. Benjamin had critiqued the upbringing, education and the legacy of German "Bildung" in the bourgeois society of the Weimar Republic as a fertile ground for Nazism. These ideas appear not only in *Berlin Childhood around 1900* but also in *Theories of German Fascism* and his last text, "On the Concept of History." In that sense, Rosenberg's series is deeply dialectical, depicting Carmen's childhood under far better circumstances. The process of remapping Berlin through Carmen's experience coincided with both mother and daughter learning German and reclaiming German citizenship for themselves. Aura also uncovered histories of her German-Jewish family from Eschwege, including the historical figure of her great-uncle, the socialist newspaper publisher and member of the Bundestag, Ludwig Pappenheim. In 1939 Rosenberg's family fled Germany for the United States and Brazil. Her father, Ernest, went to New York, where later his daughter was born. Her 1997 photograph *Bendlerbrücke* shows Ernest on one of his Berlin visits crossing this bridge with his granddaughter Carmen.

Walter Benjamin never returned to Germany, but his descendants did. While Carmen was the main character in the *Berlin Childhood* photographic series, Aura's *Berlin Childhood* film series featured Lais Benjamin Campos, Benjamin's great-granddaughter. Chantal Benjamin, Lais's mother, contacted Aura in 2004 after seeing her work in an exhibition at Haus am Waldsee titled *Schrift, Bilder, Denken: die Kunst der Gegenwart und Walter Benjamin* (Text, Image, Thought: Walter Benjamin and Contemporary Art). This exhibition included new photomontages from her *Angel of History* project. The two women became friends, and when Chantal's daughter Lais was born a few years later, Aura proposed to update *Berlin Childhood* as a series of short videos. This project led to an ongoing collaboration between Aura and the artist Frances Scholz. It captures Lais growing up from a toddler into a teenager. In 2017, I premiered this project at the Galeria Studio in Warsaw as part of Aura's *Angel of History* exhibition. Narrated largely by Lais reading her great-grandfather's texts, the films offer a rereading and rewriting of Benjamin's chronicle, a glimpse into the Berlin of Lais's generation. These videos also inspired me to study Benjamin's never-completed trip to Portugal, which culminated in the 14th iteration of my ongoing *Footnote* project, executed as *Footnote 14: Angel of History* at Casa São Roque in Porto. Participants, among others, included artists-scholars working with Benjamin: Aura Rosenberg, R. H. Quaytman, Arno Gisinger, Patrizia Bach. The show also featured artistic commissions by Chantal Benjamin and Lais Benjamin Campos and family archives from her father, Marcelo de Souza Campos Granja. This exhibition traced the movements of Benjamin in Europe, the resurfacing of a Portuguese affiliation in the lives of his descendants, and their return to Berlin.

In 1921 Benjamin purchased Paul Klee's monoprint *Angelus Novus* and he kept it with him for many years afterward. This image informs the core of his prophetic 1940 testament "On the Concept of History" and its ninth thesis. For Benjamin, *Angelus Novus* looked like the "angel of history." He is turned towards the past, where he sees ongoing catastrophe, piling ruin upon ruin. The wind blowing from paradise is caught in his wings, pushing him into the future, yet he is turned backward as the pile of ruins before him grows skyward. According to Benjamin, this wind is what we call progress. Benjamin, however, reversed the direction of progress to reveal what looks like an apocalypse. Its aftermath is ruins. In *Lectures on*

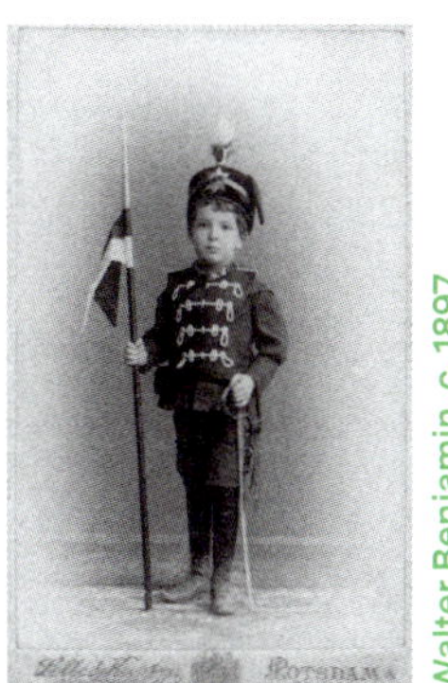

Walter Benjamin, c. 1897.

the Philosophy of History, Georg Wilhelm Friedrich Hegel described the ruin of past societies as the "good side" of history: as "the condition of the progress of spirit." Benjamin inverted Hegel to reveal the "bad side," the side of domination and oppression. Rosenberg's animated film *Angel of History* (2013) proposes a visual actualization of Benjamin's allegory in a vernacular that plays with camp and kitsch and evokes computer games. The film animates the progress of history as a ruin, compressed into five minutes, starting with the formation of planets from gas clouds and ending with the scrapheap of the present. This pile of rubble, culled from online pictorial archives and the artist's own photographs, depicts the catastrophe of determinist "progress." Only a flash of lightening at the end offers a glimpse of paradise—a hint of possible redemption. In Rosenberg's words: "A flash of original paradise interrupts the cataclysmic momentum and reminds the viewer of the dialectic of history in which the past can be recalled only in relation to the demands of the present."

Found Souvenirs and Pandora Charm Bracelets

Claire Koron Elat

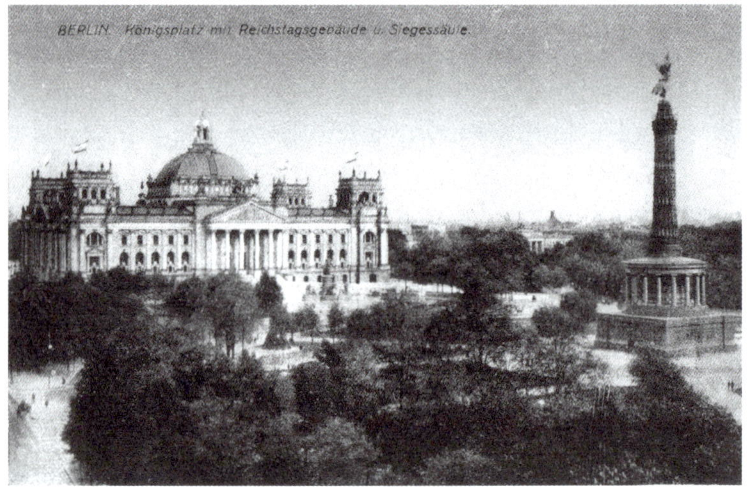

Postcard with view of Reichstag with Siegessäule in the old Königsplatz, c. 1900.

"[T]he paradox to be fully accepted is that when a certain historical moment is (mis)perceived as the moment of loss of some quality, upon closer inspection it becomes clear that the lost quality emerged only at this very moment of its alleged loss."
—Slavoj Žižek

I don't possess—or to be more accurate, own—a single souvenir. Three months ago, when I moved apartments in Berlin, I discarded everything that was superfluous, everything obsolete. Thus, a pin showing the flag of Hong Kong, a dangly Eiffel tower charm, and a rubber bracelet with a tacky lettering that said "I love Amsterdam" went to the trash. I don't love Amsterdam. Souvenirs seem to inevitably fall into desuetude. Ephemeral charms of past memories, which don't really commemorate the past but rather amass dust and remind you to get another charm ASAP, like these Pandora charm bracelets every YouTube girl was obsessed with in 2013. Souvenirs only fuel our presupposed neoliberal desire to turn everything into a product, to possess and to own experiences, memories, or observations. It's not enough to look at the original Eiffel Tower, or in Aura Rosenberg's case, Berlin's Siegessäule; the moment you are there, tactility to take home is needed. An object to touch, to feel, and perhaps to abuse is needed.

In 2001, for her exhibition at daadgalerie, Berlin, Rosenberg first conceived a set of 25 miniature models of the Siegessäule. It had not existed as a souvenir before this. Built in 1873, the monument, today popular tourist attraction, is supposed to commemorate the Prussian Victory that led to the

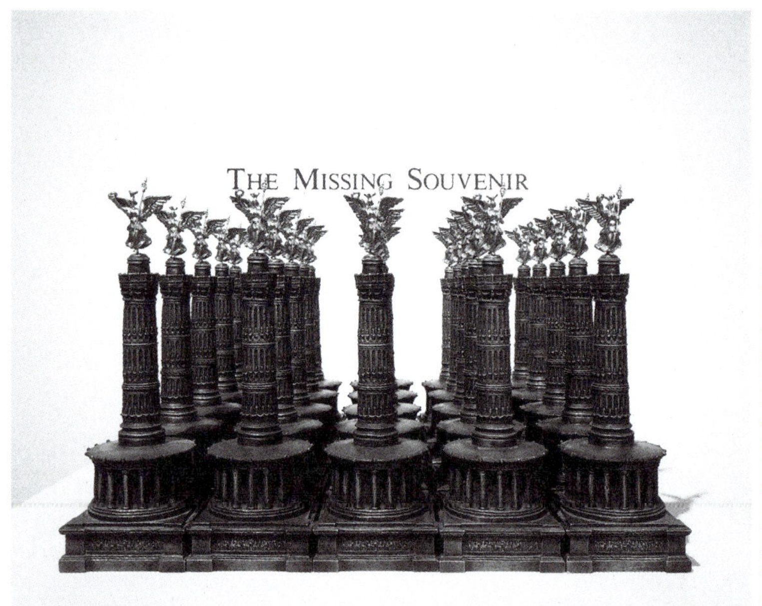

The Missing Souvenir. Installation view, Gasser and Grunert Gallery, New York, 2002.

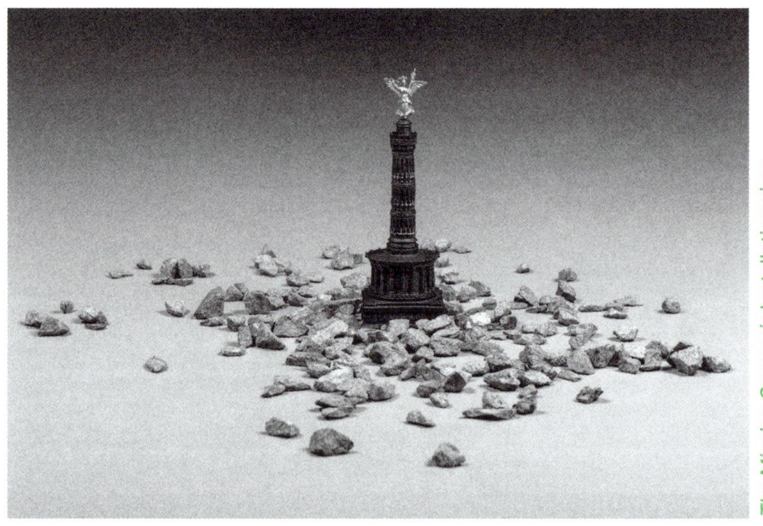

The Missing Souvenir. Installation view, Efremidis Gallery, Berlin, 2021.

unification of the German states under Wilhelm I as emperor. In the late 1930s, the monument was moved by the Nazis from its former location on the Platz der Republik to Großer Stern, where it remains today. The relocation was part of the Nazi's plan to transfigure Berlin into Germania, the megalomaniac project of the Germans' *schuldige* (guilty) past. The persistence of the enlarged version of the Siegessäule at Großer Stern seems to reaffirm this fascist history.

In the 1970s Rosenberg worked on a painting series composed of reproductions of "master-pieces" by "great" historical painters. Her work *Siegessäule* is of a similar reproductive practice. The facsimile represents the monument as it was before Albert Speer, Hitler's preeminent architect, transformed it. Thus, Rosenberg questions and revamps the Germans' perception of their history and concurrently illuminates souvenirs as pathological objects of capitalism. They are grounded in public sites that are taken to a commercial realm, privatizing an object, even if it is the miniature form, that once used to be accessible for everyone by placing them into a state of private ownership. As (historical) monuments and moments cannot be actually possessed or owned individually, they emerge, satisfying our neoliberal minds and enlarging our Pandora charm bracelets, as lost objects, forced into physical states to be taken home.

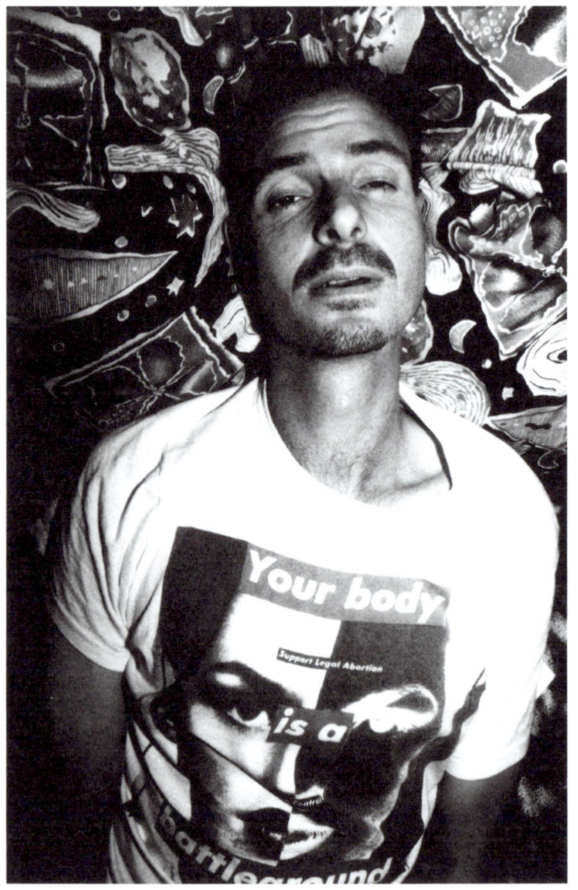

Head Shots (FW), 1991–96. Gelatin silver print, 12 × 16 in.

The point of departure is a portrait series of men. Each picture is black-and-white. Each is vertical. In most, the heads are slightly upraised, filling the frame, the eyes closed, the lips parted. The men appear to be between 20 and 40. A few are older. What's going on? Just what sort of social document does this unlikely collection present?

The exact legibility of these images, the way they might be read, is highly conditional. This latitude for dissimulation and interpretation reveals how arbitrary the expressivity of human countenance can be; as Eisenstein once suggested, a director might fire a pistol behind an unsuspecting actor in order to produce a reaction that, properly edited, would convey extreme grief. Conversely, the simple manipulation of body parts, including the face, may produce corresponding subjective effects in oneself and others. Thus, the title *Head Shots* becomes key. But this seemingly generic label insinuates a slightly pornographic potential; one might construe these faces as an index of ejaculations happening outside the frame.

Male ecstasy, male orgasm. The man who loses control of his emotions presents an exceptional figure not only in television, movies and advertising, but also in pornography—even gay pornography. The issue is charged, not the least because, beneath the gender politics, the transaction between viewer and viewed becomes purely subjective. Stripped of its emotional identifications, the whole genre of portraiture might collapse into little more than a pointless reiteration of one of humankind's universal features. But the face remains, in its own way, anonymous. Pornography necessarily operates on the basis of such anonymity. If the camera "frames out" genitalia, odors, sounds, and colors, in so doing it becomes a decisively pornographic apparatus by creating what is literally "ob-scene," i.e., outside the scenario.

"In itself," however, each portrait is rather chaste—not only because of the exact balance between what it makes explicit and what it leaves to conjecture, but also because of the tacit covenant between the photographer and her subjects on which its production is predicated. Make-believe. Usually, Rosenberg photographed the men herself. Some, however, preferred simply to send her negatives. Both the title and the steady accumulation of like images conspire to suggest, after the fact, what in most cases was never a fact to begin with. Although each picture remains a matter of some speculation, that is not the question. Rather, in all possible instances the male subject is projecting an image of himself for another. Even given the various stages of deliberate and de facto editing, the results turned out to be remarkably consistent, as if going out of control were a matter of conformity. In this respect, the difference between real and fake is trivial.

The salient aspects of the group who agreed to be photographed are easy to spot: mostly affiliated with the so-called art world and sharing a liberal resistance to certain patriarchal imperatives. Harder to discern is the rationale of those who declined to take part. Most claimed that this would somehow compromise their professional standing. (As an artist, I find the occasional request to pose before my works to be far more compromising than this ever could be.) Yet it seems that an overhaul of masculine portraiture is

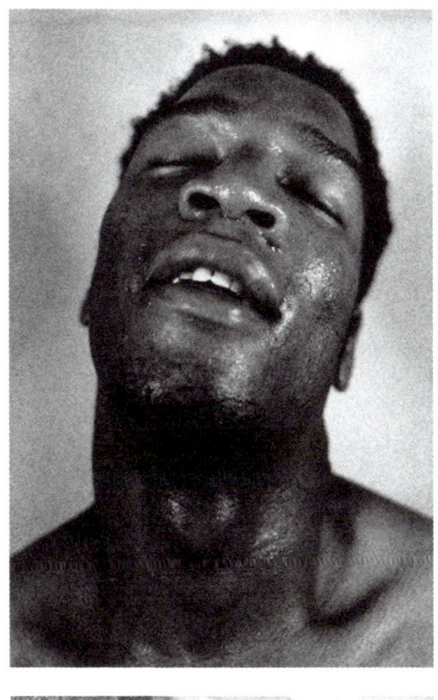

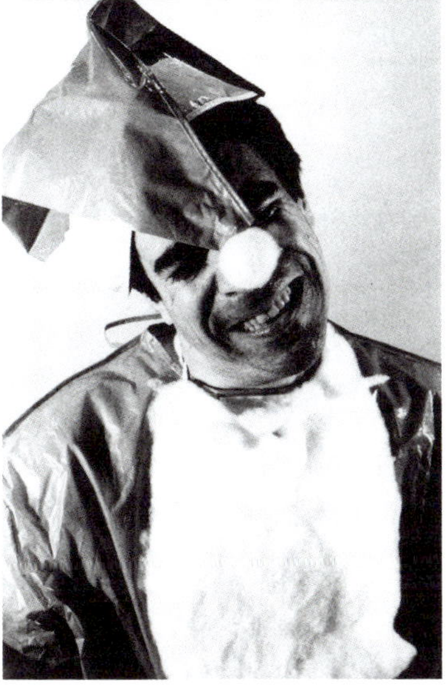

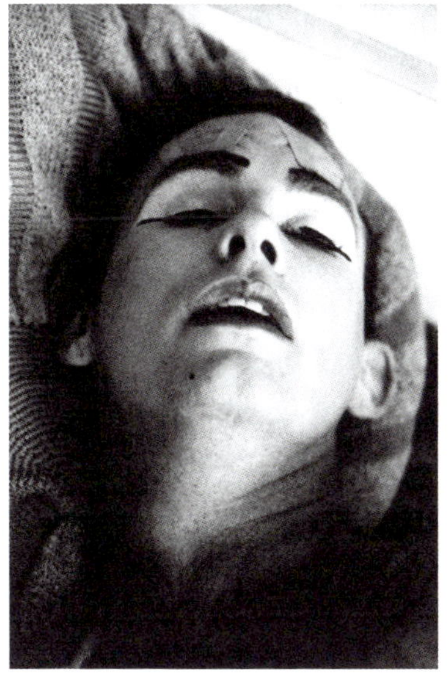

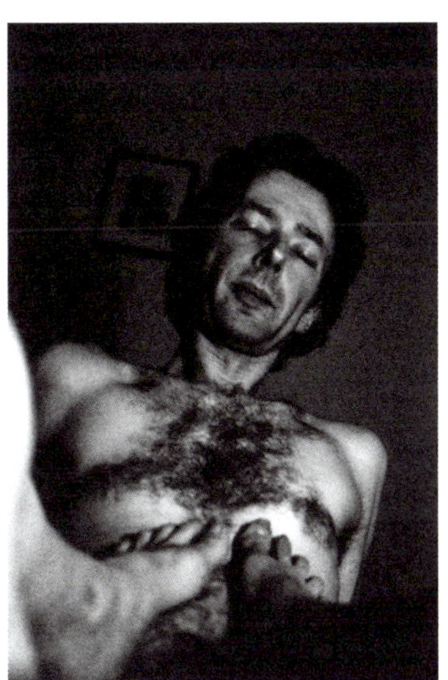

↖ *Head Shots (DL)*, 1991–96. Gelatin silver print, 12 × 16 in.
↗ *Head Shots (Santa)*, 1991–96. Gelatin silver print, 12 × 16 in.
↙ *Head Shots (Patina du Prey)*, 1991–96. Gelatin silver print, 12 × 16 in.
↘ *Head Shots (JM)*, 1991–96. Gelatin silver print, 12 × 16 in.

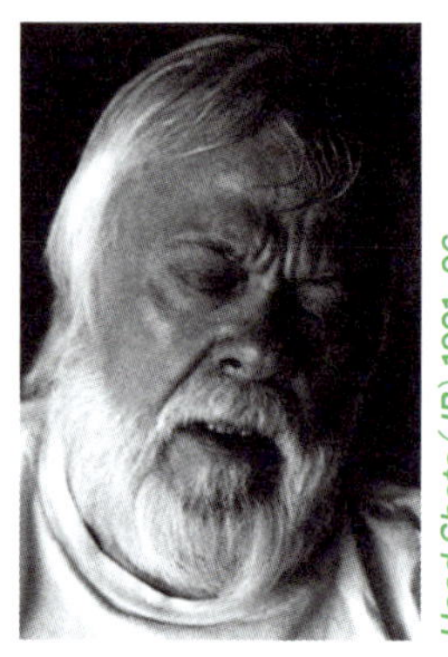

Head Shots (JB), 1991–96.
Gelatin silver print, 12 × 16 in.

long overdue. One sees it burbling under the surface, for example, in David Salle's "misogynistic" depictions of women—which Kim Gordon regarded early on as self-portraits. (Robert Gober later even forged a spread-eagled Salle "self-portrait" to be inserted as part of a pseudo art review in one of his newspaper stacks. "ARTIST REINVENTS HIMSELF IN STUNNING BREAKTHROUGH" ran the headline—or something like that.)

One of the 1950s clichés of the artist was that this figure was a man(?) who internalized the feminine paradigm of expressivity. From this odd perspective, most of the subjects are just doing their nominal job. At any rate, the social field clearly conditions the expectation of revelation vis-à-vis what these photos actually might show. Should we be surprised when "the revelation" turns out to confirm what everyone involved already believes to be true? The set of men who could be considered approachable and the subset of those who agreed to take part both represent intrinsic, pre-selection processes.

In sociological terms, then, it is more fruitful to ask, less empirically, what, under the circumstances, would constitute a perverse gesture? Because the artist enjoins participants to expose what is ordinarily prohibited, this would seem to occlude perversity from the system of representation—at least in the exchange between photographer and subject. Again, what might constitute a perverse gesture? Simply to stare straight into the camera, eyes level, mouth closed, features relaxed, no emotions evident. These are not only the classic tropes of male portraiture, but also those of that dissident masculinity, dandyism. Andy Warhol remains dandyism's best known contemporary exponent. Although his esthetic is exclusively anti-expressive, his film *Blow Job*, is the clearest precedent for this portrait series. The dandy typically fetishized the ideal of self-control to the extent that expressivity became tantamount to self-obliteration. In the mind's eye of the dandy, this fear transformed the most casual personal matters, such as grooming or deportment, into heroic struggles against the monumental forces of entropy and inertia. This price that the dandy paid for regarding himself as beautiful is only slightly higher than that demanded by authoritarian masculinity. These photos suggest that now no one need pay; it can be done for free.

To Build a Fire

Timothy Martin

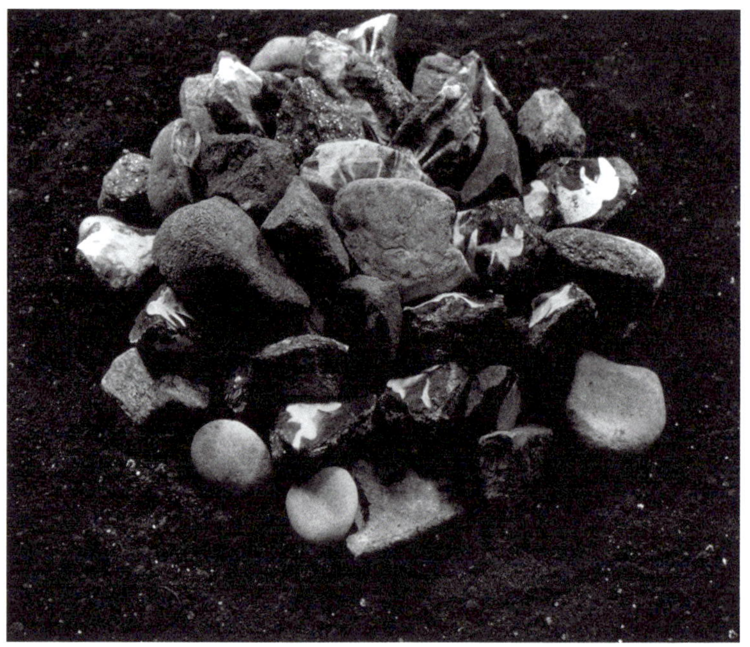

Bonfire. Installation view, Open Air, Rembertikreisel, Bremen, Germany, 1993.

If the recent histories of pornography agree upon anything it is that, in Walter Kendrick's words, "pornography" names an argument and not a thing.[6] Pornography as a regulatory category was invented in the late 18th century in response to the perceived menace of culture's emerging democratization, that is, to control the consumption of the obscene so as to exclude the lower classes and women.[7] Since its inception, pornography has denoted a cultural battle zone, the lines of which have continually shifted with the changing boundaries of private and public life, of obscenity and decency and, more recently, of victim and victimizer. To behold the pornographic image today, let alone to produce or employ it in an artwork, is to enter the divided zone, and in turn be divided by it. Upon entry, one realizes that the zone is a prison, and to indulge the pleasure of the image is to be aware of oneself as the zone's panoptical focus: as the libertine (Sade), the sublimator (Freud), the commodity fetishist (Adorno) or the fetishist of the signifier (Baudrillard), as the rapist (Dworkin), and so on. Thus, the pornographic image has become *derrière garde*, ever watchful of its exposed behind and forever formulating its next defense. Contemporary discourse on pornography, itself bound up in arguments, old and new, has given the pornographic image no recourse or future, nowhere to go besides its checkered past; it remains an aging and unreformable prisoner.

6 See Walter Kendrick, *The Secret Museum: Pornography in Modern Culture* (New York: Penguin, 1987).
7 See Lynn Hunt, ed. *The Invention of Pornography: Obscenity and the Origins of Modernity, 1500–1800* (New York: Zone Books, 1993).

Part of this bind is that pornography as a cultural form would appear to have outlived its imaginative potential. Virtually all the themes and effects of modern pornography were rehearsed, indeed, catalogued by the Marquis de Sade. In his writings, rape, incest, parricide, sacrilege, sodomy and tribadism, pedophilia, and all forms of torture and murder were associated with sexual arousal. As Lynn Hunt puts it, "No one has ever been able to top Sade because he had, in effect, explored the ultimate logical possibility of pornography: the annihilating of the body, the very seat of pleasure, in the name of desire."[8] (Thus, Sade prefigured some of psychoanalysis's more intractable mysteries as well, i.e. Freud's "death drive.") The often-heard grievance that hard-core porn "leaves nothing to the imagination" has more to bemoan than the fact that pornography has become little more than a photography-of-genital-acts. In a very real, historical sense, there is nothing left for the pornographic imagination to discover. Even a snuff film, at the extremity of transgressive effects, would excite only in spite of its lack of imagination. So commercial porn keeps recycling itself, and "pornographic" art keeps recycling commercial porn for the production of discourse. The condition is all-to-fittingly postmodern: commercial porn became image, image became code (text), so pornography became code as well, good for nothing except the breeding of more code (discourse). At times, "pornographic" art searches for something "other" in the image, some thing-in-itself, but more often than not arrives at something familiar, even retrospective: the glamour

8 Hunt, 35.

of Robert Mapplethorpe's lustful portraiture, the kitsch of Jeff Koons's monumentalized porn, and the romance of Joel-Peter Witkin's carnal *natures mortes*. The pornographic imagination in art seems permanently stuck in a salvage mode, scavenging affects of a mortified language into pastiches and recontextualizations, shunning the games of the flesh to pursue the science of the gaze.

The necrosis of the pornographic image in current art makes the vitality of Aura Rosenberg's work with pornography seem all the more startling. She too recycles commercial porn, not analytically, but literally, cutting photographs from magazines and decoupaging them onto objects, most conspicuously, onto rocks and stones. The peculiarity of this craft—which she originally contrived in order to play a practical joke on a friend—yields an even more peculiar affect: a phenomenal transformation of the lithic body into flesh and the skin of the photographic subject into a body. The transformation of the two is uncanny: unfamiliar because it confounds material categories, familiar because it approximates an imaginary process materially: the process of mind that resurrects the real of the photographic image or uncovers the body beneath its skin. At the very outset, Rosenberg's porn rocks resonate with a deep memory, an essential recognition of the synthetic mechanisms involved in perceiving a body as such. When one perceives a body, all that is given to the senses is an array of immediate surface effects—of light, texture, etc. The (inadequate) claim may then be made that a body is simply inferred from the form of these effects using the memory of past correct inferences.

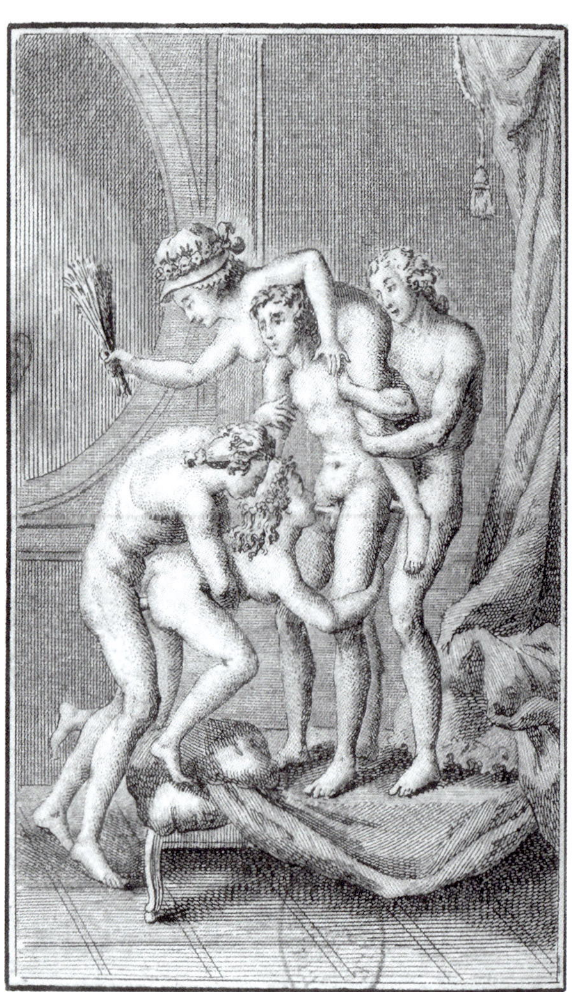

Engraving from Marquis de Sade,
Philosophie dans le Boudoir, vol. 2, 1795.

But the true recognition of a body as corporeal—and not merely formal—is always a product of intuition; intuition is the only faculty that "penetrates" another body. This is no less the case when the vehicle of the body is a photograph. The image/material confusion of Rosenberg's porn rocks takes us directly to the matrix of this intuition: the surety of our own embodiment, our own perpetual corporeality, that is its frame of reference.

This peculiar grounding of the pornographic image in a question of phenomenal embodiment is by no means a course of reduction in Rosenberg's work. It is but an opening move, an act of formal severance from prior discourses that are wont to predetermine which roles the images may play and which they may not. Although Rosenberg's first procedure may have been simply to set porn to stone, her first principle regarding the use of pornographic images in art is to drag the image out of isolation and back into the world of things. What the images then become is more a matter of how they reacquire the world or are themselves reacquired in it, and less a matter of what they have inherited. The rote (politically obligatory) objectification of the hardcore porn image as a fact of its commercial legacy then becomes, despite its airs of finality, only one of many possible objectifications to form and reform *en passant* as the image moves into the world. Rosenberg also takes at face value the formal complexion of commercial porn—its clinicality and stock devices—but, through selection and editing, derives from it a number of distinct modalities. Simply put, they fall between the two poles of the pornographic image: the facial and the genital.

In the rocks with genital images, particularly images of penetration, the modality is realism. This particular realism is not distracted by the image's "embodiment" in lithic "flesh;" indeed, it is both affirmed and supercharged by it. It is what the pornographic imagination desires, what it wants to discover in visuality: carnality, the flesh of something, a cut through the fog of desire. When Rosenberg brackets the genital image off from the rest of the body—a standard practice of commercial porn as well—and fits it to the naturally formed face of a rock, the bracketing becomes naturalized. The genital image is relieved of its conscience of the missing part or subject by the normality of the rock's own fragmentation. The rock (nature) *authorizes* the bracketing of the genitals, because it appears to cause it, thereby averting a pseudo-crisis of the subject's wholeness. The realism of the pornographic image is uncovered through this bracketing. The genital image is true, the genital is *there.* Images of penetration go further in this direction. The penetrated orifice is distorted and the partially buried penis loses its classic profile. Interpenetrated genitals cease to be iconic or symbolic and thus are disinclined to become language, to suggest other things. They are real; the documentation is authentic. Here is the hobgoblin of the proscriptive discourse against pornography: the spectacle of opposing genitals fitting together irremediably, without a care, without a thought.

The radicality of this work with respect to "the argument" is precisely this realism. The thread of realism runs throughout Rosenberg's installations and photographs: in the materials, the materiality of the photographs, and the frankness of the hardcore image. One confronts the corporeal fact of sexual bodies and is instructed to be present to it. Her working definition of pornography is insistently quite plain: pornography is merely the depiction of the carnal act, and the only form that depicts it realistically. The idea is not new, it has merely been clouded by centuries of moral and judicial smoke. Pornography as realism was an Enlightenment idea *par excellence*, having been regarded by its 18th-century advocates—Diderot himself wrote pornography and was imprisoned for it—as a pursuit of the natural and social truths of sexuality. Current discourse gives no ground to this idea, and responds with a series of "who" questions: *Whose truths? Whose gaze? Whose symptom?* The real of the pornographic image is presumed to be both an irrelevance and a politically incorrect term to bring into "the argument." In light of current discourse, the heresy of Rosenberg's realism—and therefore its value—boils down to its rather modest insistence that the genital image in hardcore porn is an adequate term for carnality, that is has truth value. This insistence becomes even more persuasive, however, when the embodied image (the porn rock) is taken out of isolation and is able to demonstrate its reality among other things-in-the-world.

Rosenberg's first installations of porn rocks in 1989 were simple sculptural groupings on the gallery floor, in which their sense as a private collection or "secret museum" was retained. But their naturalism and the similarity of the format to that of the "nonsite" gave the work a connotation of a latent externality, of wanderlust, forcibly

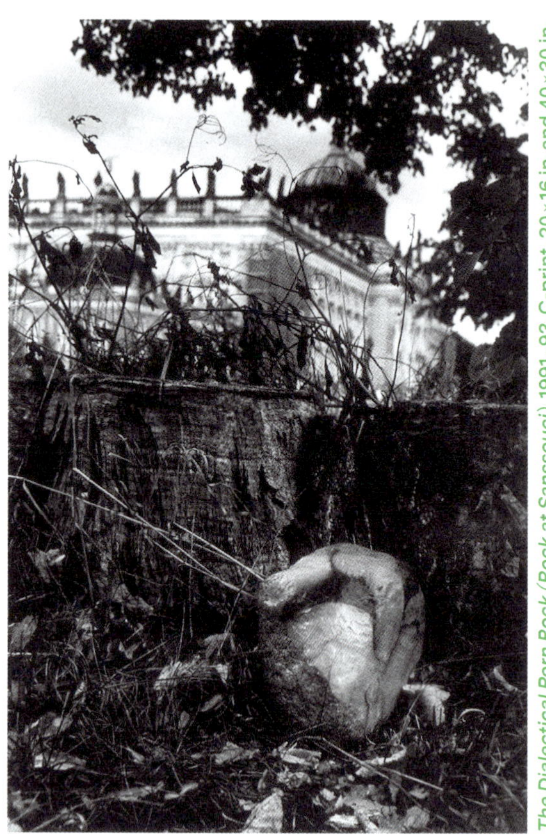

The Dialectical Porn Rock (Rock at Sanssouci), 1991–93. C-print, 20 × 16 in. and 40 × 30 in.

repressed by the interiority of the (assumed) connoisseur's "harem." The harem doors were to be flung open, however, and the pornographic subject set free to roam. Rosenberg began a photo series of the porn rocks in various exterior settings, surrounded by earth, water, plant life, etc. The first of these are reminiscent of the sharp-focused, objective nature photographs of Edward Weston, Albert Renger-Patzsch, and Imogen Cunningham, with the flesh image caught in a rather surreal reverie of the natural world. It is in the series shot in and around Berlin from 1992–93 that the serendipity of resituating the porn rocks hits its stride. For these photographs Rosenberg placed the porn rocks both singularly and in small groups at numerous sites, some anonymous, but many well-known or historically significant that would appeal to any visitor to post-unification Berlin, such as the Brandenburg Gate and the Reichstag, a remaining section of The Wall and the "anarchist encampment" nearby, Alexanderplatz, Marx-Engels-Platz, and so on. The porn rocks always appear in the foreground, shot in sharp focus with available light, with the identifying structures cast at oblique angles into the background and outlined by ample swatches of cloud-covered sky. On the whole the result is an extraordinary dual genre of documentary and tableau, charged through and through with what one could call a "situational erotics."

In *Neues Palais Restoration* (1993), for example, nature, the built world and political history converge around a porn rock of anal penetration. It is a tableau of impossible visual consistency and realism. The problem this startling convergence presents to the mind is insoluble, impossible to think through without grasping for allegorical straws, or denying the documentary trace of the real, or pulling back from the carnal vortex of rock-flesh. The rock gives the tableau a tumescent urgency that is ill-disposed to let go of the beholder's sense of embodiment; it says: "Be present, be aroused, be historical, split yourself...watch out for the police!"[9] For those whom

9 This photograph resonates so strongly with Hans Belmer's rare outdoor doll photos that I can't not mention them. In Plate 7 from *The Games of the Doll* (1935–37), the doll (headless and mostly naked with four legs and double genitals sprouting from a single central belly) leans seductively against a tree as the partially obscured figure of a man looks on in the background. The elements in Rosenberg's photo correspond so closely to Belmer's that it's eerie. By comparison, the porn rock becomes the doll and the Neues Palais becomes the man, an ominous father/state/Big Other overlooking the scene of an excruciatingly private affair.

the porn rock affects—this particular flavor or porn may not be for everybody—there is a complex exchange immanent in this image, motored by its confounding realism and raw carnality, its phenomenal unreason (uncanniness), and the desire of the beholder to hold all of its pieces together. Therein lies a strange and fertile pleasure for the body that thinks. One's dialogue or reckoning with the image becomes so entwined in a phantasy-exchange that for all intents and purposes the two processes become indistinguishable. For the prospective "reader" of the photographic "text," the image is pregnant with possible meanings, but the perplexing dynamics of the image are rooted in the body of the participant, not the eye of the reader. Here, to read is to sit out the dance, or worse: to join the ranks of what Nietzsche called "the despisers of the body."

This is not the case where Rosenberg employs the other pole of the pornographic image: the facial. Here, a certain kind of reading is presumed—the reading of faces—and the notion of phantasy-exchange takes a different connotation. The face is the locus of pornography's theater, the place where the other person's pleasure is supposedly reflected and read. That is, it is the site of pornography's defining lie. The "pleasure" of the pornographic subject exists only as a pleasure-face, a *language*, to solicit the pleasure of the beholder. Pornography is never about the pleasure of the other. A phantasy cued on the expression of a face is either a projection—whether for the comfort or voyeuristic titillation of the beholder—or a reading/misreading: open mouth and closed eyes merely signify pleasure; they never testify to it. The pornographic face always registers a doubt, a self-reflection on the grounds of one's empathies and identifications, and a conscience about the indeterminability of the other's interior. When facial rocks appear in Rosenberg's work—as they have from the start, often in groups of a kind—the modality is contrary to the realism of the genital rocks.

This sense of conscience and reflexivity, as well as the facial image's embodiment in rock-flesh, becomes entangled with political history and monumentalization in several photographs of the Berlin series. For one image, Rosenberg placed a small group of facial rocks atop a Holocaust memorial among the collection of stones already there; for another, scattered a larger group over a pile of construction rubble at the Alexanderplatz U-Bahn station. In both, the faces of pleasure become *momenti mori*; the "little deaths" of sexual orgasm become the big deaths history buries and monumentalizes. The Jewish tradition of placing stones on a grave marker overlaps with the local phenomenon of the "rubble monument" indigenous to Berlin (i.e. Prinz-Albrecht-Terrain), and overlaps again with the omnipresent rock-rubble of the post-war city—in which Rosenberg has situated porn rocks in a number of other photographs. In these two images, commemoration is given the immediacy of flesh. But, like pornography's face of pleasure, the interior of history is no less unknowable for its outward incarnation. Here, the reading of faces demands allegory, as it is through allegory that the disparate and unknowable past becomes, at least, thinkable. The facial rocks present the problem as one of self-reflection and embodiment, in which the embodiment of the beholder, that corporeal link to history, is called upon to testify, regardless of personal connection or non-connection to events. The shibboleth "nicht vergessen" in this instance may be directly translated to the body: "never forget *being*," the only connection to all those who *have been*.

By incorporating the complete polarity of the pornographic image in her work, signified by the genital and the facial, Rosenberg permits the beholder a certain degree of disengagement and pulling back to view the broader positionings of her project. But doing so closes still more escape routes to the comforts of reading. For example, one may view the whole Berlin project as superimposing upon the built world of the city a "pornotopia"—Steven Marcus's term for the utopian phantasy implicit in pornography. Pornotopia is a world that resists external or social reality and "moves toward independence of time, space, history, and even language itself,"[10] a world defined by the repetition of sexual encounters and the reduction of bodies to sexual parts to be recombined in infinite variation. Seeing the built world through a pornotopia, one must make the unavoidable inference that it is not only in art—pornographic or otherwise—that the libido is sublimated; it is in all the works of *homo faber*. With sublimation as the underpinning of the entire built world, any complaints about its local effects seem picayune and redundant. Must all civilization burn to rid ourselves of a stack of magazines? Andwhere is the *difference* to be found by which pathology may be determined? The animal

10 Steven Marcus, *The Other Victorians: A Study of Sexuality and Pornography in Mid-Nineteenth-Century England* (New York: Basic Books, 1974): 268.

kingdom? The symptom is so broad a category that there is nothing left to measure it against, no outside symptom of consequence.

If Rosenberg is indeed making a link between sexual pleasure and the built world, it would appear to connect on a more concrete level. Again, it is a matter of embodiment. The hand, for example, is as much the phenomenal organ of the caress as it is the organ of labor and, as Gaston Bachelard has pointed out, even to the primitive mind, caress and work must have been associated. The linkage is embodied and in a real sense *known* through the hand; experience both bears this out and is itself born out of it. Bachelard's description, coincidentally enough, focuses on the working of stone, from chipping ("tormented stone") to polishing ("caressed stone") with its progressively gentle, rhythmic, and seductive movement: "The man who works away with such patience is encouraged both by a memory and by a hope, and it is in the domain of the affective powers that we must look for the secret of his reverie."[11] Rosenberg, too, has "worked" the surface of a stone to a seductive sheen—the lacquered skin of the porn rocks—and has elsewhere in her art located sexuality in the organ of the hand. In a small series of untitled sculptures (1989), she decoupaged collages of porn faces onto the fleshy forms of surgical gloves filled with cement. The fetish quality of these objects is quite pronounced—the latex material of the gloves being, like leather, a signature fabric of sexual fetishism—and this quality is reinforced by the collage's connotation of a private collection.

11 Gaston Bachelard, *The Psychoanalysis of Fire* (Boston: Beacon Press, 1964): 31.

The faces, as always, are open to reading, reflexive, but resistant to interior penetration except through phantasy. In this sense, they are a type of prophylactic as well, like the latex skin of the glove; they make the intuitive linkage—of caress to work, pleasure to manipulation—but hold us back at the barrier where the body of the other is encountered.

So pornography in Rosenberg's work is never reduced to a disembodied argument or critique. Nor is it seen as an untainted reflection of the sexual real—although she does manage to discover the real within it and insist that this real be reckoned with. Nor is it in any sense monolithic or Cyclopean. It is more a site than a thing or argument, a site of genuine multiplicity and difference: of the facial and the genital, of reflection and incarnation, of history and being. The defining intuition of her practice has been to pose the pornographic image as elemental material, notwithstanding its multiplicity. As such, it is never wholly answerable to language, and must be approached and understood through one's own embodiment, which is, of course, the common reference point of both the real and imaginary realms of sexuality. Rosenberg's work, while bracketing the real and imaginary off from each other in order to pursue certain articulations of affect—such as those produced by the pornographic modalities of the genital and the facial—ultimately dwells in the place of their eternal exchange, where we live and breathe.

To pose pornographic images as elemental material—merged with stone, submerged in water, illuminated by the sky—is to insist upon an interplay of the real and imaginary; it is to build a fire. The "element" which most intimately corresponds

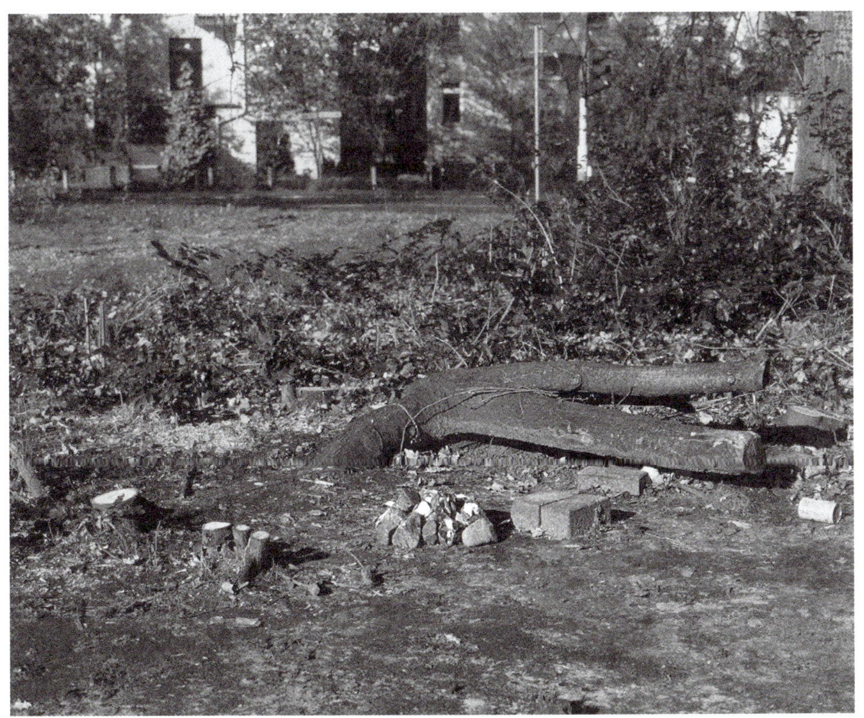

Bonfire, 1993. Installation view, *Open Air*, Rembertikreisel, Bremen, Germany, 1993.

to carnality is fire, as intuition and the whole of human history would appear to affirm. (Is not Prometheus the ur-protagonist of an *Oedipal* drama?) Indeed, sexual response *is* phenomenal fire: the fertile, capricious, self-reproducing, consuming and enlightening flame. To date, images of fire are the only non-pornographic images to appear in Rosenberg's rock decoupage. In the smoldering circle of *Bonfire* (1993), the multiplicity of individual genitals and faces threatens to converge, as at some point it is bound to. Inner and outer fire, like sexual bodies, desire to meet, that is, to meet again, for it is certain that they have already met before. But Rosenberg's fire-rocks are more than essentialized porn rocks, and fire is more than phenomenal carnality. As Bachelard put it, "fire is precisely the first object, the *first phenomenon*, on which the human mind *reflected*; among all phenomena, fire alone is sufficiently prized by prehistoric man to wake in him the desire for knowledge, and this mainly because it accompanies the desire for love."[12] By the same token, the realization of inner fire would be the first realization of the fundamental dialectic of subject and object, of inside and outside. If the conquest of fire is a sexual "conquest," the dialectic too must be sexualized in some way, and thus subject to the eternal desire and irresolution that come with the territory. The outer fire must be continually stoked to maintain the inner, and so on. While it exercises considerable license to refer to "first" things in the context of Rosenberg's ersatz *Bonfire* the analogue of photographic fire and pornographic carnality remains valid and compelling, and turns up the heat under all her images. Until the fire ceases to radiate and reflect, whether only in the imagination, we are loath to turn our backs on it.

12 Bachelard, 55.

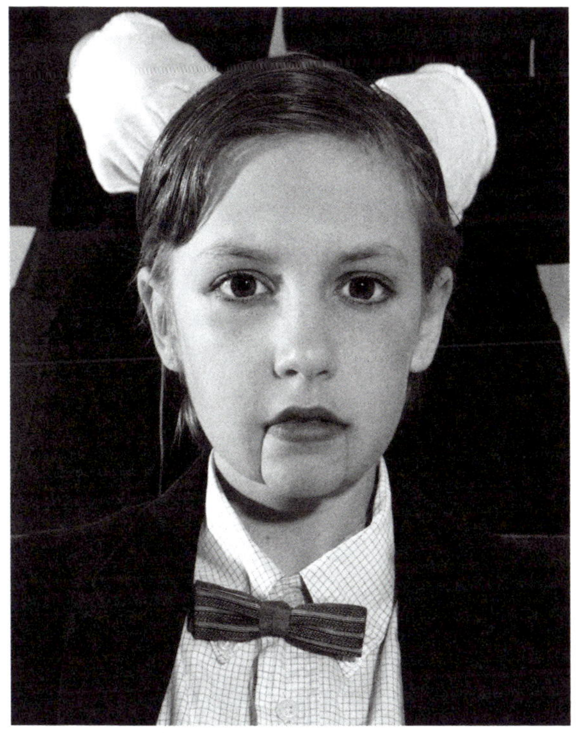

Laurie Simmons/Lena, 1996–98, from *Who Am I? What Am I? Where Am I?* Inkjet print. 46 × 36 in.

I must have been seven or eight when I realized that I could make myself look like a ventriloquist dummy. I was in the bathroom in our loft on Broadway, flossing in the mirror, when a slip of the hand revealed a trick that resembled a hinged jaw—floss pulled tight over either corner of my bottom lip and down my chin. I ran into my mother's bedroom to show her and she seemed genuinely impressed.

There were lots of ventriloquist dummies who lived in our house, along with other dolls and props that my mother, Laurie Simmons, photographed. Her studio was two floors down and I loved bringing my friends down there almost as much as I loved helping her scour flea markets for the best deals on antiquated dollhouse furniture and puppets. I never really questioned her interest in these things—to me, she was just a big (albeit glamorous) kid and to her I was a tiny (albeit needy) adult and our hobbies and interests met somewhere in the middle.

People often ask if my mother took lots of pictures of me. I always laugh and say, "No, actually." Because my mother took photos of inanimate objects—and did it for a living—she documented our childhood less than the non-artist parents I knew seemed to (although she did keep our family photos and negatives very organized in the same thick brown albums she used to preserve her own work.) As a child with a penchant for dress up and a desire to perform, I often begged her to take pictures of me—and sometimes I resorted to taking them of myself, carefully making my face up like I had learned to from the Kevin Aucoin how-to book she bought me.

A year or so after the floss discovery, my mother approached me with an idea—her friend Aura

Rosenberg was doing a series of images of children (including her own daughter, Carmen, a younger girl I knew from around the neighborhood) as reimagined by artists. Some—like Louise Lawler or James Sienna or my mother—were to transform their own kids. Others chose children of friends as subjects. We all got the chance to be dressed fantastically (my mother bought me a little boy's suit jacket and selected a clip-on bow-tie) and made up (I had red lipstick and hair gel, strictly forbidden unless I was alone on the weekends) and we got to sit in front of the bright lights and Aura's patient camera. It's the first time I really understood the magic that could be created with a story and a camera, how I could place myself both within the narrative and use the lens to refract a very different image of myself—and in many ways that's the process I've committed my life to, in no small part because of the buzz I felt on set that day.

Aura remembers me telling her it was "the best day of my life" and I wasn't lying. Not only was it a fresh diversion with a lipstick reward, but it's the first time I remember being a part of the work instead of party to the work. I felt proud and

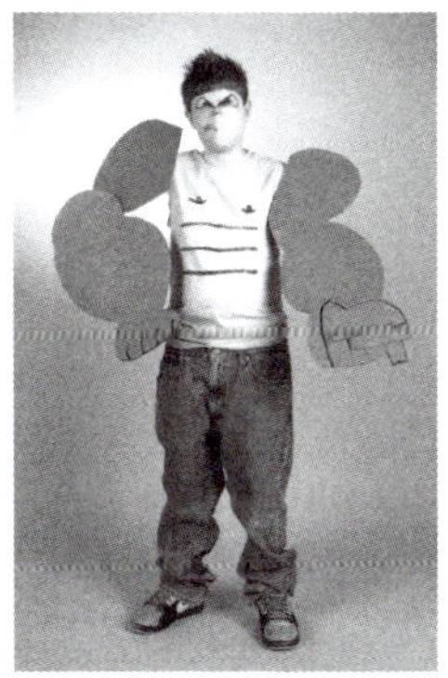

Amy Sillman/Isaac, 1996–98, from *Who Am I? What Am I? Where Am I?* Unprinted photograph.

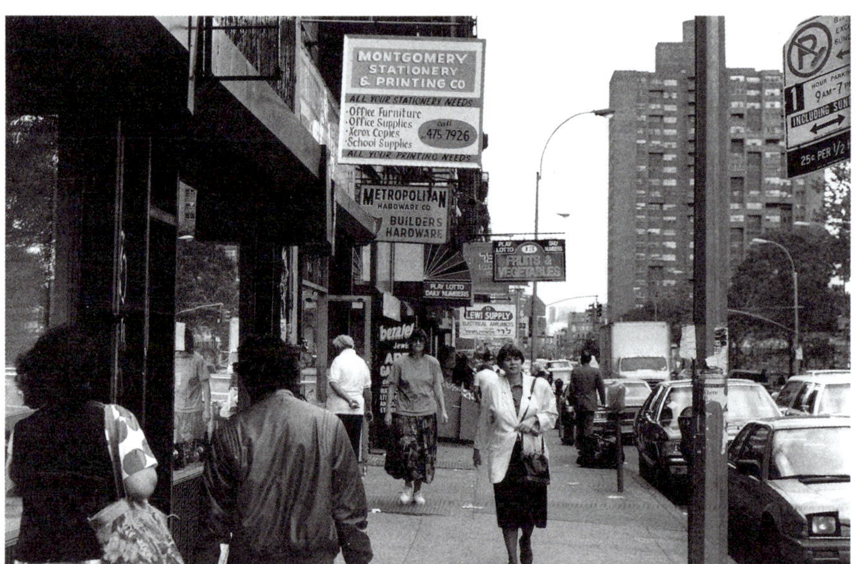

Lower Manhattan, 1990.

indispensable, smart and cool. I think that every artist's child, no matter how adored they were—and I was adored—knows the ghostly feeling of watching your parents make work. No matter how much they love you, there is always a part of them you don't have access to, the part reserved for the great mystery of their artistic life. Art is more than a profession, and it has the power to take your parent away, if not in body then in mind, and no child really likes that even if they admire it. And while my parents always let me spend hours in their studios, if they were working a kind of church-like hush fell over the scene and I felt them drift up and away. It was the part of my mother that was the most magical, and also the part I knew the least. But on that day, with her hands holding the dental floss like the strings on a puppet, I was both her child and her collaborator. We still collaborate—in a sense it opened a trap door that never closed.

Looking at the series now, almost 30 years later, I am struck by its genius—the way that Aura turns children, both so unaware and so hyper-attuned, into both props and creators, objects and fully formed creatures. The pictures respect the autonomy of children while also demanding that they submit to the whims of adults. There is something both haunting and hilarious about the photos—Carmen as a Tony Oursler, peeking out from a fleshy donut. Marilyn Minter's Willa, freckled with a bagel. Amy Sillman turns Isaac into a demented cartoon, part child superhero and part abstraction. It's also a very giving series—Aura making the space for other artists to express themselves within her work (not the norm) and for the children they love to claim a place in that too. I remember lots of these kids from the neighborhood, where we'd recognize each other in the throngs of chatty grownups, catching eyes through our parents' sea of black-panted legs. It makes me emotional, thinking of a time and place that was so particular to grow up in—Soho in the 80s and 90s—that is technically there but will never exist again, converted as it has been from artists' community to Mall of the Americas. Back then, your parents saw everyone you knew on the street on Saturday—and you saw their kids—and whether they liked each other or not they had this grand mission in common.

In a review of Aura's show in *Time Out New York*, Robert Mahoney said, "It seems that Laurie Simmons has become blinded by her own ego; she thought it would be funny to present Lena as one of her signature puppets. Finally, what mother would let Mike Kelley anywhere near her daughter?"

It's hilarious for me to read now, not only because it seems oddly conservative for a downtown art critic—Mike Kelley's imagination would have been a gift to any child, and the reviewer talks about artists more like deviants who shouldn't be allowed to parent—but because he misses out on the central thesis: Aura (and my mother) weren't dressing us up like pageant girls (a much more harmful practice than having Mike Kelley smear your face with ghoulish paint). They were empowering us to be part of the process we saw every day—the same way they empowered us simply through the act of creating as women in that time in history. My mother showed me I could be an artist, but Aura showed me that I had a subject—it wasn't me, exactly, but I was in there, standing in front of the bathroom mirror, figuring out how to look like someone or something else.

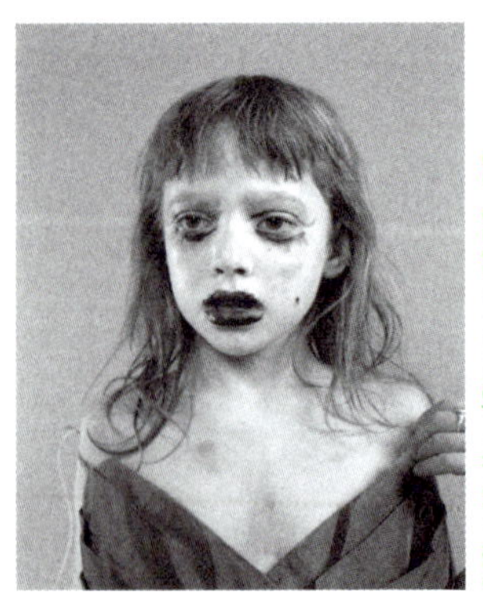

Mike Kelley/Carmen, 1996–98, from *Who Am I? What Am I? Where Am I?* Unprinted photograph.

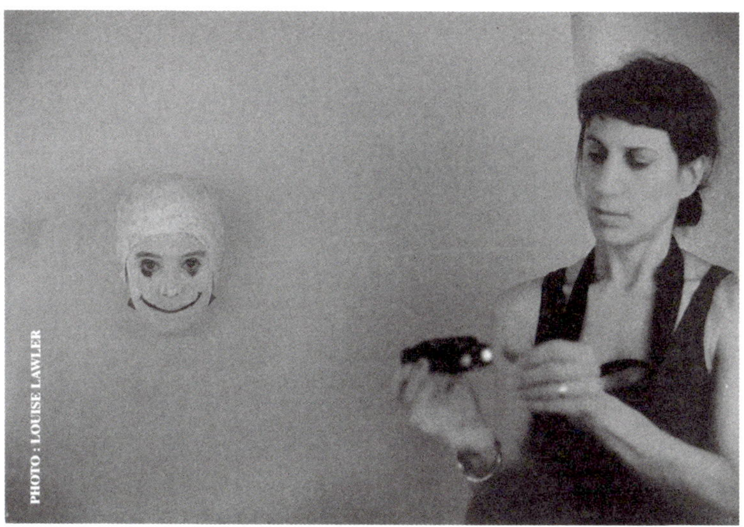

Announcement for *Who Am I? What Am I? Where Am I?* at Windows, Brussels, Belgium, 1998.

When we think of "private performances," the phrase often describes what we do in the safety of our homes, actions we take for ourselves without the judgmental gaze of others. If there is an audience, it might be a mirror, or someone who shares in our domestic space such as a lover or a caregiver. In early interventions engaging both performance work and media in the 1970s, artists such as Dara Birnbaum and Adrian Piper radically brought these clandestine gestures into public view. These artists frequently played with the expectations of gender and racial identity to explore what it meant to be "seen" by a camera and the unknown audience which existed beyond—long before the dominance of social media. Two photographic series by Aura Rosenberg, *Head Shots* (1991–96) and *Who Am I? What Am I? Where Am I?* (2008–ongoing), address private performances that might seem wildly disparate in their initial concepts, but which clearly share her values of collaboration and agency in working with her subjects and expand upon ideas of what constitutes performance for the camera.

In *Head Shots*, Rosenberg homes in on the expressions of men at the instance of orgasm. While these images are unified formally as small-scale black-and-white prints, there is an incredible range derived from this simple prompt. Although the majority of these men appear alone, traces of a partner periodically make their way into the frame. The men appear in bed, outside, in public, possibly at work; they are naked, dressed, in costume; some look in twisted pain, others in ecstasy. These are expressions that the subjects may never see of themselves—in this moment of release, they could also be

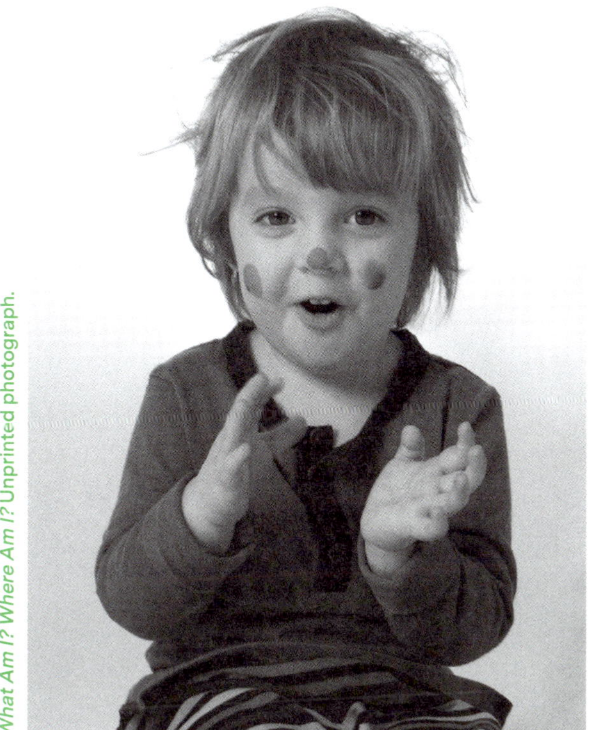

Lawrence Weiner/Henry, 2008, from *Who Am I? What Am I? Where Am I?* Unprinted photograph.

holding back, exaggerating, or perhaps faking it all together. Despite the intimate situation, Rosenberg was friends with only some of the subjects; in some cases, she did not even take the photograph. Yet, the conditions she created complemented the desire these men had to be seen—but not *exposed*. And because *we* know *they* know they are being photographed, it causes us less discomfort to partake in this voyeuristic position.

The adult men of *Head Shots* are understood as making a choice to render themselves more vulnerable or indulge in exhibitionist fantasy; the children in *Who Am I? What Am I? Where Am I?* are often read as powerless subjects forced to work at the whims of professional artists. For this ongoing

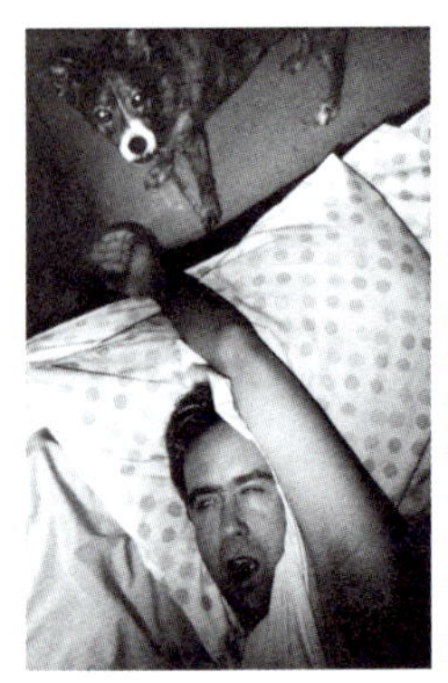

Head Shots (TO), 1991–96.
Gelatin silver print, 12 × 16 in.

series, Rosenberg was initially inspired by children's face-painting, and asked artist friends to collaborate with children which could include their own, Rosenberg's daughter Carmen, and the children of friends. Many of the works do take face-painting as a starting point, but others become more elaborate and recognizable manifestations of the artist's work, such as *Laurie Simmons/Lena* (1996–98) or *Tony Oursler/Carmen* (c. 2000). Like the portraits of *Head Shots*, these photographs recognize the face as a locus of personality; many artists chose to obscure them completely, perhaps in response to how we understand these subjects to be undeniably authentic, incorruptible. There are no forced child-model smiles here, only reflections of deeper emotions such as confusion and compliancy that come with the serious considerations of their role.

The title of this series points to how "make believe" is of great emotional and psychological importance to children in processing the adult world, and Rosenberg has remarked on how this collaboration re-introduced the element of play into a professional artist's work, allowing all three parties involved to break out of conventional roles. Yet "make believe" is almost never referred to as performance because it is an intrinsic part of childhood, and most commonly shared between children and their family, or other children, instead of a "public." The title of *Head Shots*, in contrast, is shared with the term for the highly regimented portraits performers use to get hired for gigs. These series cannily demonstrate the entanglement of values and assumptions in the relationship between the camera, self-representation, and an artist's subject. Our contemporary understanding of the photographic image has moved far beyond its conveyance of veracity; it is equally, or arguably even more so, associated with the liberation from that truth through its power to transform our behavior.

In "The Performativity of Performance Documentation" (2006), scholar Philip Auslander disputes the concept that the "documentary" mode of photography—evidence of an event that was performed for an audience—is more truthful than the "theatrical" mode of performance for the camera. Arguing against the "you had to be there" doctrine that accompanies the ephemerality of performance, he assigns such importance to the photograph as to write, "The act of documenting an event as a performance is what constitutes it as such." Continuing on to dispute the importance of the live audience as witnesses, he writes:

> Perhaps the authenticity of the performance document resides in its relationship to its beholder rather than to an ostensibly originary event: perhaps its authority is phenomenological rather than ontological.... These pleasures are available from the

> documentation and therefore do not depend on whether an audience witnessed the original event.... It may well be that our sense of the presence, power, and authenticity of these pieces derives not from treating the document as an indexical access point to a past event but from perceiving the document itself *as a performance* that directly reflects an artist's aesthetic project or sensibility and for which we are the present audience.[13]

Even if Rosenberg's photographs fall squarely into the "theatrical" mode of photography, Auslander's use of "pleasures" here applies to how, in our reception of these series, we are invited to focus on the experience of viewing, and the unresolved feelings provoked from that experience. The photographs are not merely proof of mundane or exceptional private performances. Rosenberg's approach is equally invested in the arc of negotiations as the final result; as we study these static images, we can imagine the conversations, the cajoling, the trust, the process, and the potentially messy aftermath. Rather than furthering divisions between authoritative roles on either side of Rosenberg's camera, the images compel us to recognize the complex desire for performance in the in-between spaces of the everyday.

13 Philip Auslander, "The Performativity of Performance Documentation," *Performance Art Journal* 84 (2006): 1–10

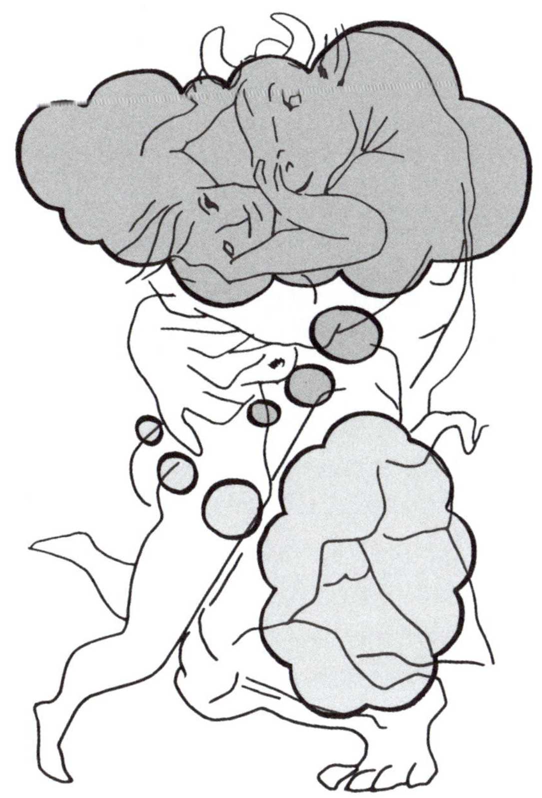

You'll Never Know How Much Your Words Mirror My Thoughts, 2021. Lenticular print, 71 × 47 in.

In Wilhelm Jensen's novella *Gradiva: A Pompeian Fantasy* (1903), archeologist Norbert Hanold becomes so enthralled by a young woman represented on a Roman bas-relief that he travels to Pompeii after dreaming of her walking its pebbled streets shortly before the eruption of Mount Vesuvius. During the otherworldly midday hours, Hanold encounters Gradiva in dreamy flesh, later discovering that the girl in the marble relief was, in fact, his childhood neighbor, Fräulein Bertgang, for whom he felt an overwhelming desire he couldn't face, thus unconsciously congealing her into a statue.[14]

Like Jensen, Aura Rosenberg has a wondrous sense for the passions set in stone. In 2019, she completed *Statues Also Fall In Love*, a series of lenticular prints in which classical sculptures transform into pornographic images that hold similar poses. The idea came to her while shooting a film with a child actress whom she observed enacting a conversation between the figures of ill-starred lovers König Wilhelm III and Königin Luise at the Tiergarten in Berlin as if she could hear their petrified lament. The girl's magical ear opened Rosenberg's eye to the fiery kernel of the stone, like the vision she had when she started her sculptural series *The Dialectical Porn Rock* (1989–93). In it, she decoupaged porn photographs onto rocks and took them back to nature, bringing to mind the lust-ridden, bucolic rendezvous of Greek gods on Mount Olympus.

Sigmund Freud was fascinated with Jensen's story and dedicated to it a famous psychoanalytic

14 See Wilhelm Jensen, *Gradiva: A Pompeiian Fancy* (Amsterdam: Leopold Classic Library, 2015).

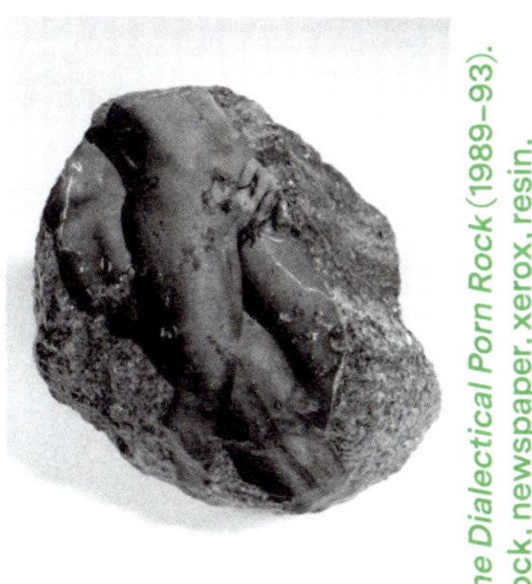

The Dialectical Porn Rock (1989–93). Rock, newspaper, xerox, resin, dimensions variable.

study: *Delusion and Dream in Jensen's "Gradiva"* (1907). Among other insights in line with his magnum opus *The Interpretation of Dreams* (1900), he found the burial of Pompeii, in which elements become at once inaccessible and preserved, a perfect analogy for repression of unseemly drives—a hardly coincidental choice on Jensen's part.[15] The city's excavations during the 18th century shed light on the bustling erotic life of the ancient Romans, revealing plentiful and marvelously preserved frescoes of copulating couples, and well-endowed polychromatic sculptures of gods. This scandalous discovery contested the Neoclassical view of the Classical world put forward first and foremost by Johann Winckelmann. Art historian Reginald Wilenski refers to this as "Greek prejudice"—the idea that Greek and Roman cultures were as restrained, white, and pure as the colorlessness presumed of their statues.[16] In *The Birth of Tragedy from the Spirit of Music* (1872) Friedrich Nietzsche questioned this premise—which had come to define the Western

15 Sigmund Freud, *Delusions and Dreams in Jensen's "Gradiva,"* (London: The Hogarth Press, S. E.), 40.

16 See Elizabeth Prettejohn, *The Modernity of Ancient Sculpture: Greek Sculpture and Modern Art from Winckelmann to Picasso* (London: I. B. Tauris, 2012), 174.

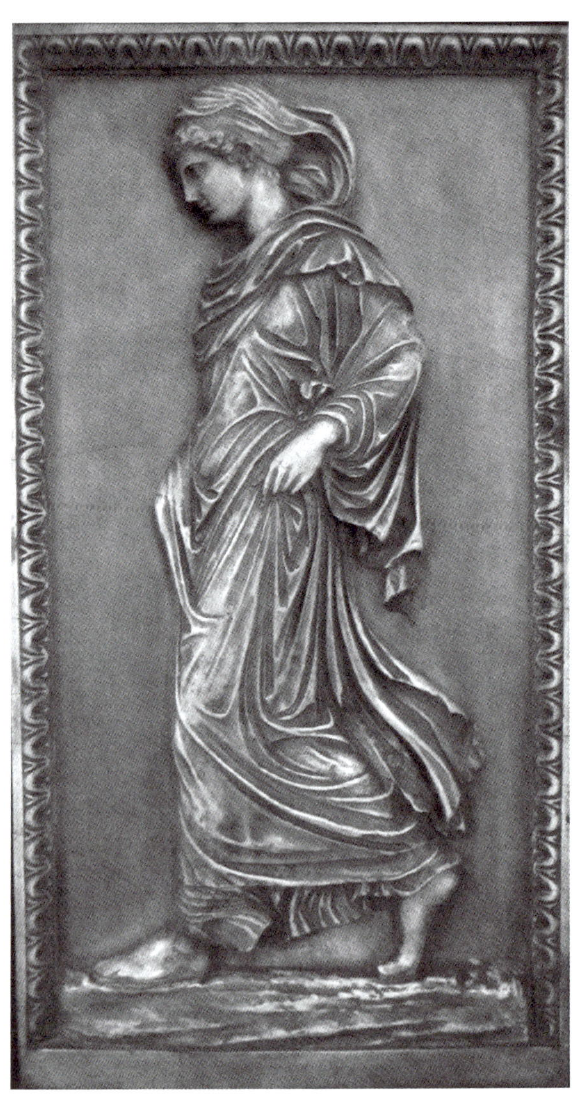

Unknown artist, Relief of Gradiva, c.1908. Bronze Cast. Freud Museum, London.

artistic tradition. Nietzsche identified two opposing tensions in our culture: the Apollonian (idealized, rational, monochromatic) and the Dionysian (base, erotic, colored). Unlike Neoclassicists, he didn't regard classical culture as the epitome of the Apollonian, but saw Greek tragedy as the interplay of both forces, thus advocating a more integral and profound view of the human condition.[17] Therefore, the burial of Pompeii could be interpreted as the metaphorical repression of the Dionysian—which resulted in a Western culture characterized by idealism, grandiosity, and universalism.

Throughout her career, Rosenberg's oeuvre has aligned with Nietzsche's defense of the integration of this polarity in art, consciously or intuitively keeping a bond with Greek culture that recurs in her work. Indeed, turning noble marble sculptures into found porn is a counter-Winckelmannian gesture, even more so considering that some of the figures shift into people of color—which opens up a very contemporary debate on the *whiteness* of the Western, Eurocentric tradition. Likewise, *The Astrological Ways*, a series of body imprints that she made different versions of since the 80s, is inspired by a famous black-light poster from 1972 in which men and women posed in sexual positions representing the signs of the Hellenistic zodiac. Interestingly, her series *Scene/Obscene* (2013) refers to classical drama. These paintings of photographs belonging to the so-called "Golden Age" of pornography (the 70s and early 80s) focus explicitly on the concept of the "obscene" in Greek theater—the elements outside the "scene" or action.[18] The source material depicts salacious acts in very specific settings: usually living rooms or bedrooms adorned with the colorful geometric patterns of the time,

17 See Friedrich Nietzsche, *The Birth of Tragedy* (New York: Dover Publications, 1995).

18 This etymology is put forward by D. H. Lawrence in his 1929 paper *Pornography and Obscenity*. Nevertheless, the Oxford English Dictionary says the etymology is obscure. See David Isaacson, "Dilemmas in Balancing a University Literature Collection," in *Selecting Materials for Library Collections*, ed. Linda S. Katz (New York, London: Routledge, 2004), 6.

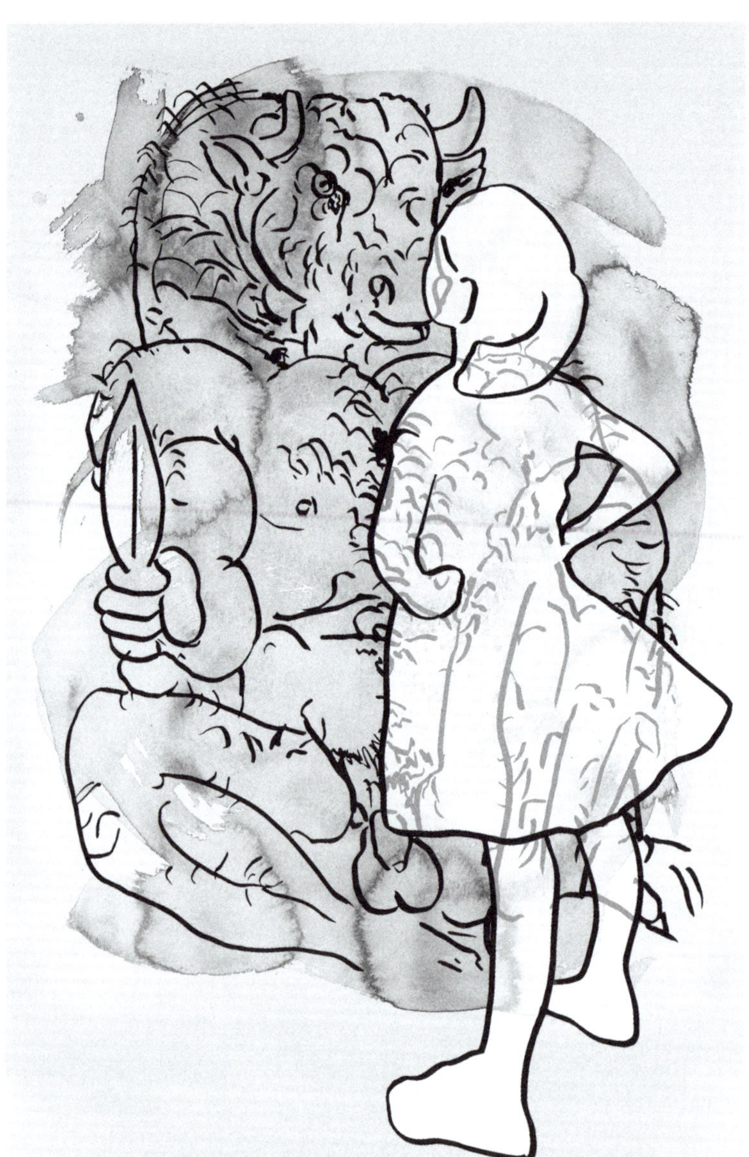

You Seem to Look Right Through Me, 2021. 3D Lenticular print, 71 × 47 in.

Moroccan decor, and where liquor bottles and tacky glassware abound. These details are the true protagonists of this series, and in them, curtains play a star "obscene" role explicitly evoking theater representations. Another direct allusion to classical antiquity can be found in her 2022 lenticular prints dedicated to two popular—and sometimes controversial—sculptures: Arturo Di Modica's *Charging Bull* (1989) and Kristen Visbal's *Fearless Girl* (2017). Almost 30 years after Di Modica surreptitiously dropped his bull in front of the New York Stock Exchange, Visbal confronted it with a defiant girl, creating a destabilizing semantic plateau for the new sculptural couple, which was dissolved after Di Modica won his long battle to remove the new, unwanted partner. Before their estrangement, Rosenberg sensed the silent yet charged dialogue between the bull and the girl, perceiving in them the echo of Ovid's myth of the Minotaur and Ariadne, in which the human-hungry beast dies at the hands of Ariadne's beloved Theseus. Nevertheless, in Rosenberg's fantasy, this story is traversed by Cortázar's and Borges's reinterpretations of the narrative, rendering the monster Ariadne's paramour, or a lonely soul who welcomes its murderous fate as a final redemption to its solitude.[19]

Apart from eroticism, Rosenberg's work has often tackled the topic of motherhood, for instance in A *Berlin Childhood* (1993–ongoing), inspired by Walter Benjamin's chronicle of his bourgeois upbringing in Berlin around 1900. In tandem with Benjamin's texts, Rosenberg began a documentation

19 Julio Cortázar's play *Los reyes* (1949) and Jorge Luis Borges' short story "La casa de Asterión" (1947).

of her own daughter's experiences growing up in Berlin a century later. *Who Am I? What Am I? Where Am I?* (1996–2008) is a series of photo collaborations between Rosenberg, another artist, and a child (often her own daughter Carmen). Her interest in both eroticism and fecundity is in line with the paramount role ascribed to women in Greek mythology as custodians of the continuity of the cosmos. Nevertheless, while Greek gods remain under the patriarchal rule of Zeus, Rosenberg inverts the power balance by gaining agency through her most efficient weapons: sensitivity and kindness. This unaccustomed position is manifest in *Head Shots* (1991–96), now a cult collection of photographs in which men in her social circle are portrayed seemingly mid-orgasm. These black-and-white prints are restrained and austere, and the men's surrendered countenances evoke the soulful erotic exposure of Bernini's *Ecstasy of Saint Theresa* (1647–52). When Rosenberg shot these portraits, men's beauty in this profound act of abandonment had not yet been deemed worthy of contemplation—the vulnerability it implies threatens certain understandings of masculinity. It is indeed a revolt against patriarchal canons through love and compassion.

One of the subjects of this series was Rosenberg's friend and collaborator Mike Kelley, whose oeuvre, like hers, often indulged in base materials and themes as a rebellion against the "Apollonian" heritage. In his text "Playing With Dead Things: On The Uncanny" (1994) he addresses the topic specifically, suggesting that this tradition sought to find essential and universal truths, while Surrealism and, later, Pop Art would effect a change of direction by examining the truthfulness of an image in relation to daily experience and cultural clichés. After psychoanalyst Janine Chasseguet-Smirgel, he argues against the mendacity of idealization, and for a humbler truth—a position that Rosenberg, Kelley, and many artists of that generation such as John Miller, Paul McCarthy, or Jim Shaw, among others, could subscribe to. He unsurprisingly illustrates his argument with another reference to classical antiquity: a quote from Shakespeare's *Troilus and Cressida* (1602). In this play, and in line with Rosenberg's position, Shakespeare puts forward a satire of the supposed heroism of the Greek world, and advocates a more precarious and minor, yet more genuine, notion of beauty:

> Whilst some with cunning gild
> their copper crowns,
> With truth and plainness I do
> wear mine bare.[20]

20 Mike Kelley, "Playing with Dead Things: On the Uncanny," in *Foul Perfection: Essays and Criticism*, ed. John C. Welchman (Cambridge, MA: MIT Press, 2003), 80–81.

Images Animées de Désir: Aura Rosenberg's Lenticular Photographs

Bob Nickas

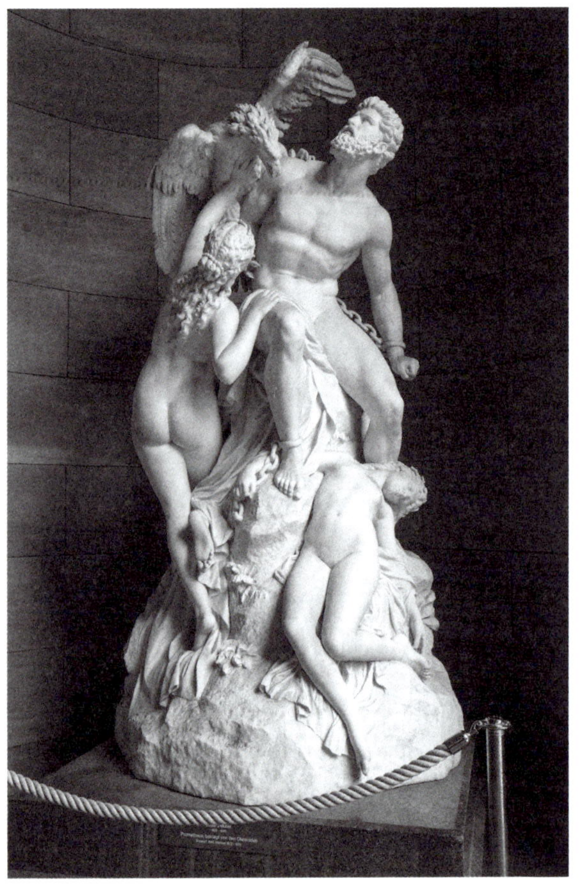

Prometheus Bound, 2019, from *Statues Also Fall in Love*. Lenticular print, 71 × 47 in.

What are animated images of desire? A still photographic image that we bring to life in our mind's eye? A figurative sculpture, a statue or a mannequin, that we similarly endow with movement, or even sentience, whether in a museum or in a shop window? Does this activity establish a libidinal space into which we project ourselves? Haven't we done this from an early age, from childhood, when imagination is set free, as we moved from the illustrations in comic books to cartoons on television or movies in the theater? And isn't a movie, a moving picture, a succession of still images projected at 24 frames per second, larger than life, the cinematic experience we have all shared, no less than a ritual in the dark? In Jean Cocteau's Surrealist film, *Le sang d'un poète* (*The Blood of a Poet*, 1930), a mouth that has been drawn by an artist, when transferred by him to that of a statue, white marble and female, played by the photographer Lee Miller, allows her, semi-animate and with eyes closed, to speak. This opening is preceded by a title that reads: "The sleeper seen from up close or the surprise of photography, or how I got caught in a trap of my own film." The artist, both in the film and Cocteau himself, is in a dream state, clearly, and film, moving pictures, is the surprise of photography—the medium, as if almost supernatural, by which still images and inanimate objects are brought to life. *Le sang d'un poète*, along with *Les statues meurent aussi* (*Statues Also Die*, Chris Marker and Alain Resnais, 1953), and *L'Année dernière à Marienbad* (*Last Year at Marienbad*, Resnais, 1961), where the actors are sometimes frozen, sculptural, and inanimate, may be brought to bear on Aura Rosenberg's series of lenticular photographs, *Statues Also Fall in Love*.

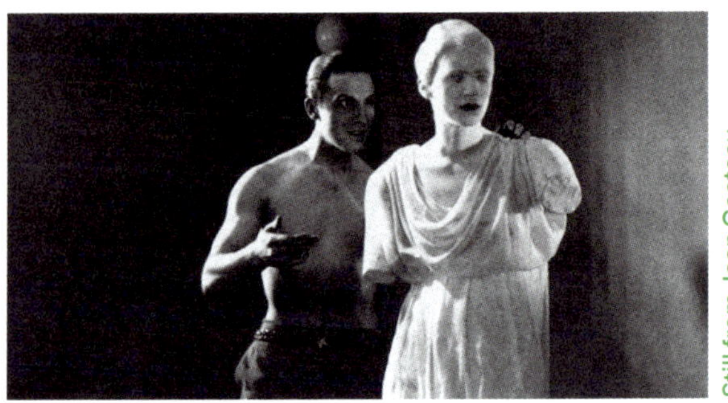

Still from Jean Cocteau, *The Blood of a Poet*, 1930.

Desire is not always for *itself*. There is desire for respect, for equality, enlightenment, liberation, and so on. Desire is not always corporeal, not a matter of lust, of physical want, but of what we need or require, and where this is contested, in the larger anatomical sense, within the body politic. The visual language to raise and articulate these debates may take the form of surrogates, body doubles—as in the movies, when one actor stands in for another, the star, in a scene involving danger or nudity. Many of the classical figures we encounter today are copies, based on earlier works, or composed of sculpted prosthetics, a lost limb, by way of restoration. The figure in marble, stone for flesh—antiquity from the vantage of the present mostly thought of as milky white—has not prevented offense or deterred violence; witness the many disfigured and headless statues throughout history, and its erasure, those destroyed in our time. Statues, as we ourselves identify them, are referred to as male and female—not forgetting the *Sleeping Hermaphroditus* in the Louvre, an embodiment which often elicits a double take among viewers—yet statues are neither. They have no gender. Still, in terms of forbidden fruit, well-placed folds of drapery and a fig leaf suggest propriety was meant to be maintained, and where all is bared, with male figures so-called, endowment is rarely if ever impressive. Sculpture is not pornographic; not even those works "made in heaven," leaving little to the imagination. (A philosophy not of the bedroom but of the marketplace.) The pornographic resides in the worlds of photography and literature, and even then it may not be prurient at all, more a matter of social and political critique, which is what it truly intends to arouse.

Aura Rosenberg, who works primarily in photography, has since 2018 photographed sculpture in New York's Metropolitan Museum, the Alte Nationalgalerie in Berlin, and Sanssouci, the summer palace built by Frederick the Great in Potsdam. Her subjects include many well-known from mythology: Cupid and Psyche, Aphrodite, Perseus and Medusa, who he decapitated. Rosenberg presents her photos as lenticulars, works in which two images have been overlaid so that as we pass by, an initially unseen second image is revealed. In this way she transforms, for example, Hercules into a Black man, and Fragilina, sculpted by Attilio Piccirilli in 1923, as a Black woman. Piccirilli believed that "every person has his own ideal of beauty stored away in his subconscious mind." In Rosenberg's transformation, fleeting but repeatable, this ideal opens more widely as it registers consciously. Within the doubled images of the lenticulars, she suggests as well that photography is only skin deep. Photographing *Fragilina* from behind and replacing the head with one turned subtly in the direction of her camera, the woman appears to be aware of us without any need to acknowledge our presence: a form of empowerment. With *Prometheus Bound*,

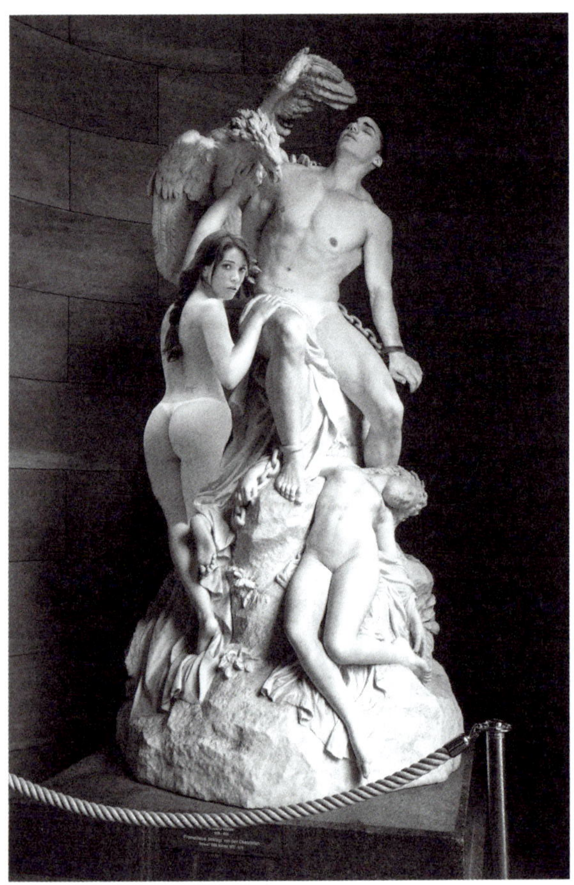

Prometheus Bound, 2019, from *Statues Also Fall in Love*. Lenticular print, 71 × 47 in.

Rosenberg's inserted female figure, unlike the sculpted one that reaches toward the devouring eagle, does return our gaze, to engage the otherwise passive viewer in the wild scene as it unfolds. She animates the figures and the action, implicating the viewers. She and we, mere mortals, are witness to the consequences for defying the gods, those who represent the law and administer its punishment. Rosenberg's images, do not always present the full figure of their sculptural subjects. At times she draws our attention, as hers was, to the face of a statue, in parallel to how it would be approached in a museum for closer examination. With *Lucretia*, based on a photograph of Philippe Bertrand's c. 1704 sculpture, depicting the suicide of Lucretia after her rape, the statue is only seen from the left breast up to the tilted head. We do not see that, in anguish, she has just thrust a knife into her chest; in close proximity she appears serene. Has the violence visited upon her, and that which was self-inflicted, been undone?

Passing before *Lucretia*, the marble face shifts to one human, with makeup and jewelry: dark eyelashes, bright lip gloss, and an earring. In this we are reminded that the classical sculpture which for centuries has been regarded as white marble, may at one time have been adorned with paint or gilding, and semi-precious stones. In other words, more lifelike, more naturalistic, less cold. White marble came to be seen as a sign of purity, praised as such, and not only in terms of aesthetics but ideologically. In monochrome, the human figure may be thought of as a person, flesh and blood, turned to stone. Modest renderings in clay from which life-size and monumental figurative marble sculptures would have been realized were based either on models posed in the studio, or on life drawings. Rosenberg, in a sense, allows the model or its surrogates to inhabit the image of the sculpture, to be immersed within it in the way the human form was thought to emerge from a block of raw stone. We wonder: from where does the artist draw her human actors? From models she herself has photographed, or appropriated from fashion advertising? As in past work, Rosenberg's source is commercial pornography, straight and gay, representations as staged as those from life and publicity. Her photos, always black-and-white, carefully aligning the contours of the inserted image to the body or face of the sculpture, make the internal shift of the doubled image nearly seamless, while the representation appears documentary up until the second reveal. These images play off of and simultaneously undermine the ideal of "purity," particularly as its human subjects have been liberated from what may be considered impure and exploitative acts. At the same time, the artist summons and amplifies the eroticism implicit in much of classical art.

There are instances of levity in this series, most notably when Rosenberg, although she has not added human figures or faces to those of the sculptures photographed, suggests sentience and human desire. In *Hercules and Aphrodite*, the two statues are paired in the photograph, with Aphrodite in the foreground turned slightly to the right, where Hercules stands a few feet away, seemingly lost in thought. The reveal in the lenticular is a stylized cartoon bubble over his head. In it, the naked Aphrodite is seen from behind, from his exact point of view in the photo, beholding her as an object of beauty and sexual desire—attributes for which the Greek goddess was revered.

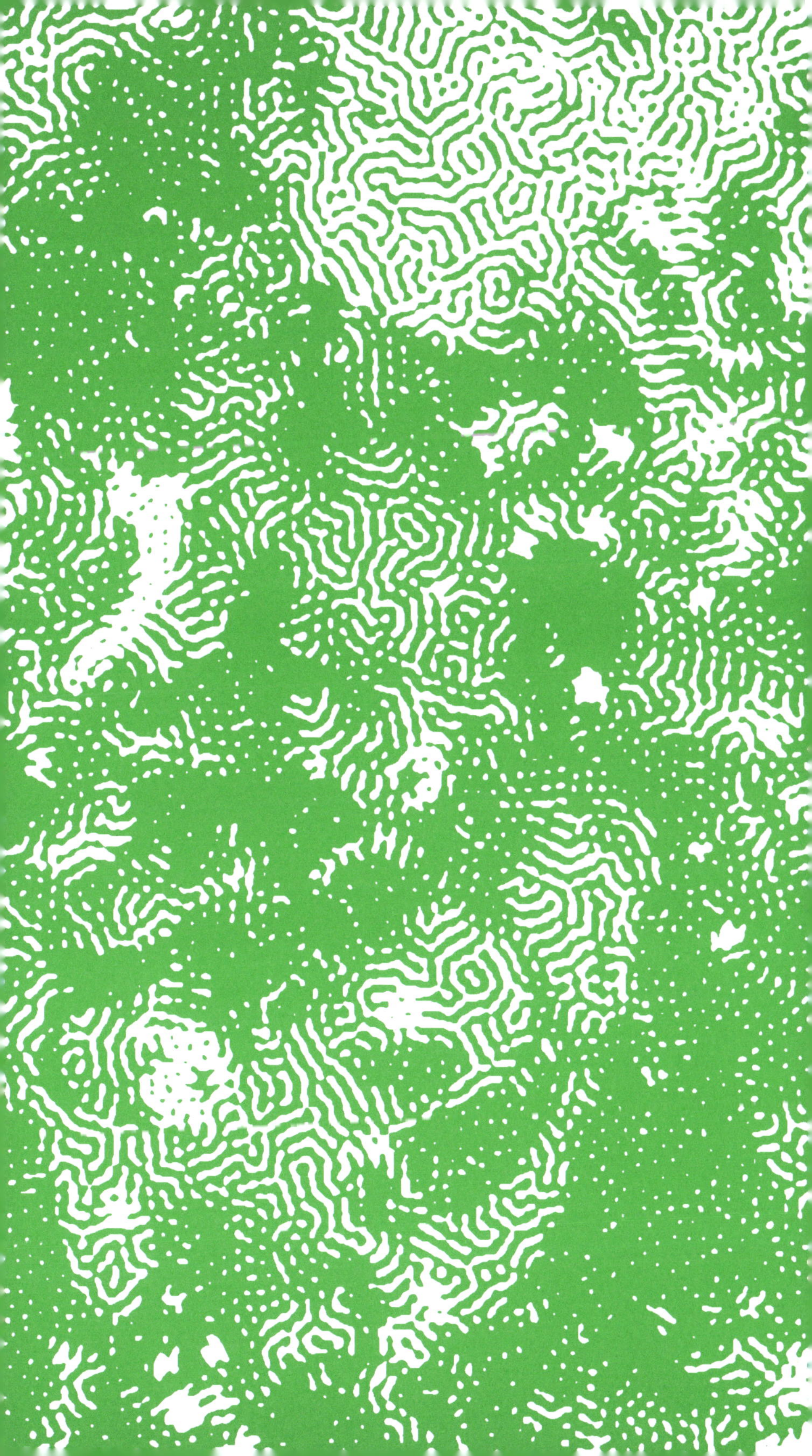

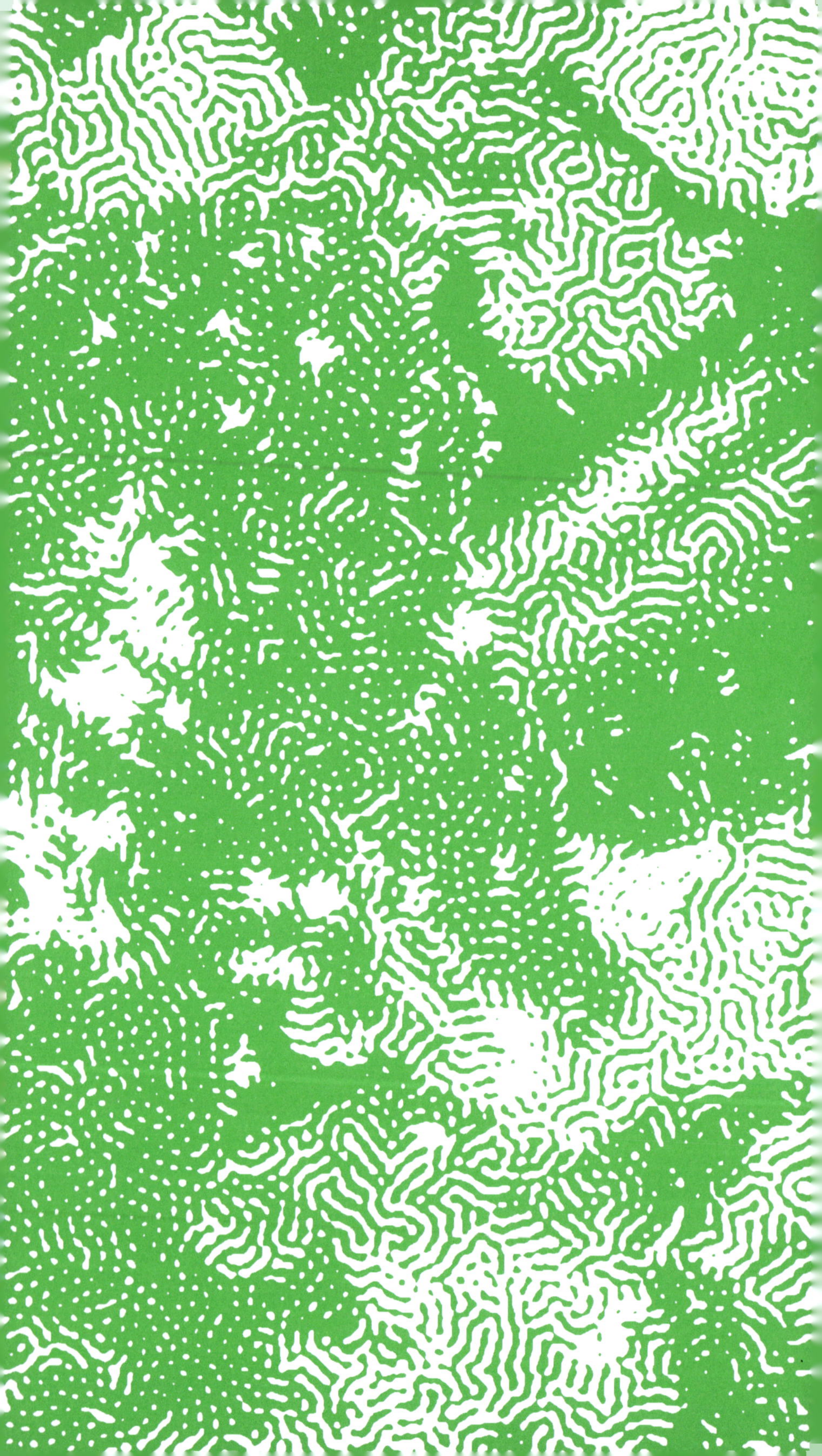

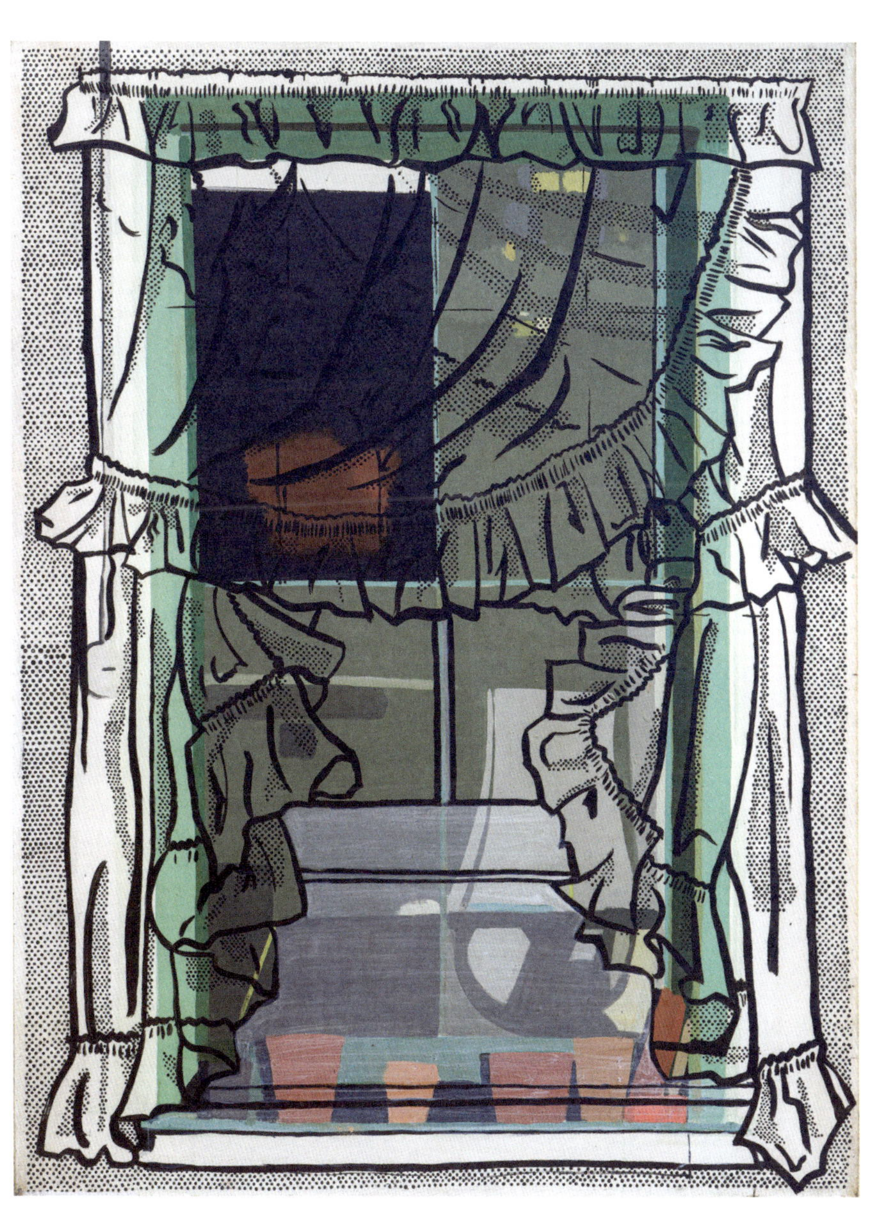

The Window
c. 1975. Acrylic on canvas.
77¼ × 57 in.

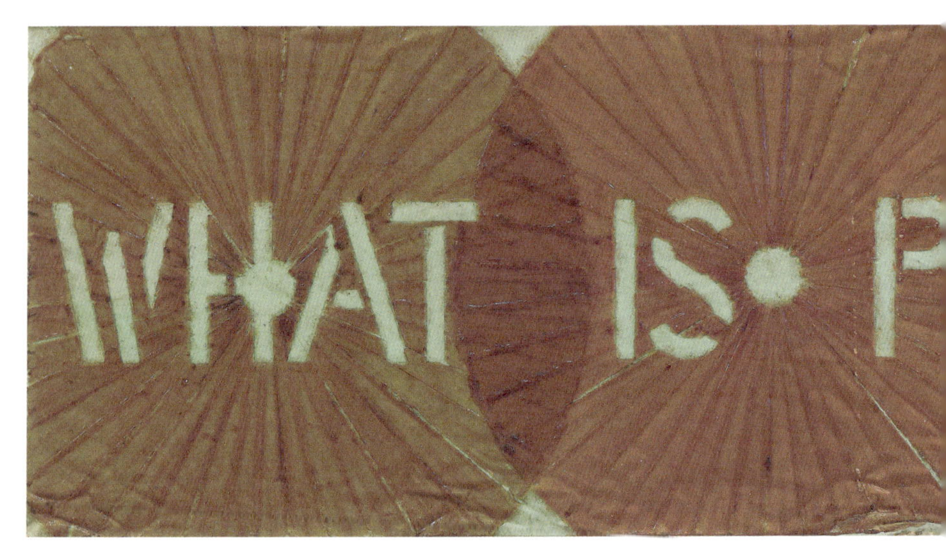

What Is Psychedelic
1973. Acrylic and acrylic gel on canvas.
32 × 120 in.

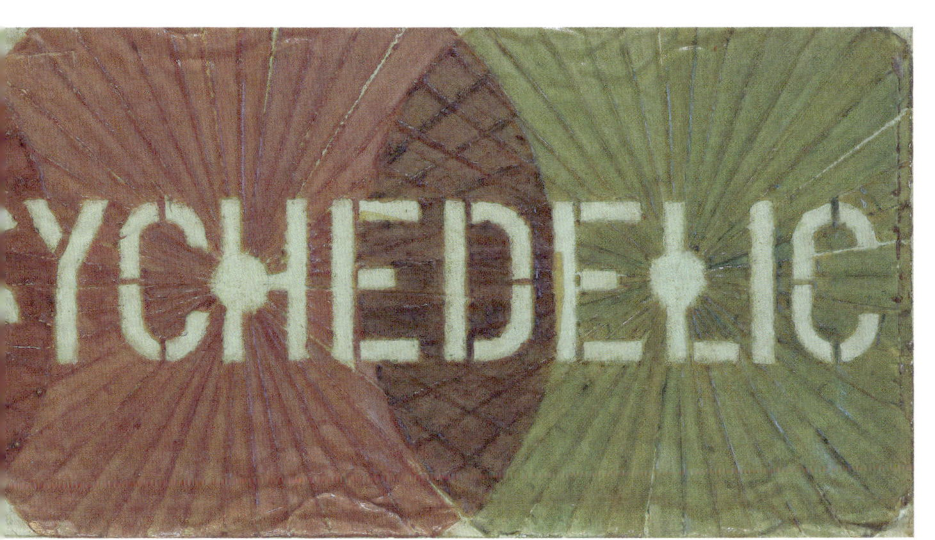
YCHEDELIC

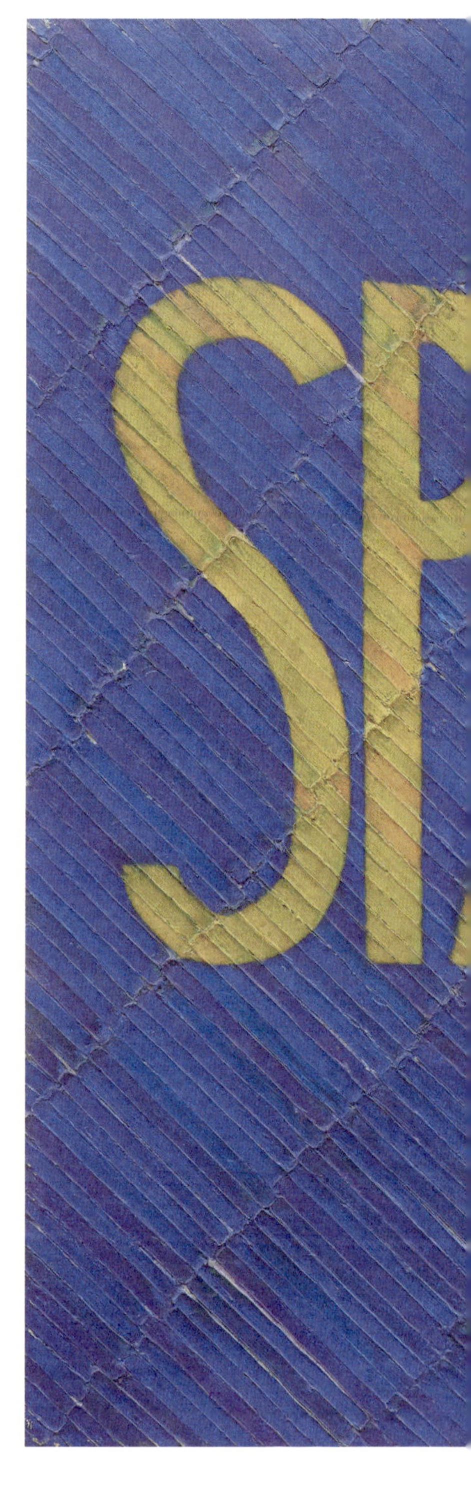

SPACED
1973. Acrylic and modeling paste on canvas.
75 × 77 in.

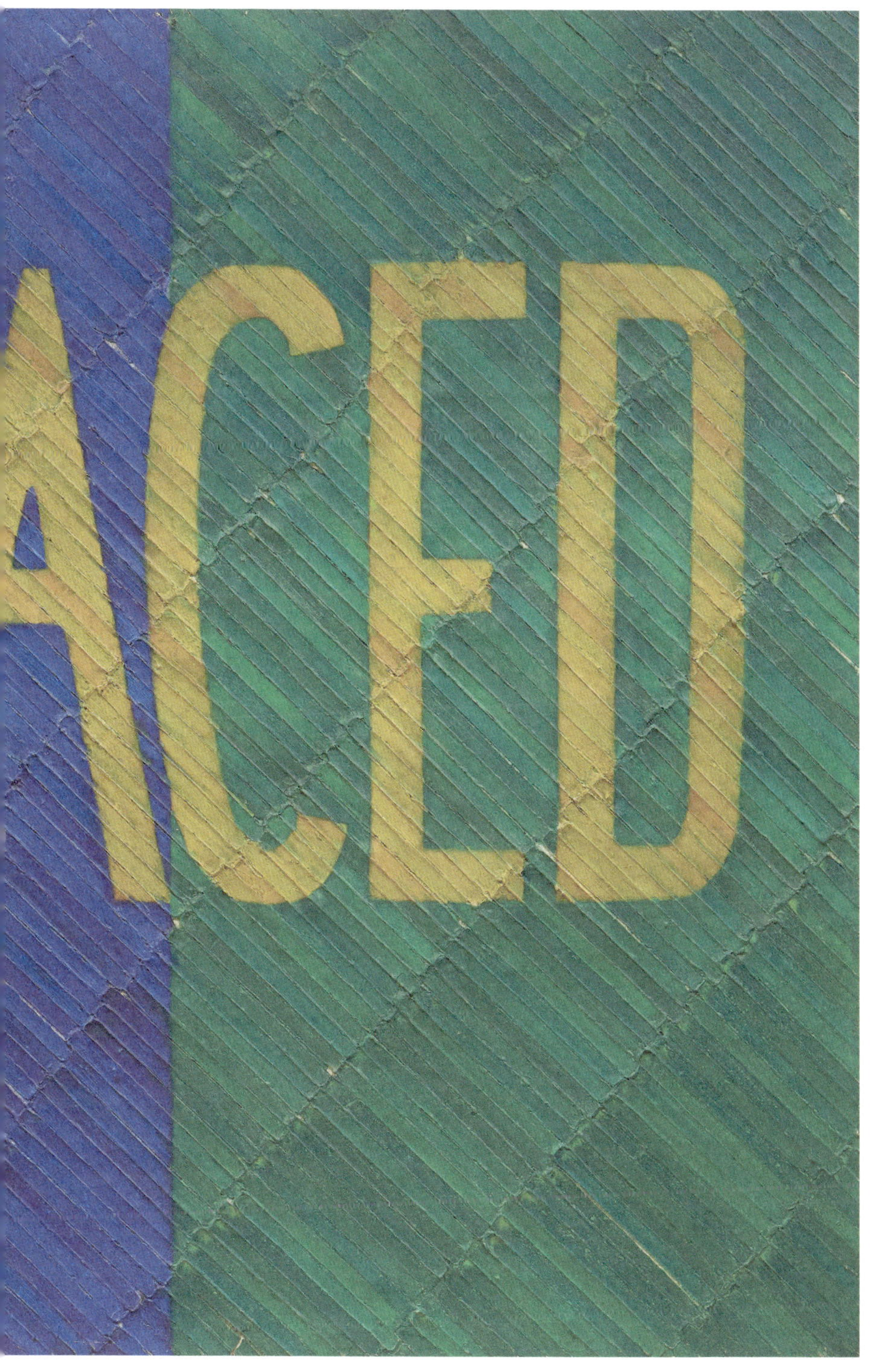
ACED

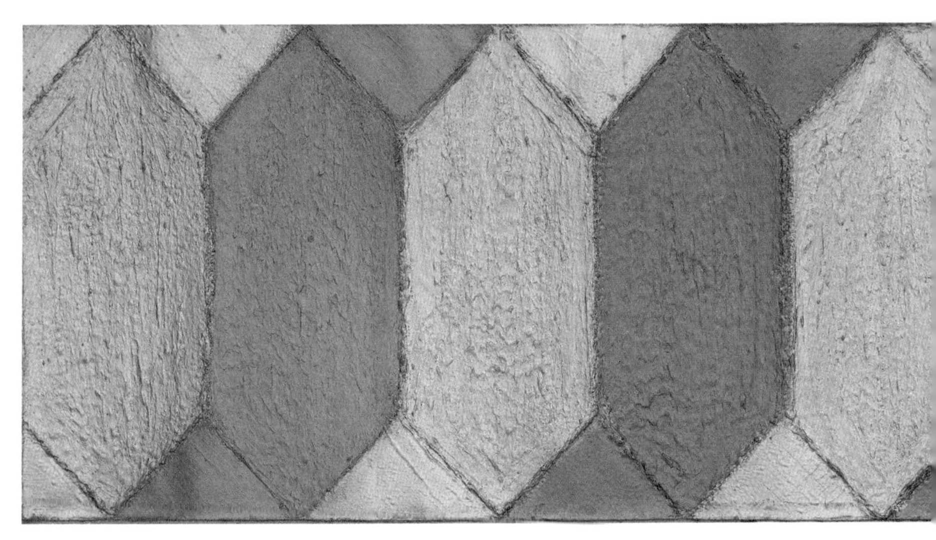

Headboard
c. 1973. Acrylic and aluminum pigment on canvas.
24 × 89 in.

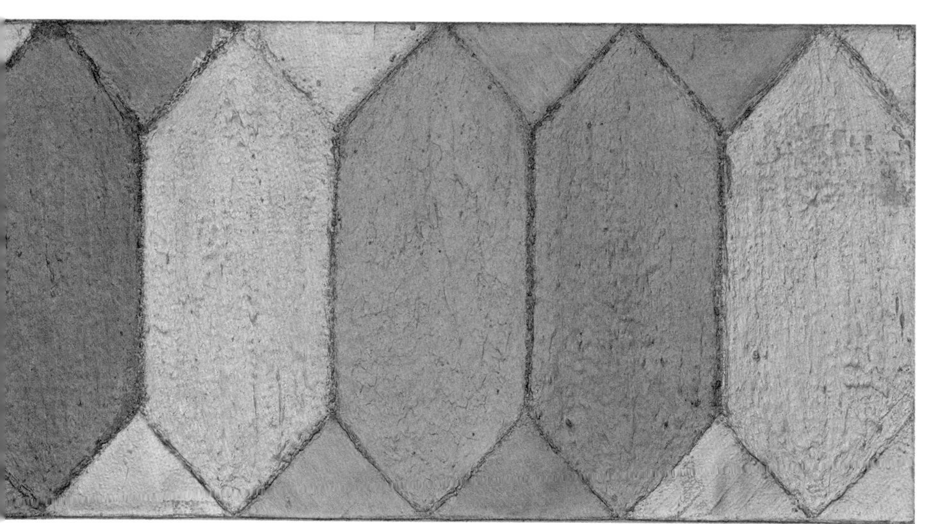

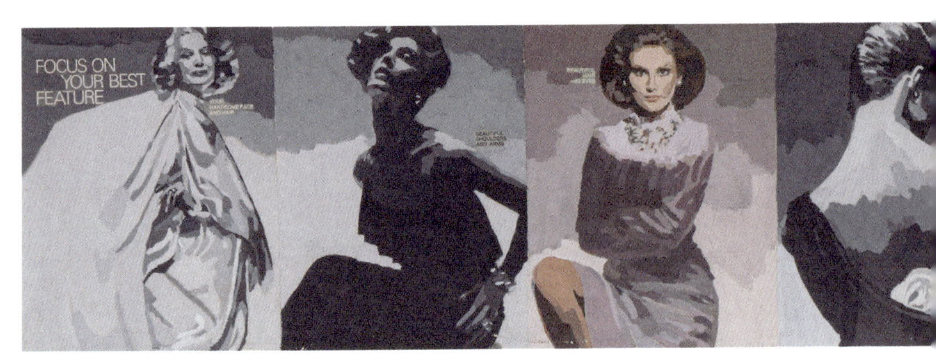

Focus On Your Best Feature
n.d. Acrylic over newspaper clippings on canvas.
14 × 74 in.

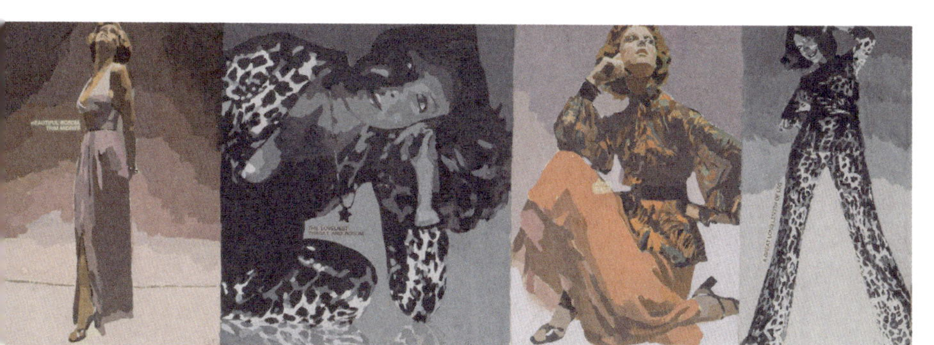

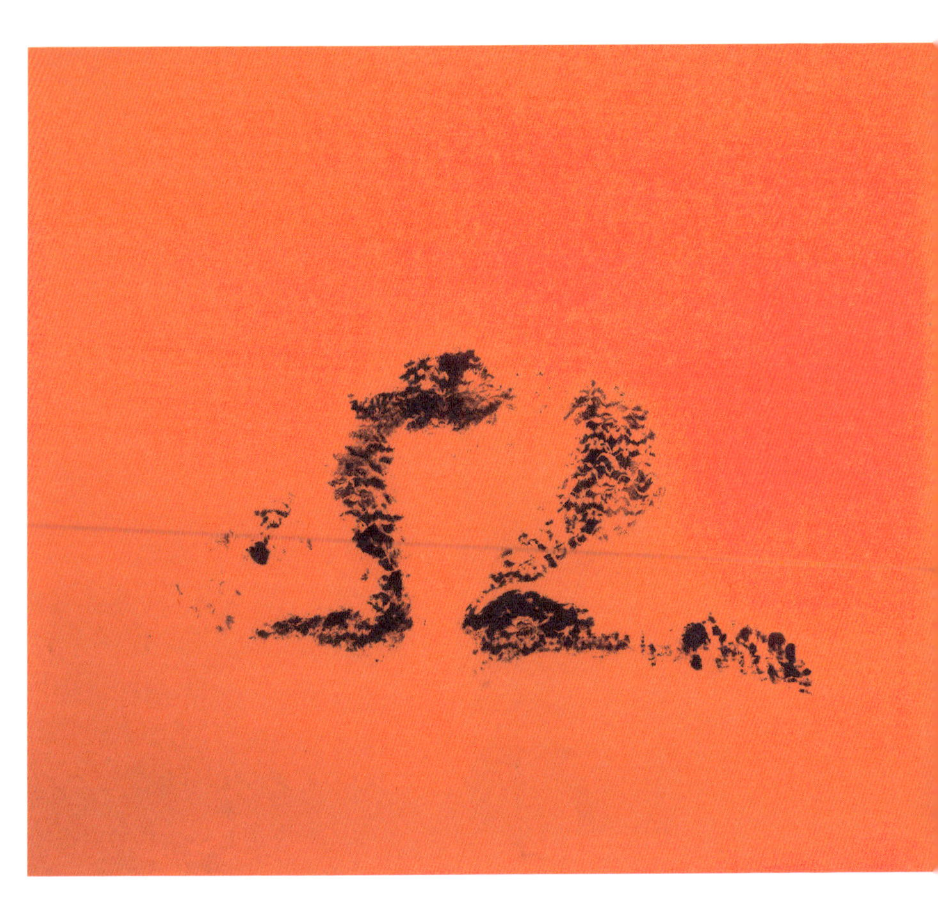

Calligraphs
c. 1984–85. Acrylic body imprints on vinyl.
48 × 118 in.

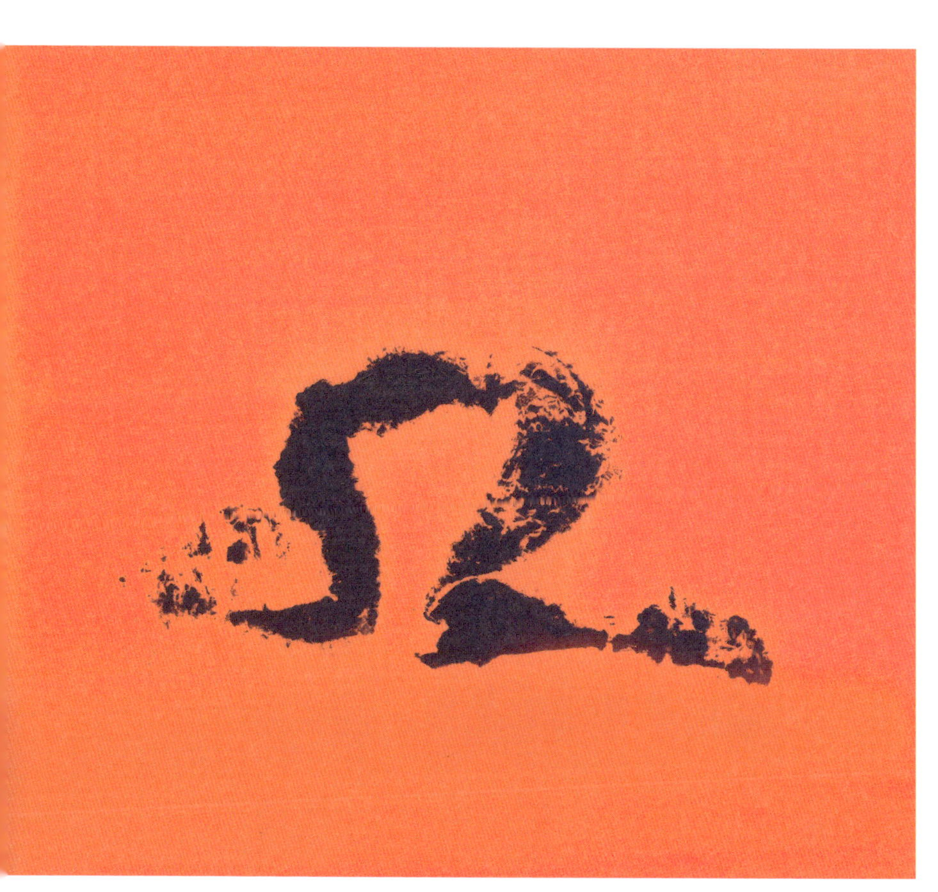

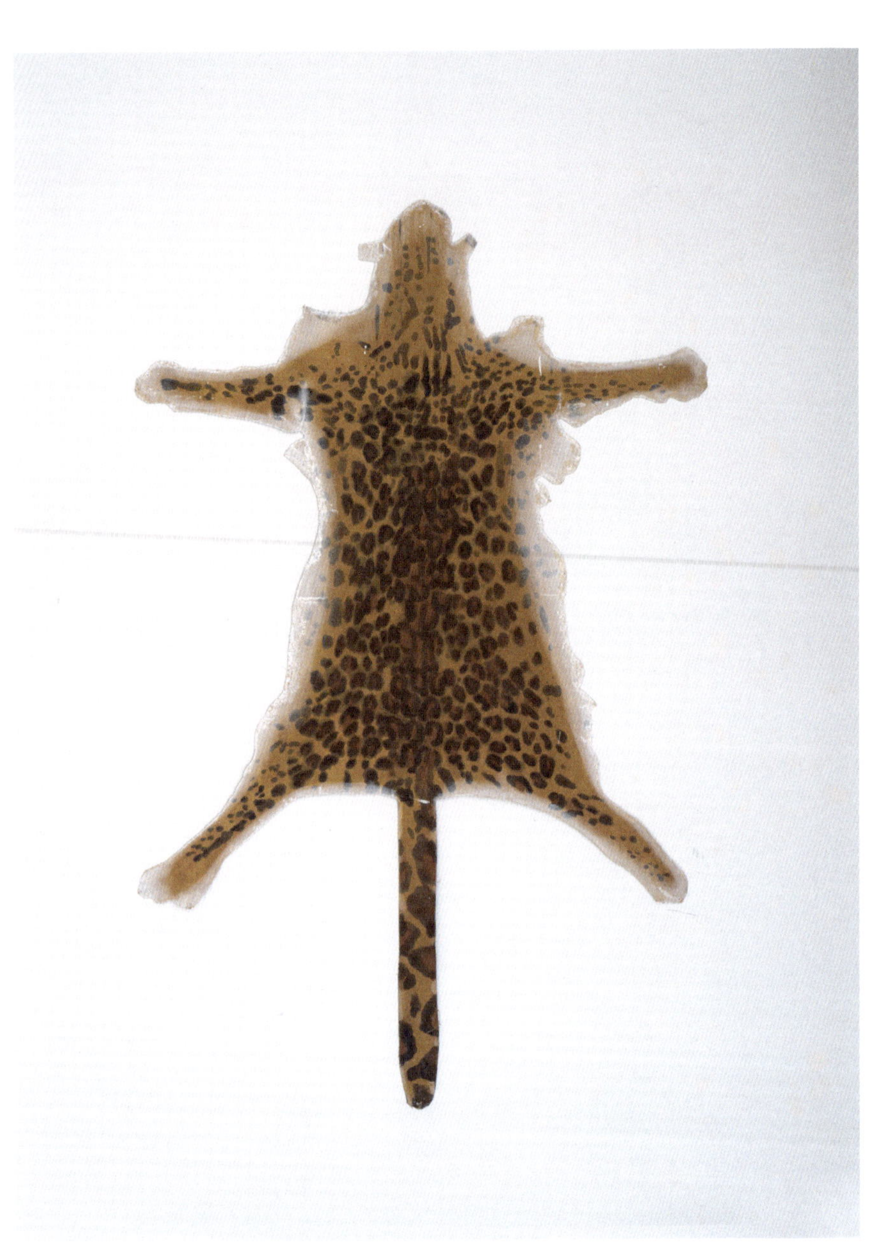

Leopard Skin
1982. Acrylic on canvas.
81 × 50 in.

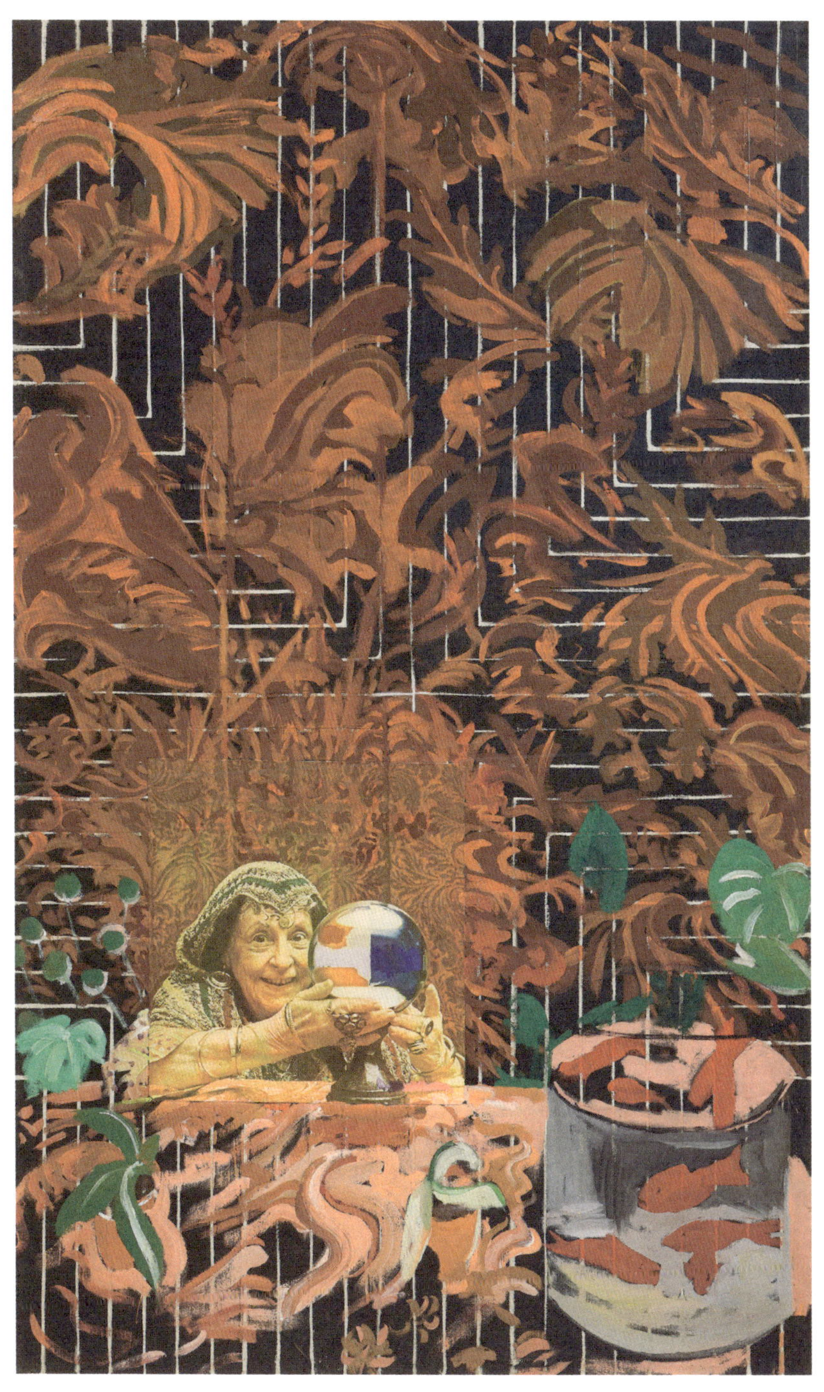

He Who Asks Fortunetellers the Future Unwittingly Forfeits an Intimation of Coming Events
c. 1970s. Acrylic and found poster on canvas.
87½ × 53 in.

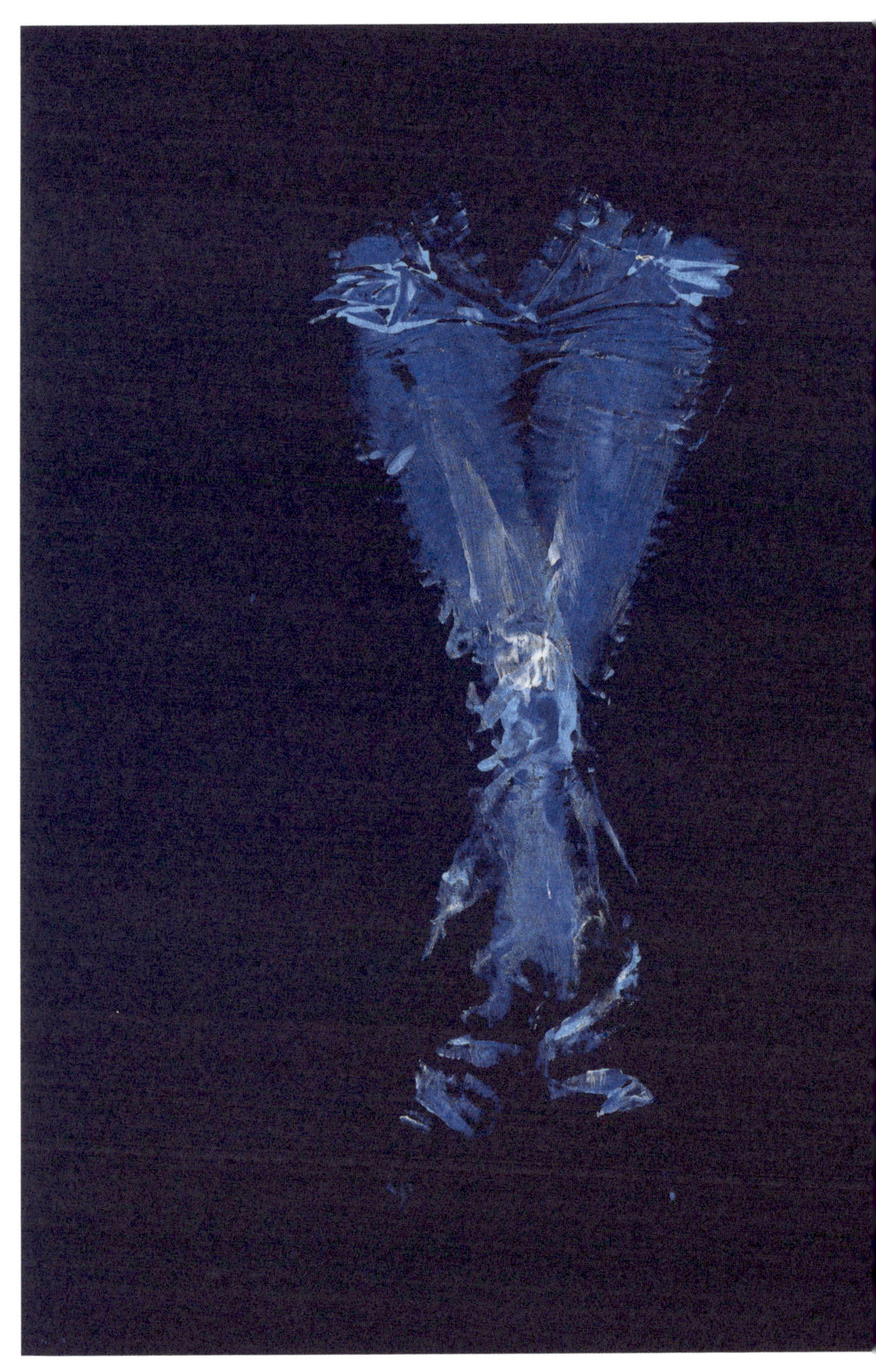

Untitled
n.d. Acrylic jean imprints on black velvet.
58½ × 67 in.

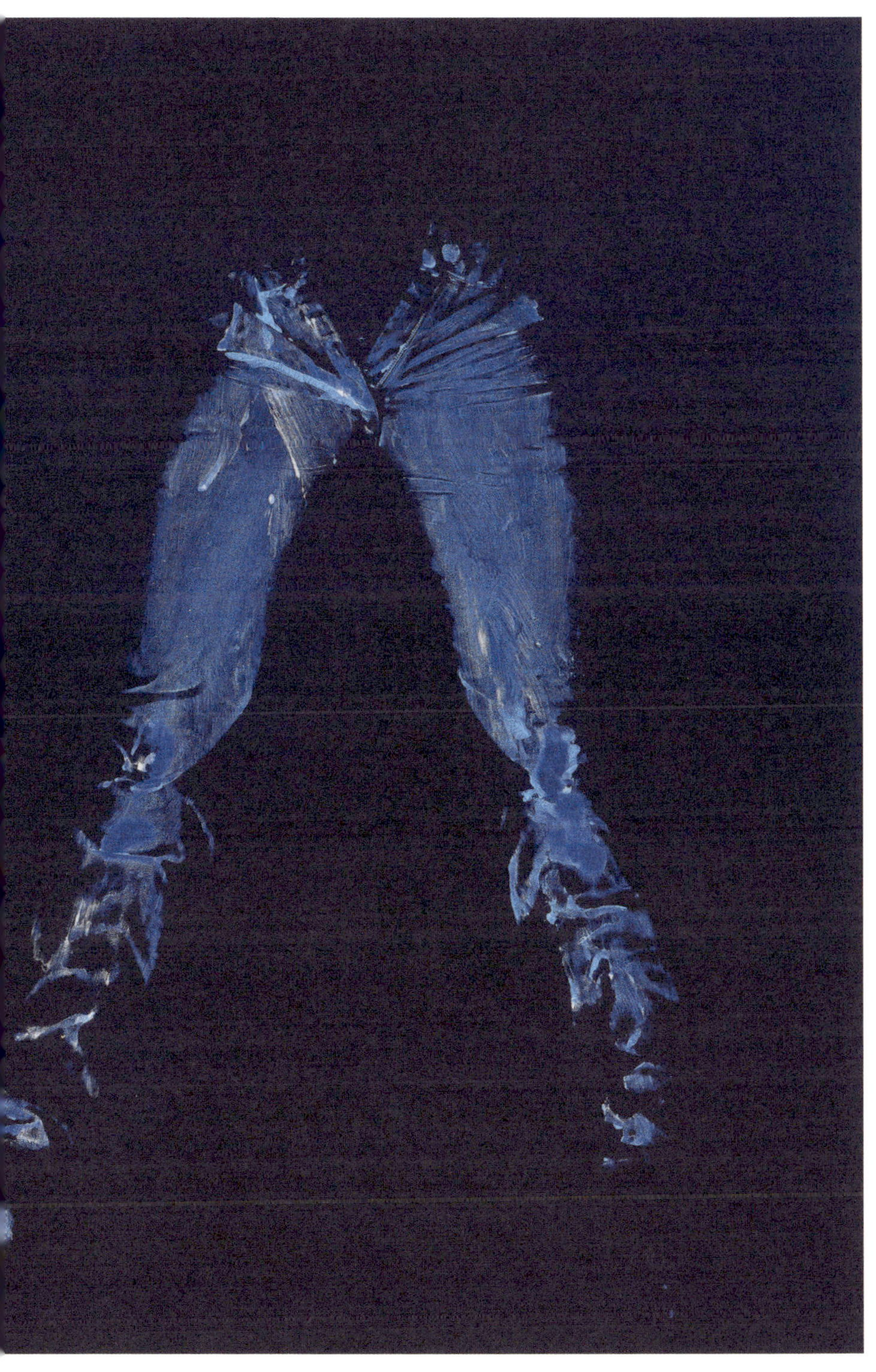

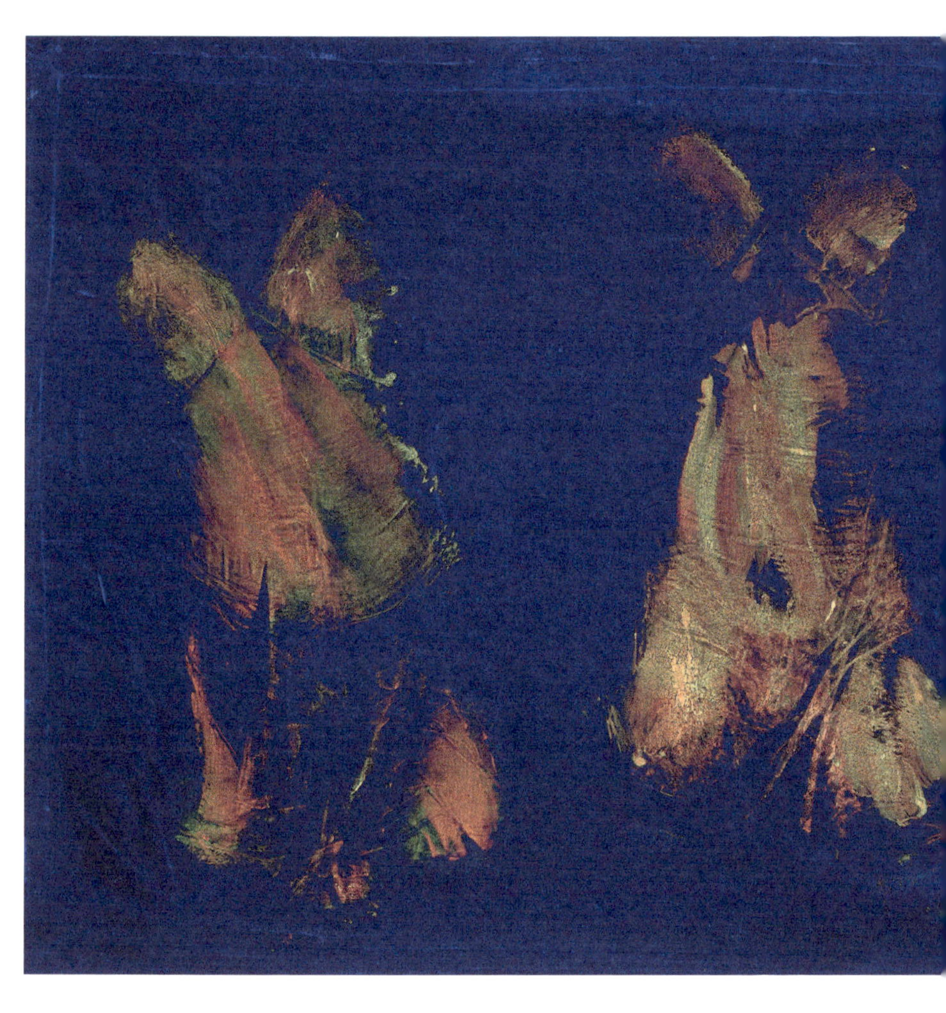

Slips
n.d. Neon acrylic slip imprints on blue velvet.
85 × 40 in.

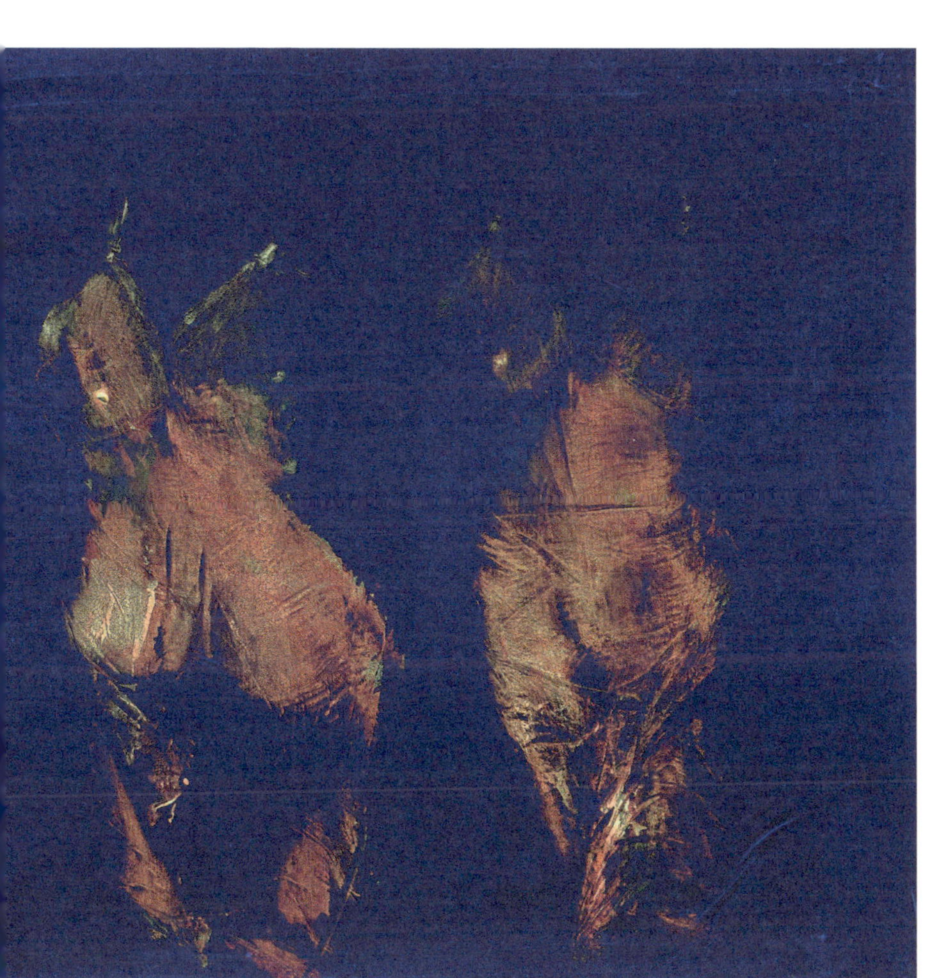

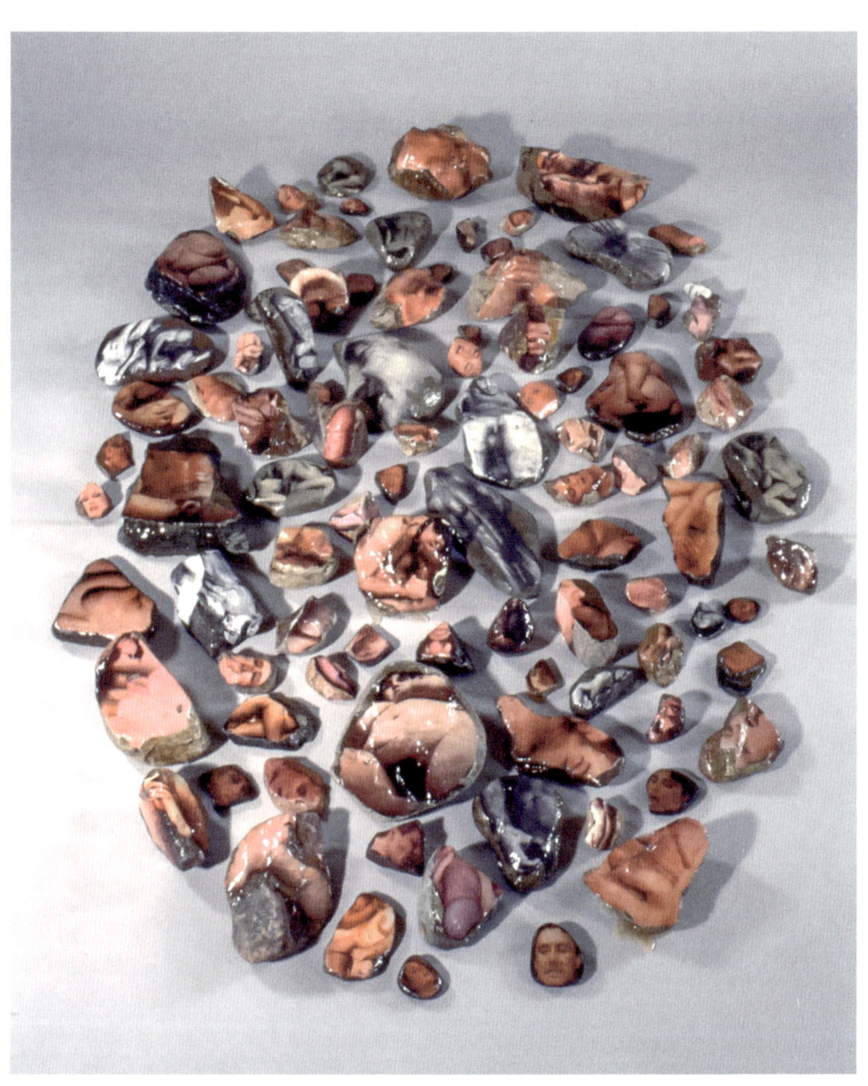

Untitled installation
1989, *The Dialectical Porn Rock.*

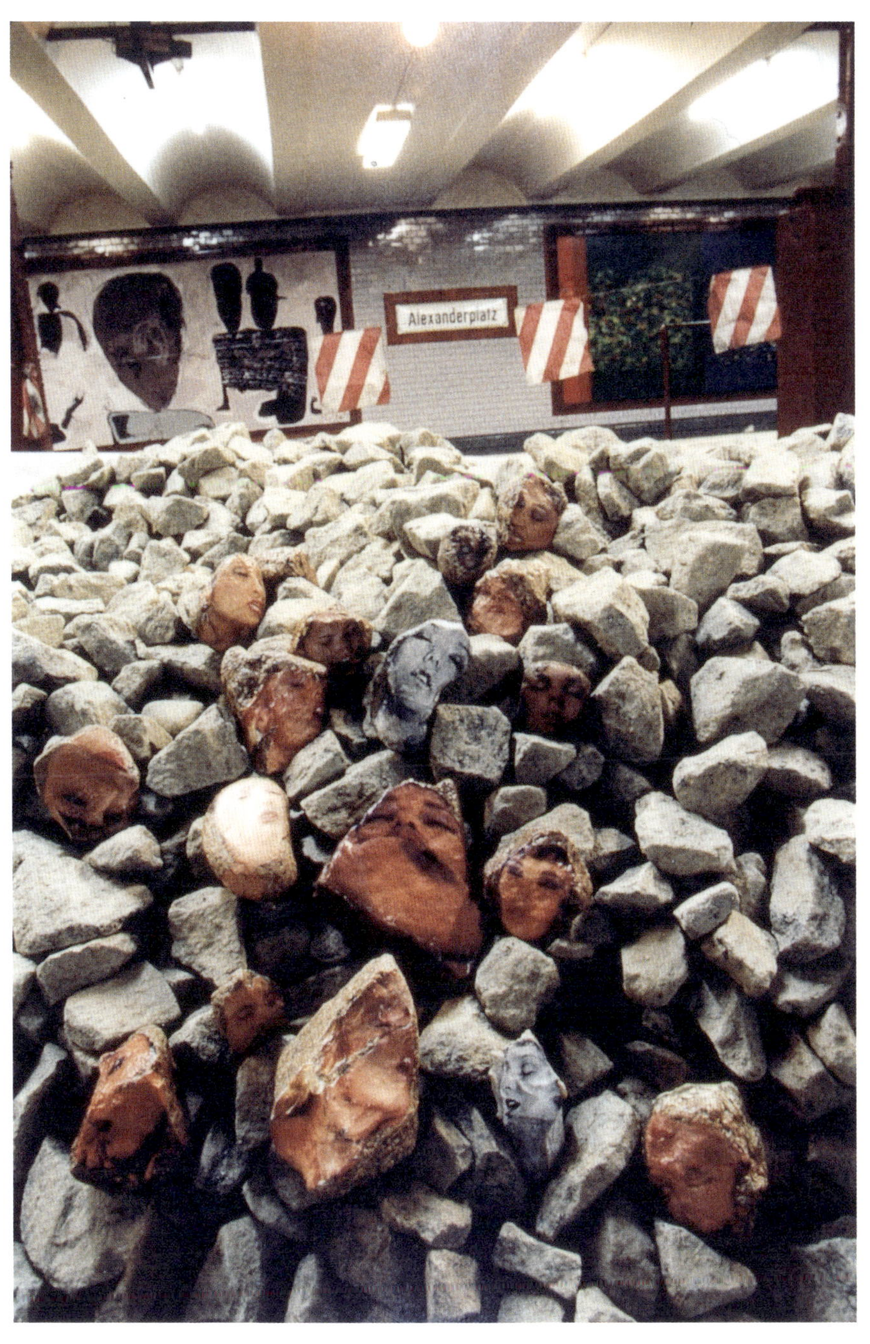

The Dialectical Porn Rock
(Alexanderplatz U-Bahn Station)
1993. C-print.
20 × 16 in. and 40 × 30 in.

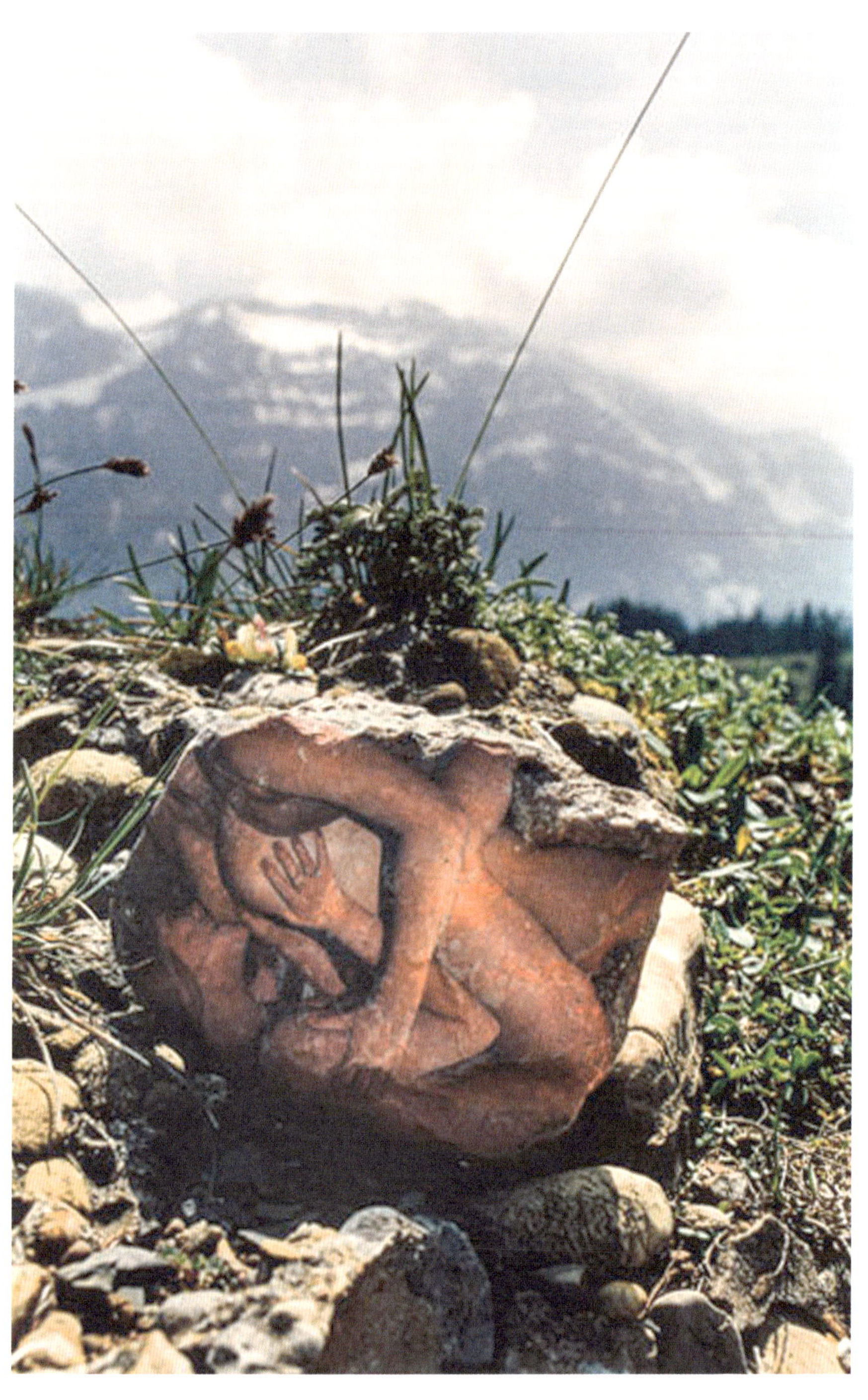

The Dialectical Porn Rock (Opposite Säntis)
1993. C-print.
20 × 16 in, and 40 × 30 in.

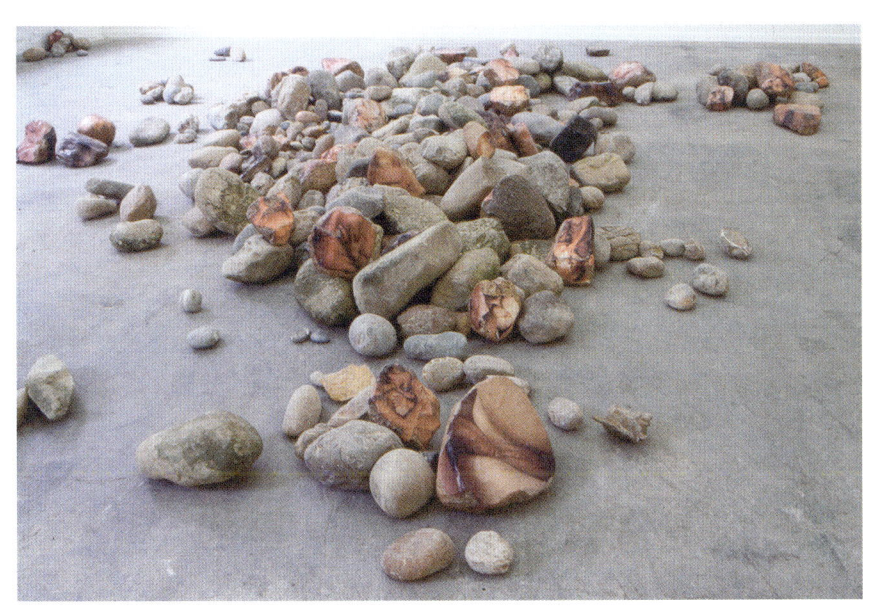

The Dialectical Porn Rock
Installation view, Kunst Halle Sankt Gallen, St. Gallen, Switzerland, 1993.

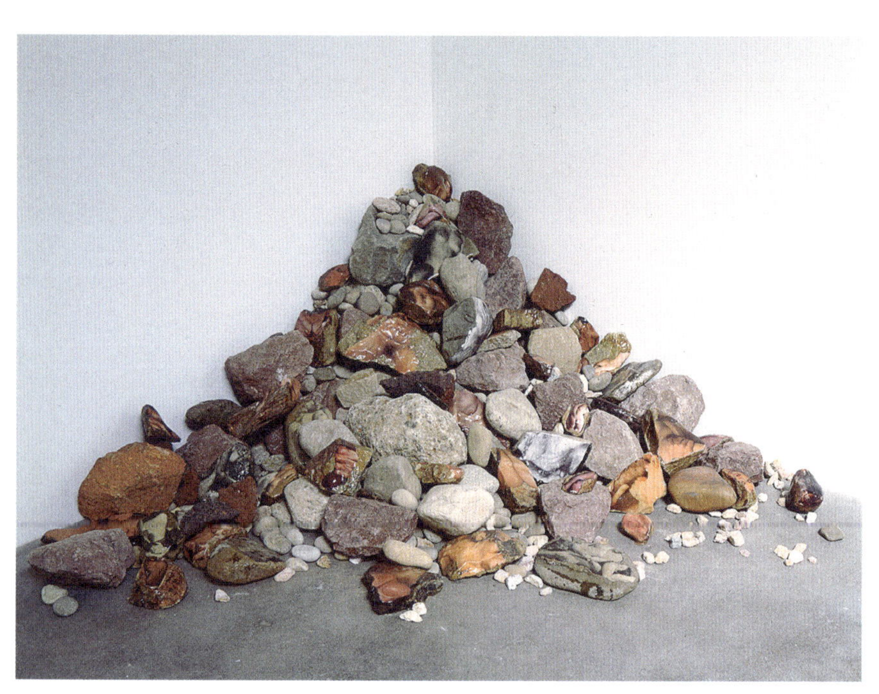

The Dialectical Porn Rock
Installation view, Roy Boyd Gallery.
Los Angeles, 1992.

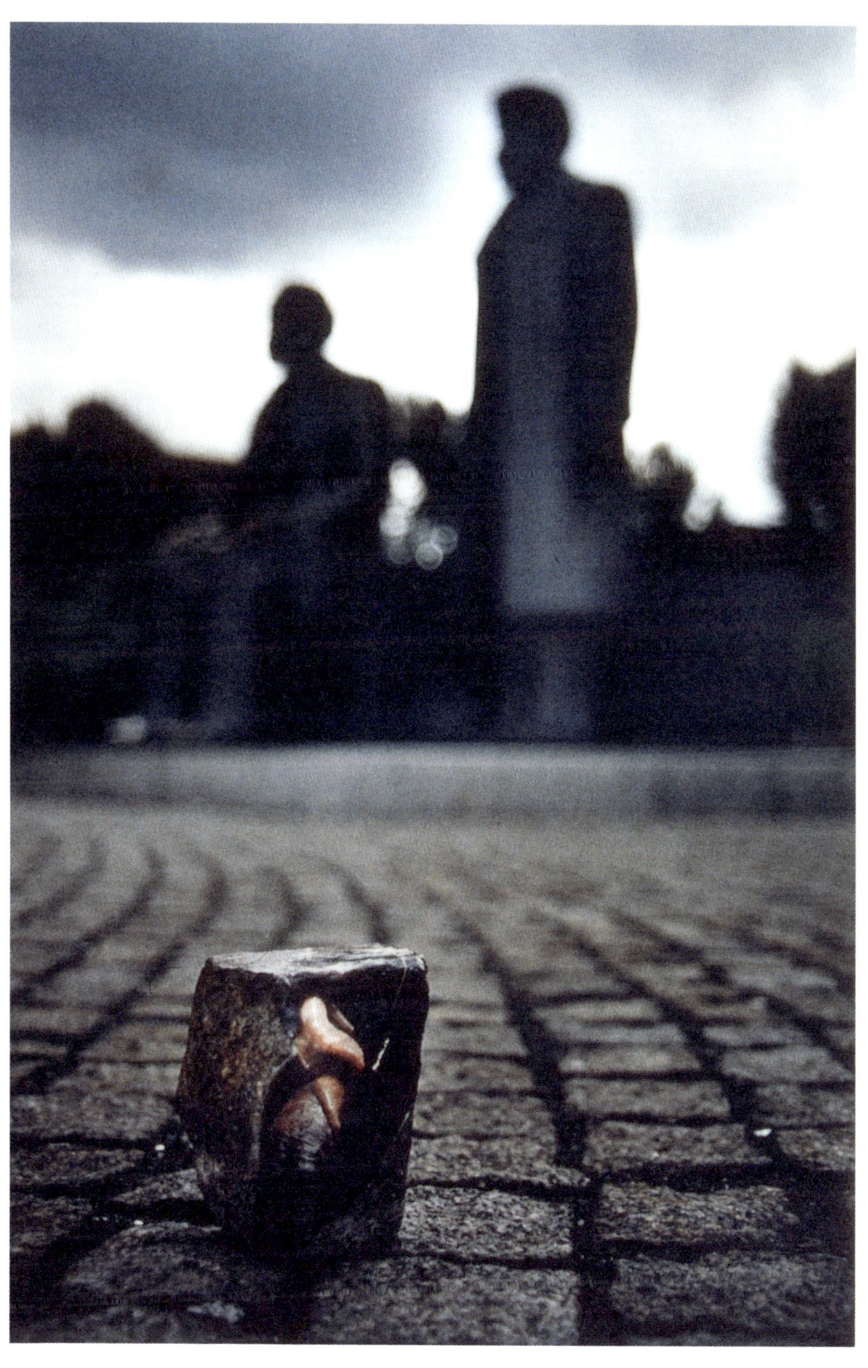

The Dialectical Porn Rock
(Marx Engels Platz, Berlin)
1991–93. C-print.
20 × 16 in. and 40 × 30 in.

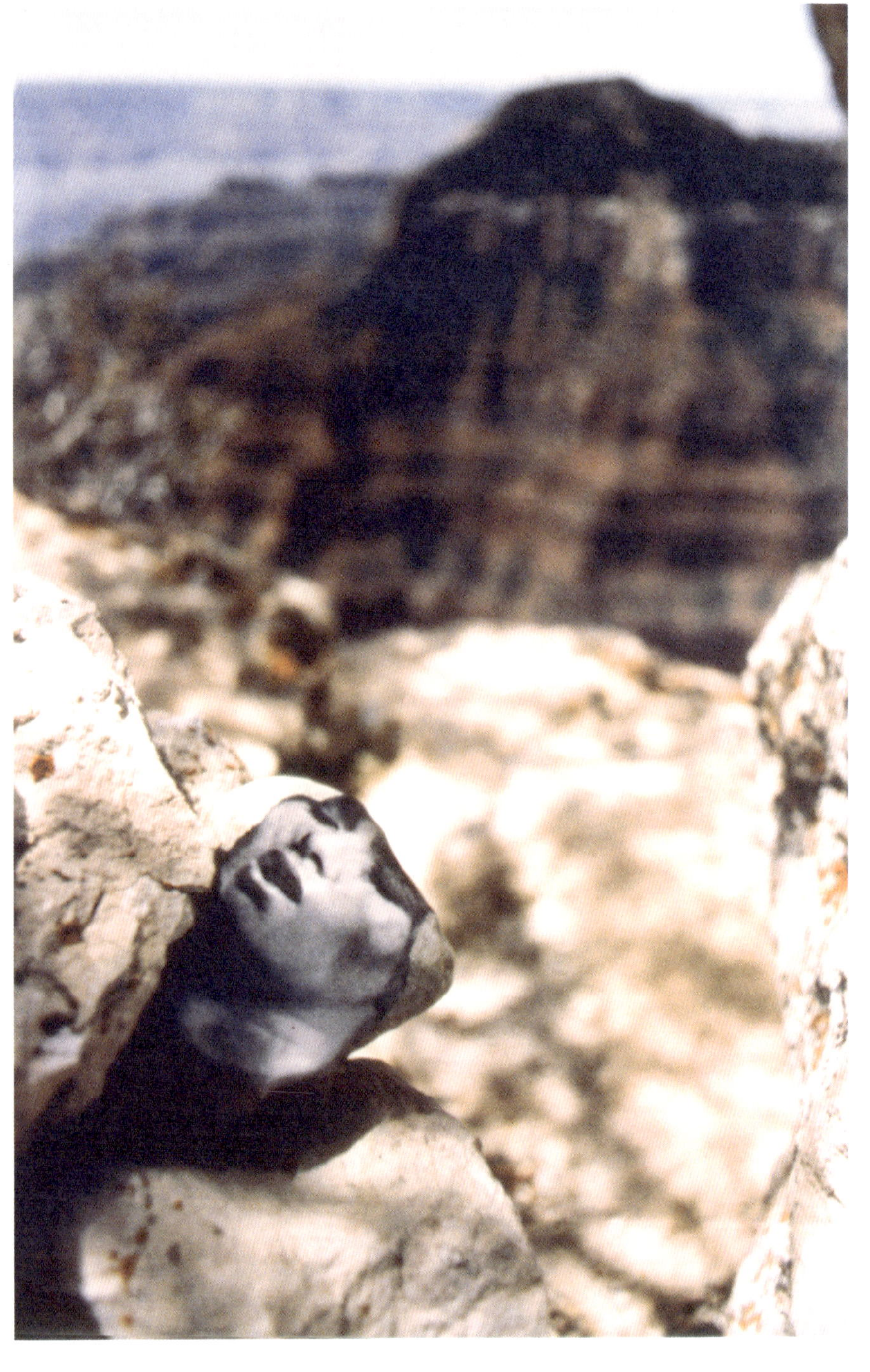

The Dialectical Porn Rock (Grand Canyon)
1989. C-print.
20 × 16 in. and 40 × 30 in.

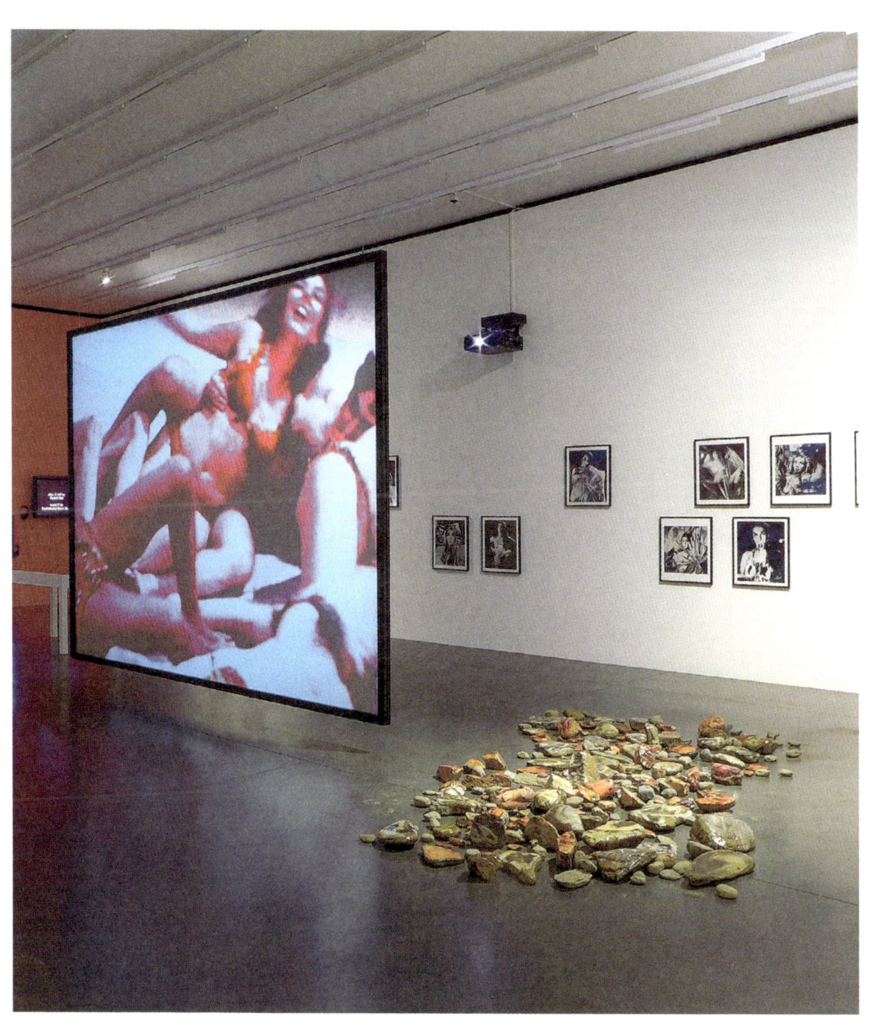

The Dialectical Porn Rock
Installation view, *Up to and Including Limits: After Carolee Schneemann*, Muzeum Susch, Susch, Switzerland, 2019–20.

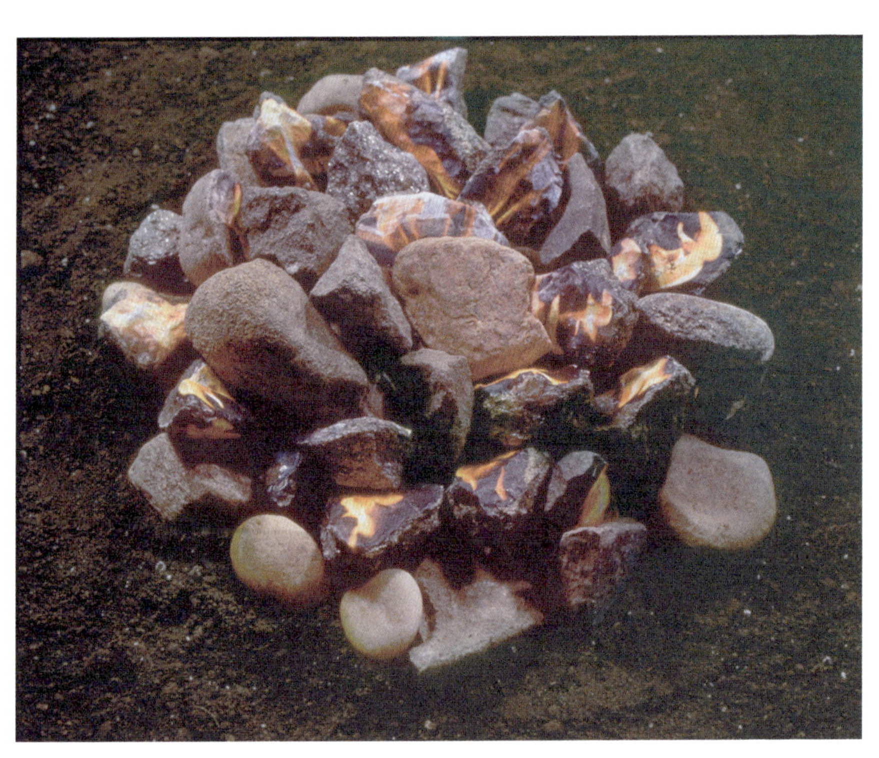

Bonfire
Installation view, *Open Air*, Rembertikreisel, Bremen, Germany, 1993.

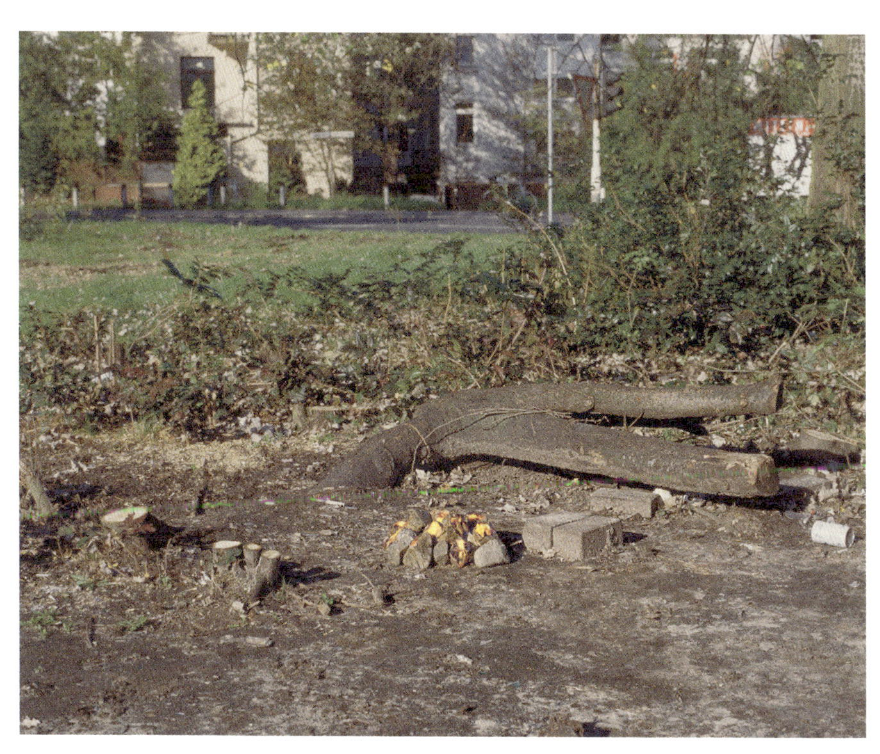

Bonfire
Installation view, *Open Air*, Rembertikreisel, Bremen, Germany, 1993.

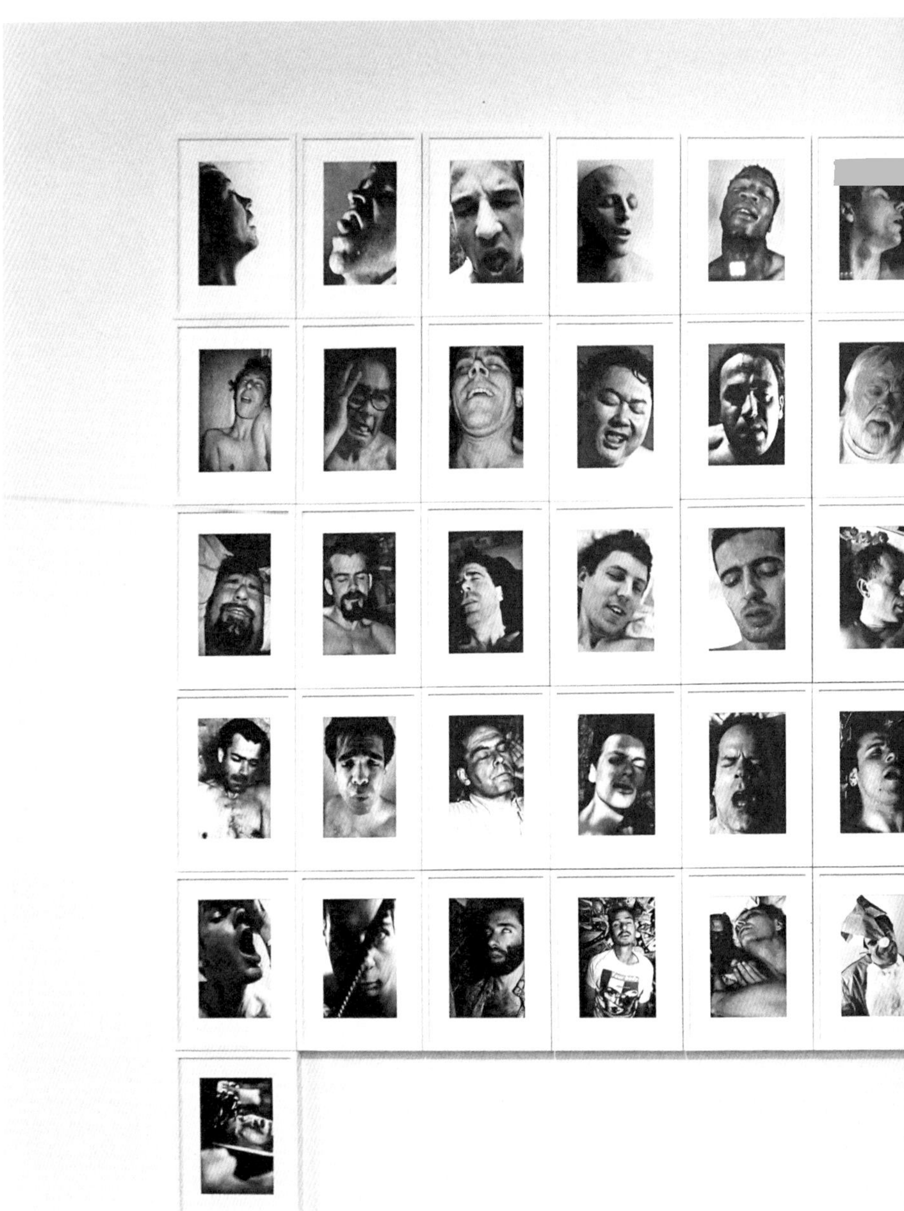

Head Shots
1991–96. Installation view, *Ektase*, Kunstmuseum Stuttgart, Germany, 2018.

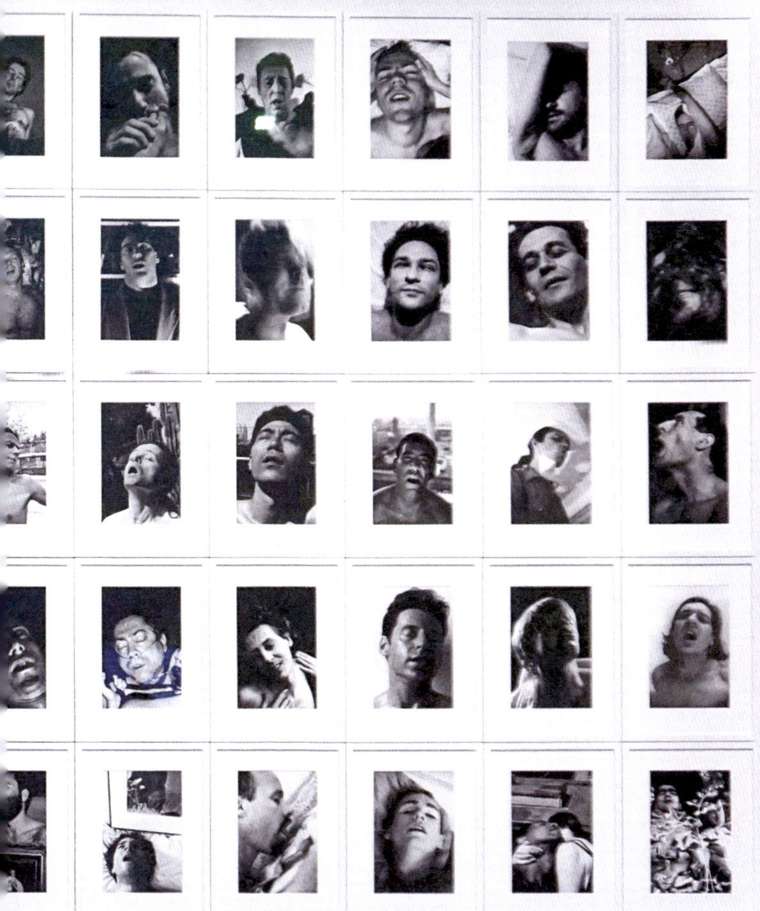

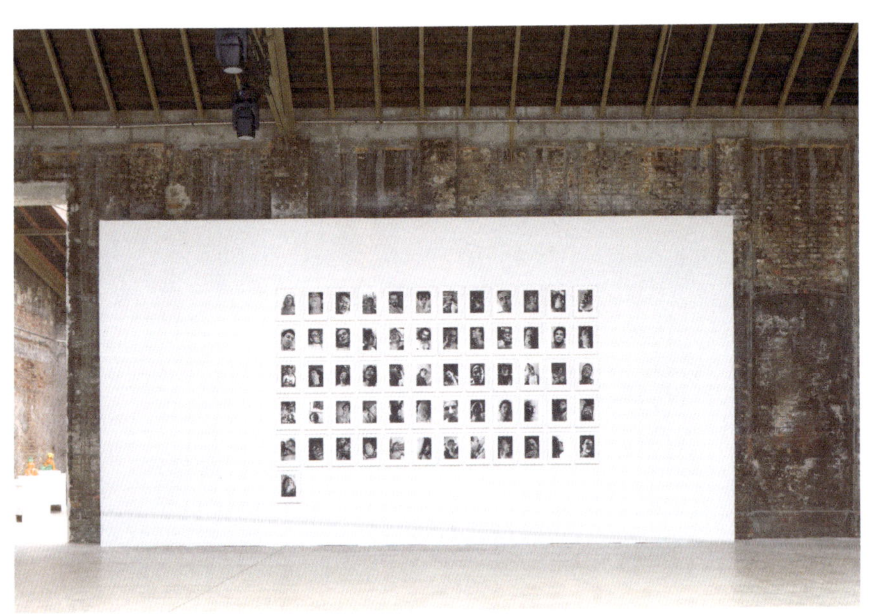

Head Shots
1991–96. Installation view, Wilhelm Hallen, Berlin, Germany, 2022.

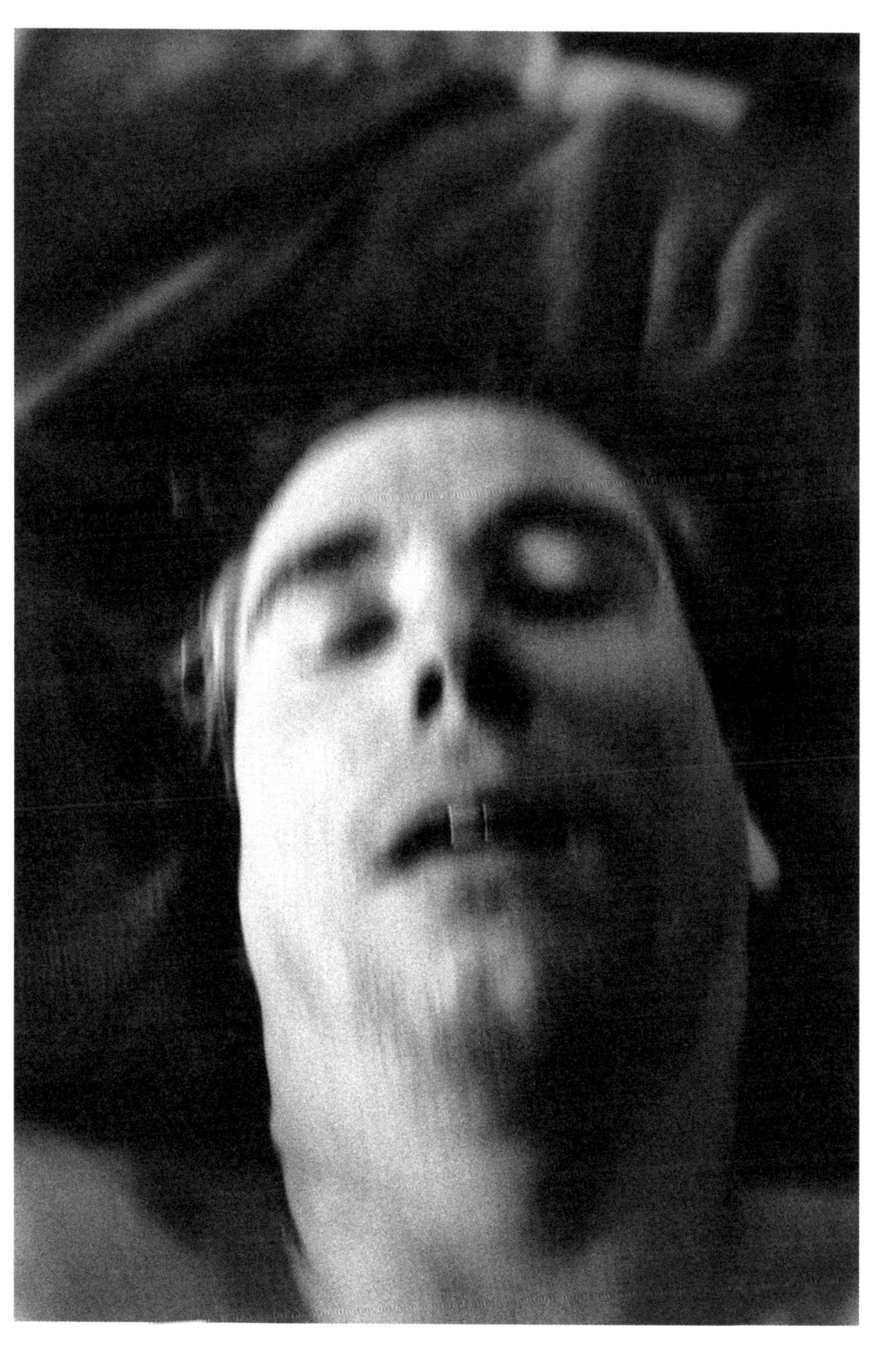

Head Shots (MK Outtake)
1991–96. Gelatin silver print.
12 × 16 in.

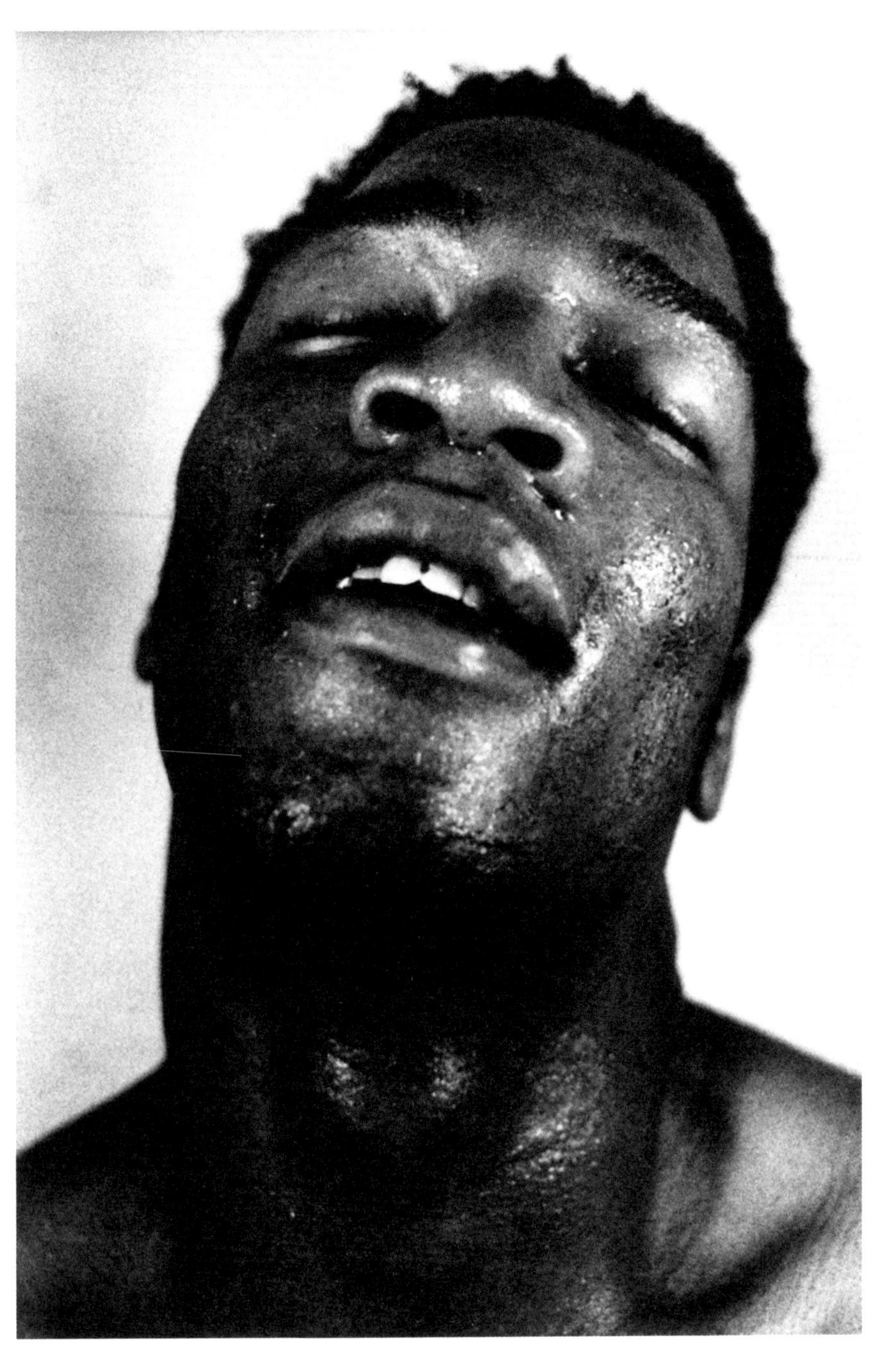

Head Shots (DL)
1991–96. Gelatin silver print.
12 × 16 in.

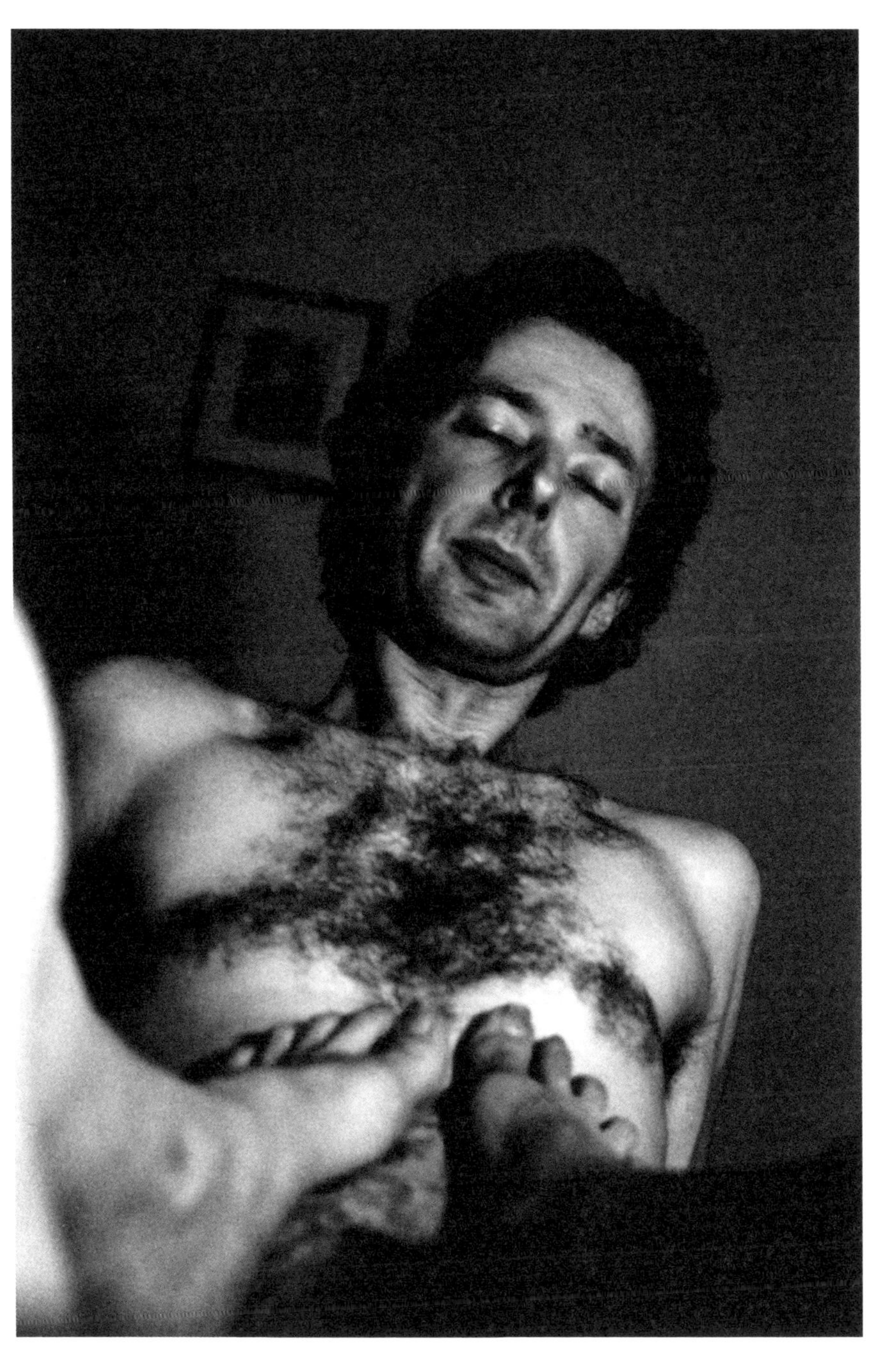

Head Shots (JM)
1991–96. Gelatin silver print.
12 × 16 in.

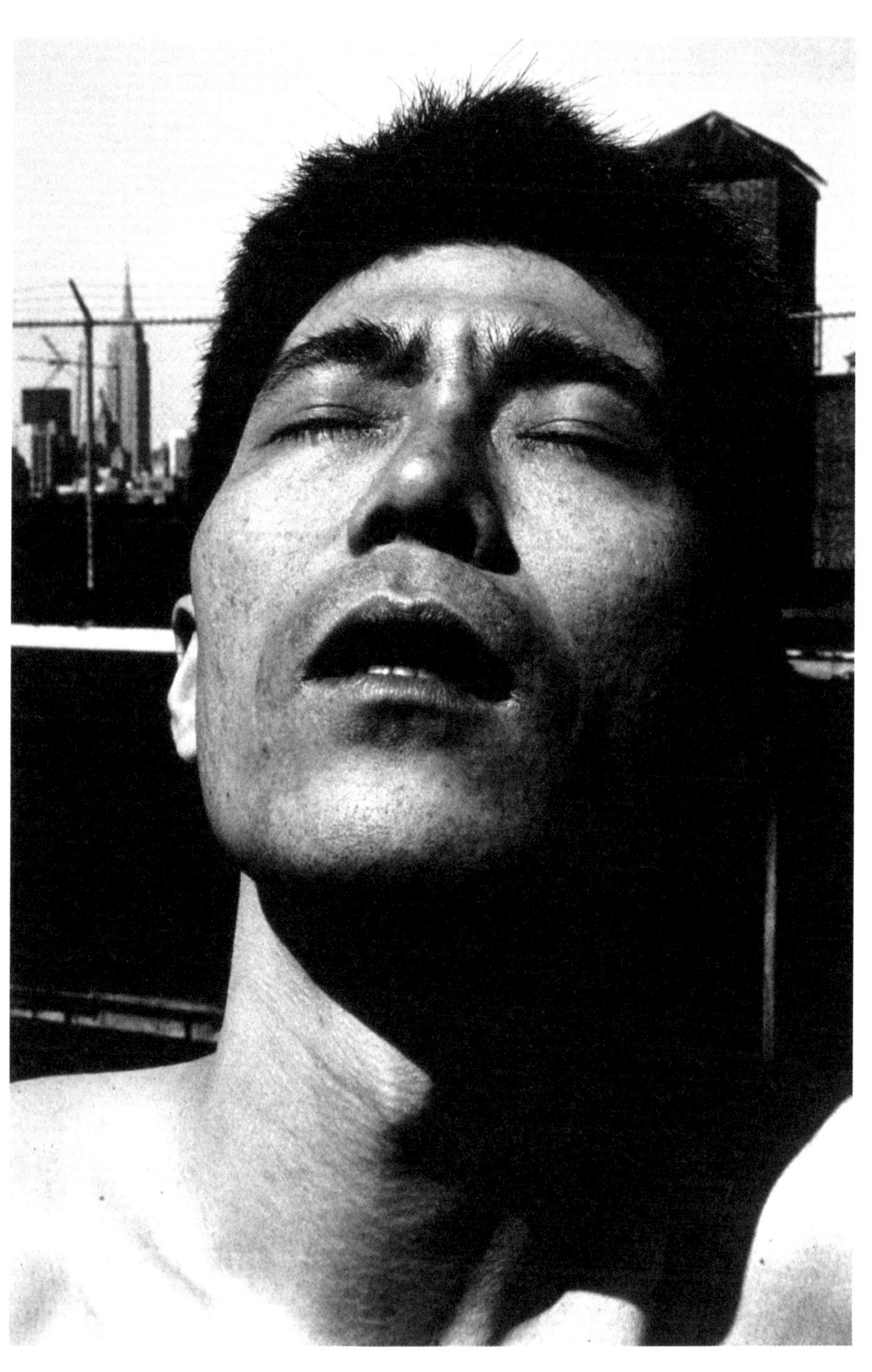

Head Shots (JMu)
1991–96. Gelatin silver print.
12 × 16 in.

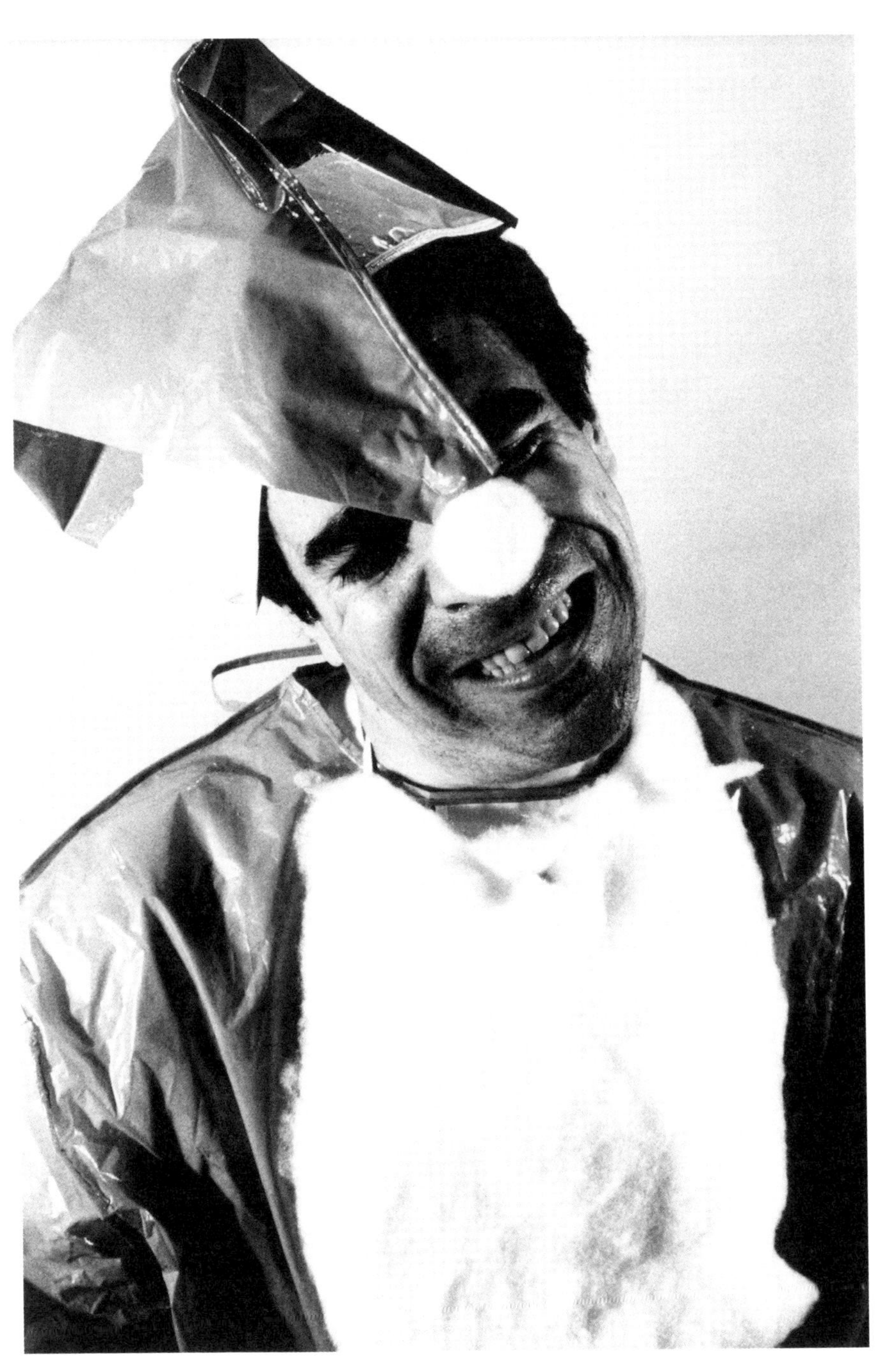

Head Shots (Santa)
1991–96. Gelatin silver print.
12 × 16 in.

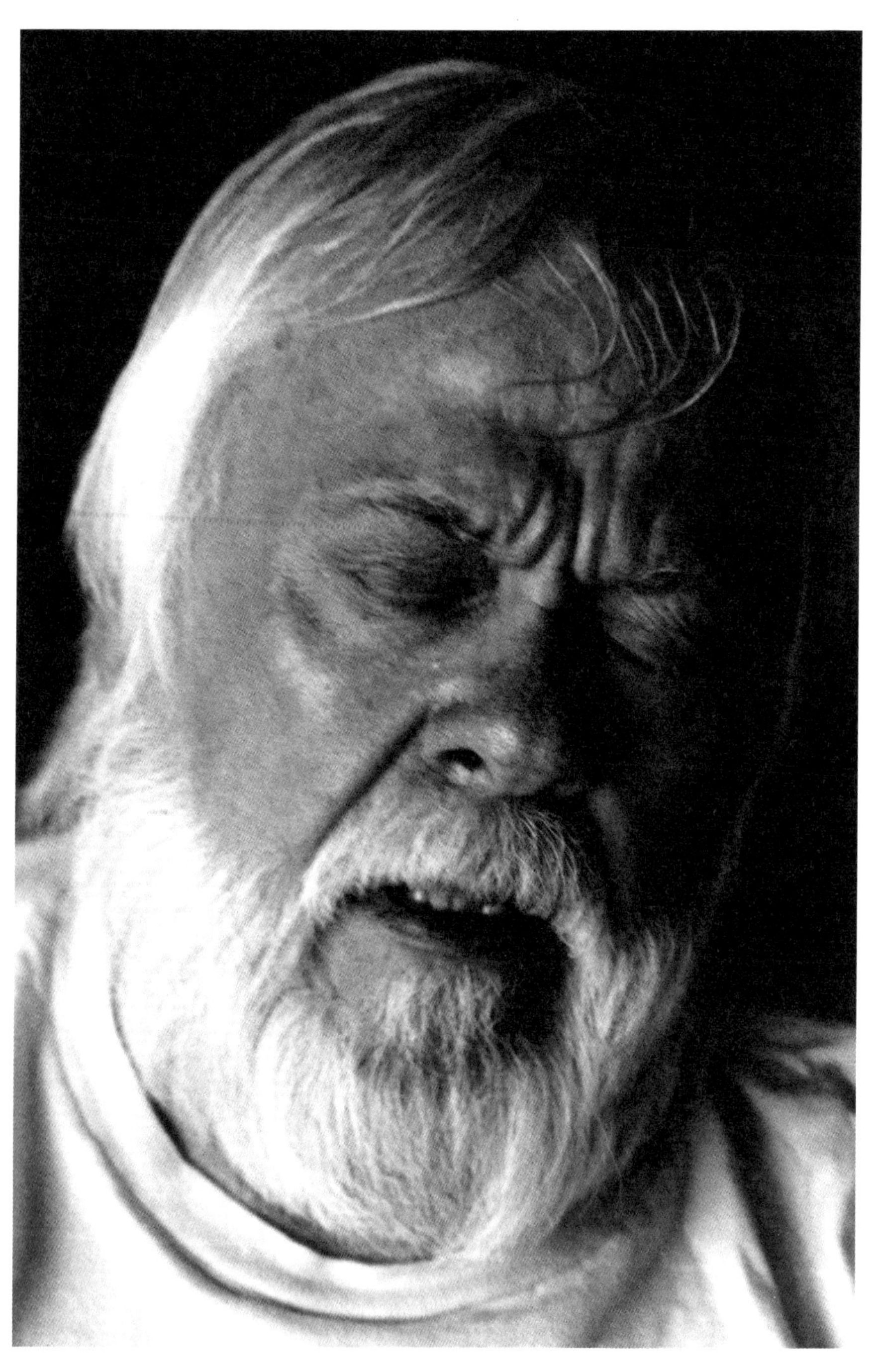

Head Shots (JB)
1991–96. Gelatin silver print.
12 × 16 in.

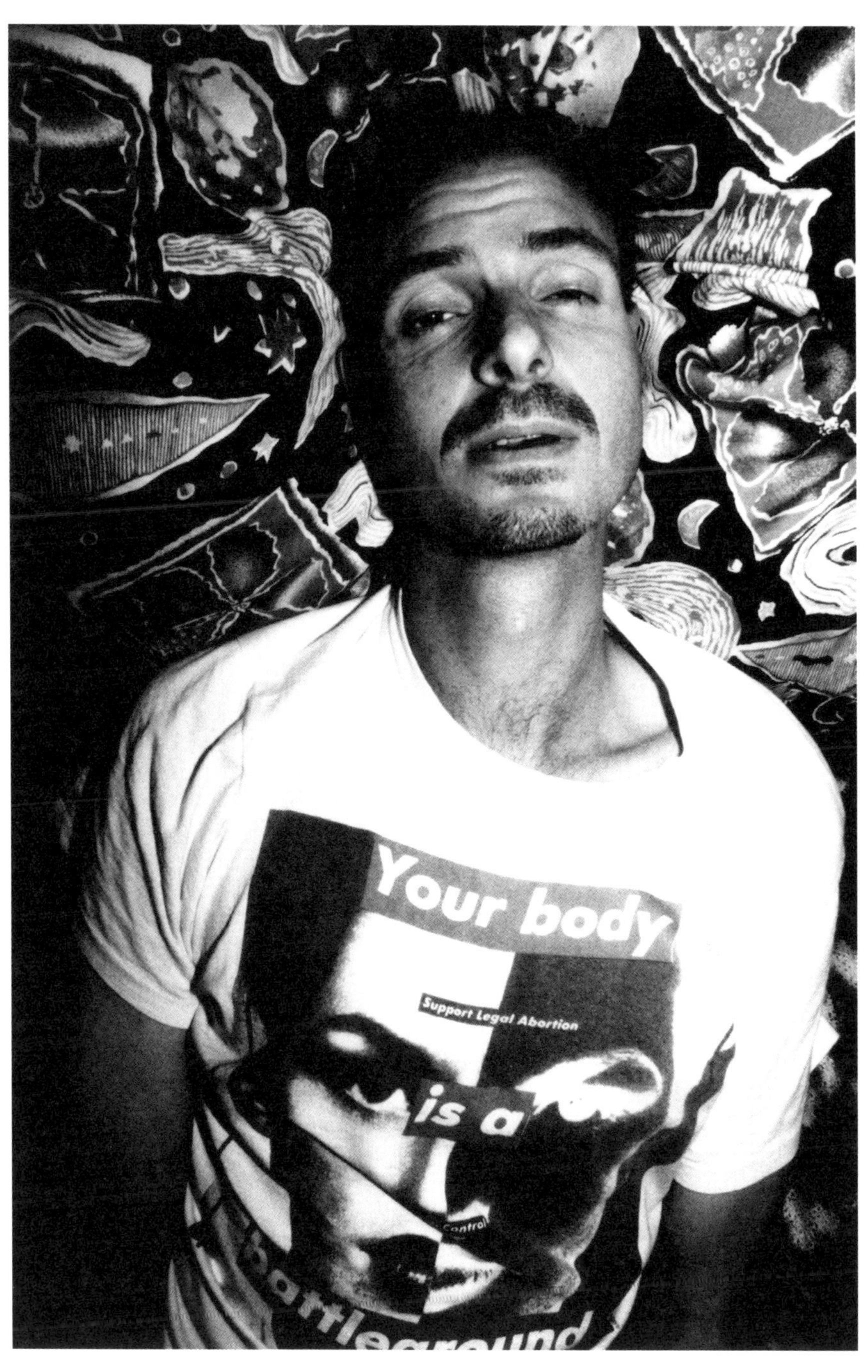

Head Shots (FW)
1991–96. Gelatin silver print
12 × 16 in.

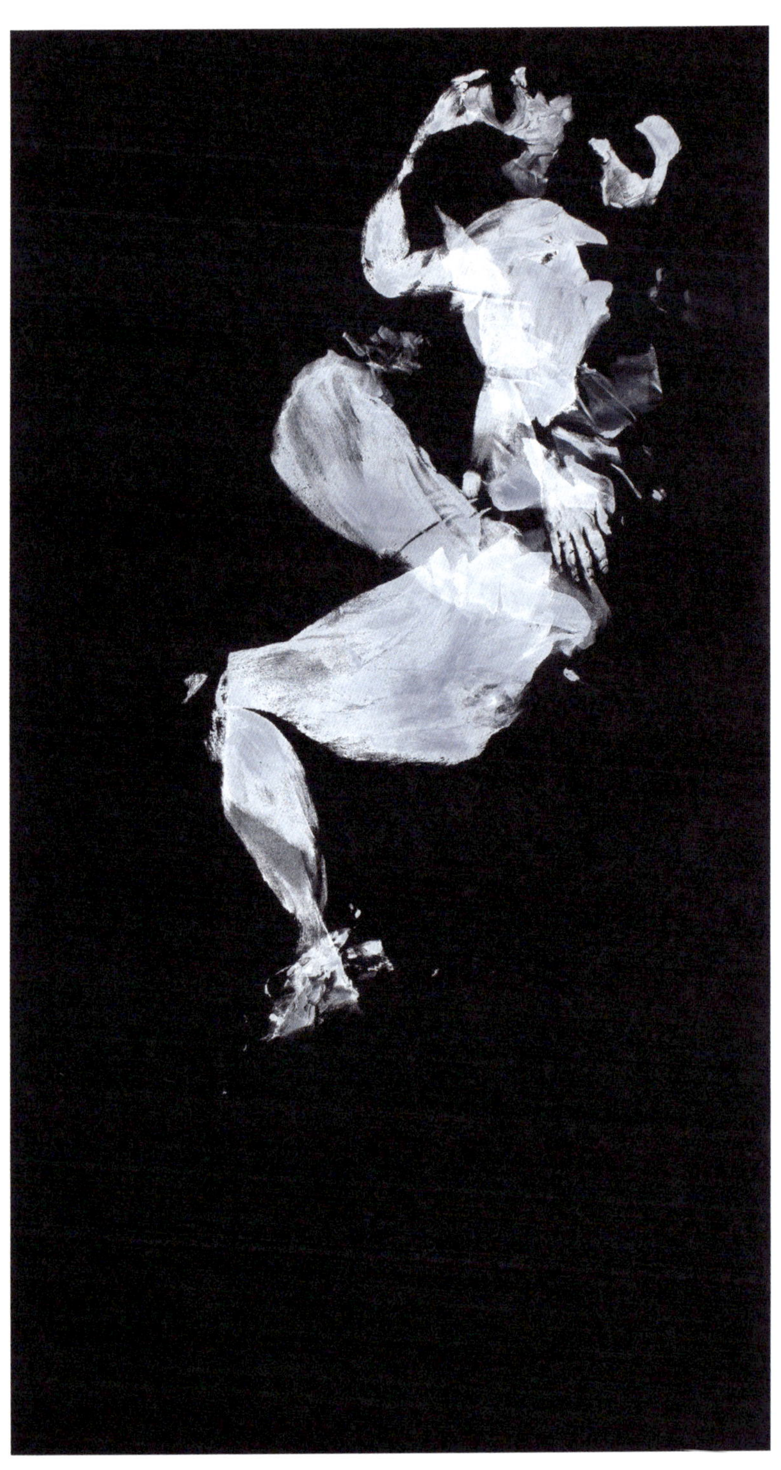

Sagittarius (Liz and Seth)
2012, from *The Astrological Ways*.
Acrylic on black velvet, 84 × 48 in.

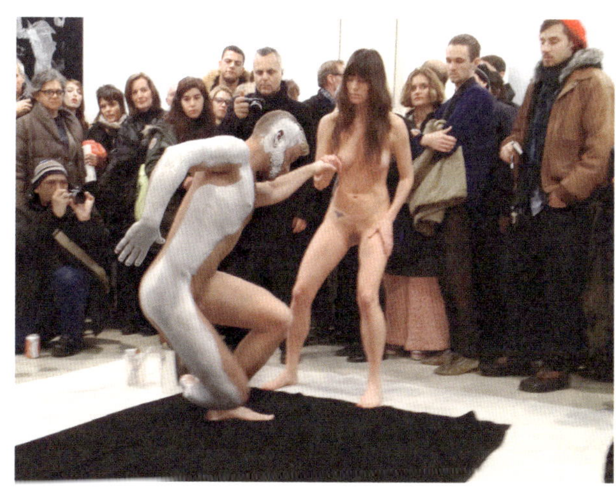

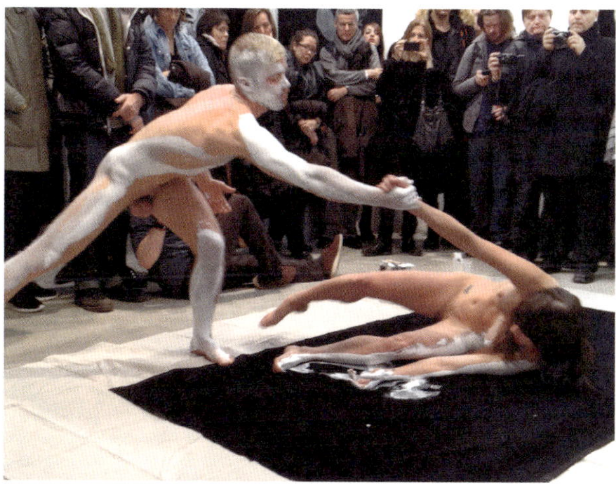

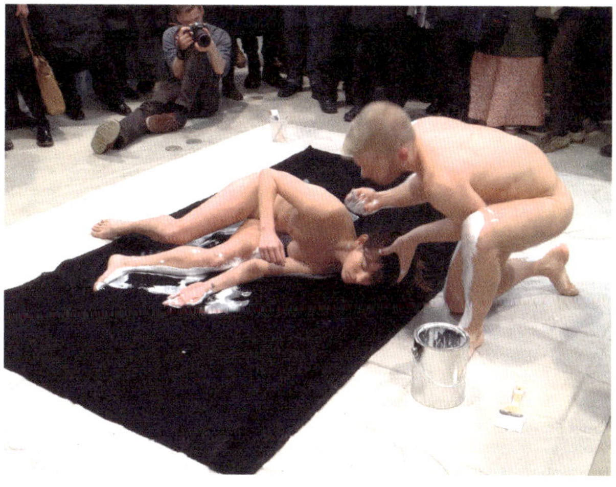

I Know It When I See It
2013. Performance.
Martos Gallery, New York.

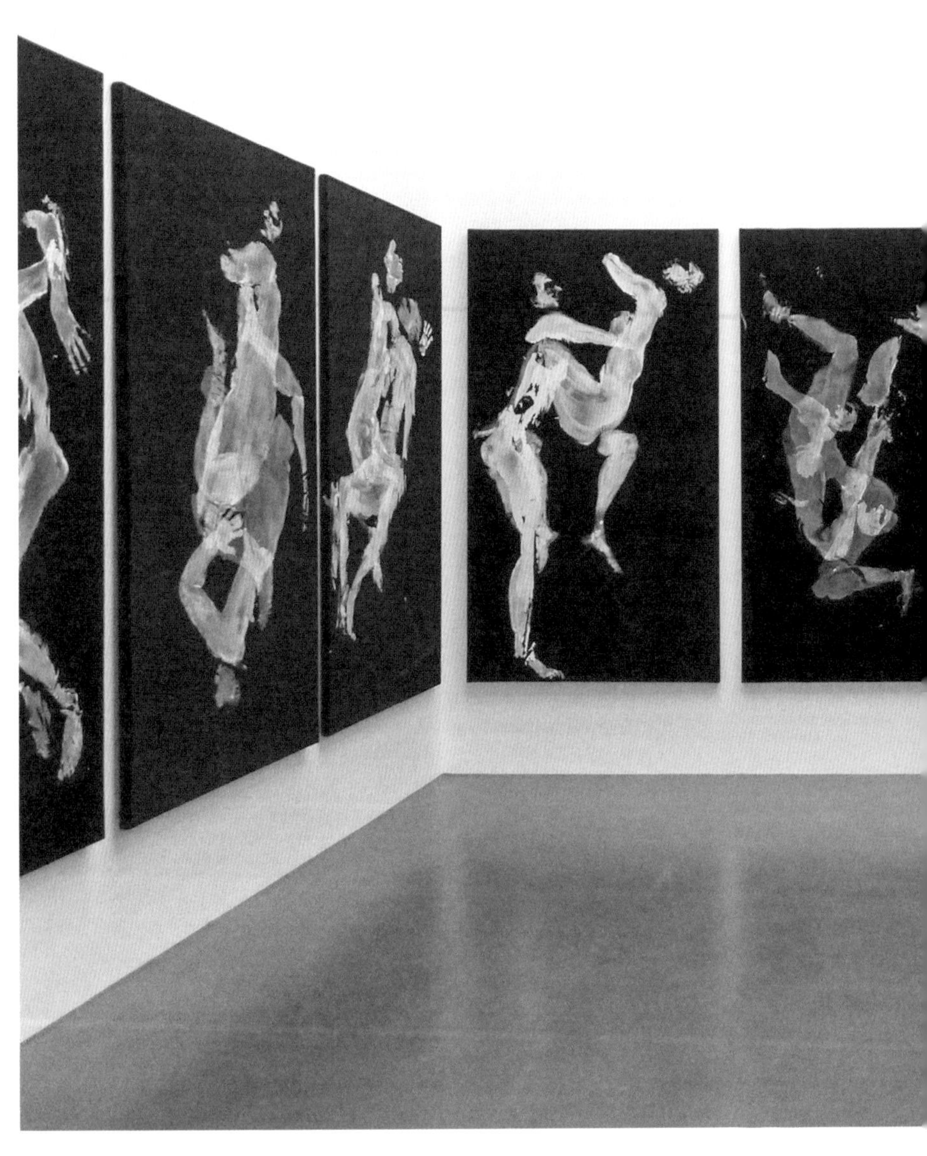

The Astrological Ways
Installation view, *Up to and Including Limits: After Carolee Schneemann*, Muzeum Susch, Switzerland, 2019–20.

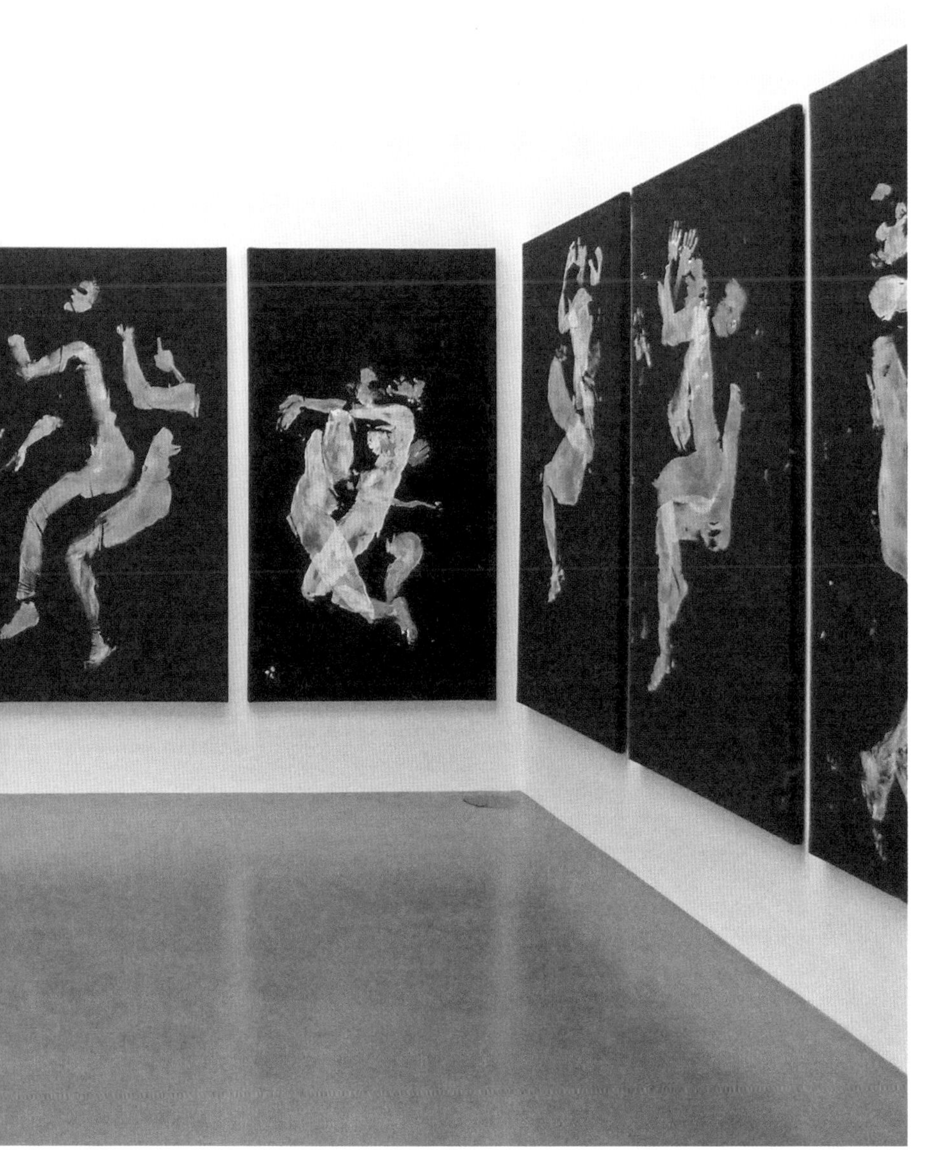

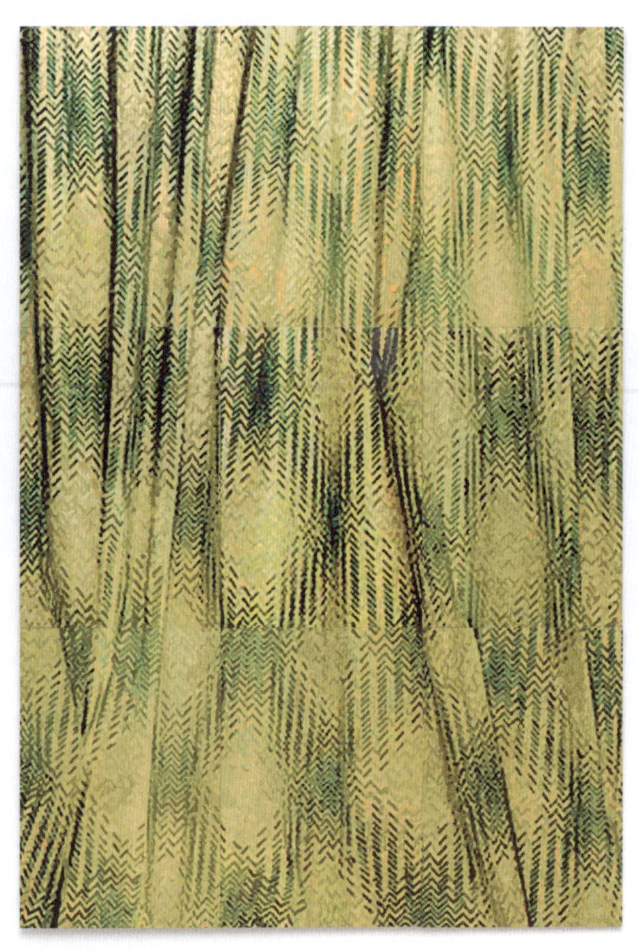

Obscene: Gold-Green Curtain
2014, from *Scene/Obscene*. Acrylic and inkjet print on gold metallic photo paper mounted to dibond, 10 × 6 in.

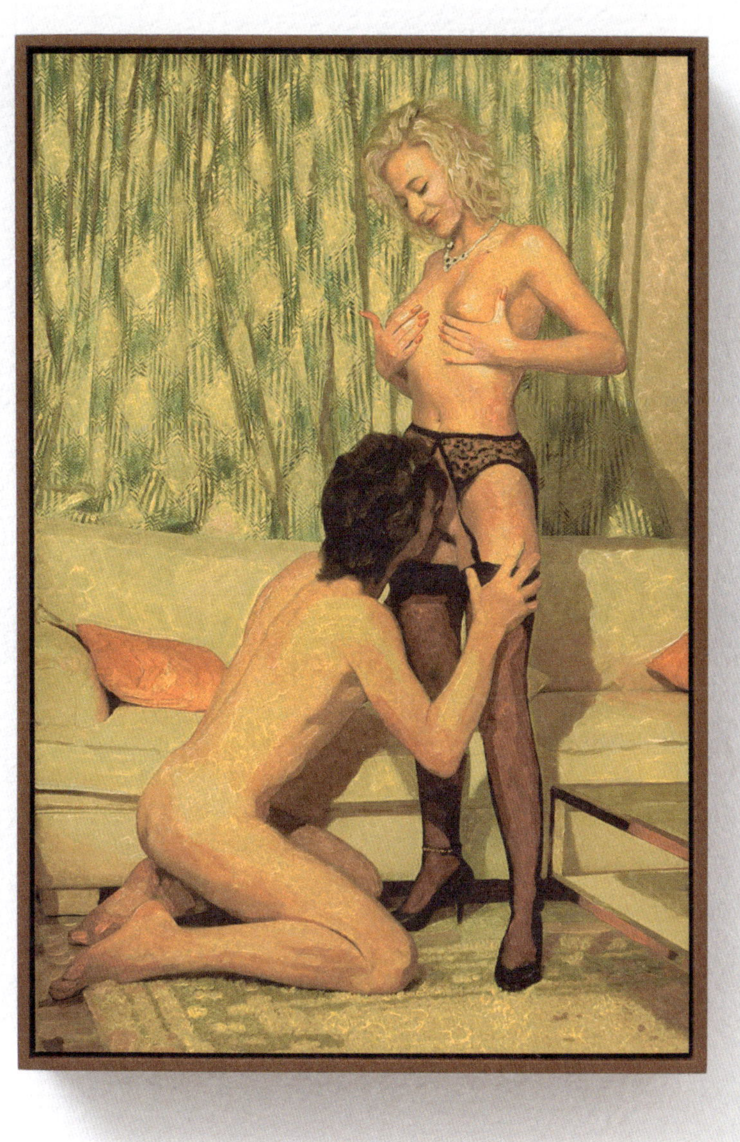

Scene: Naked Man
2014, from *Scene/Obscene*. Acrylic and inkjet print on gold metallic photo paper mounted to dibond, 10 × 6 in.

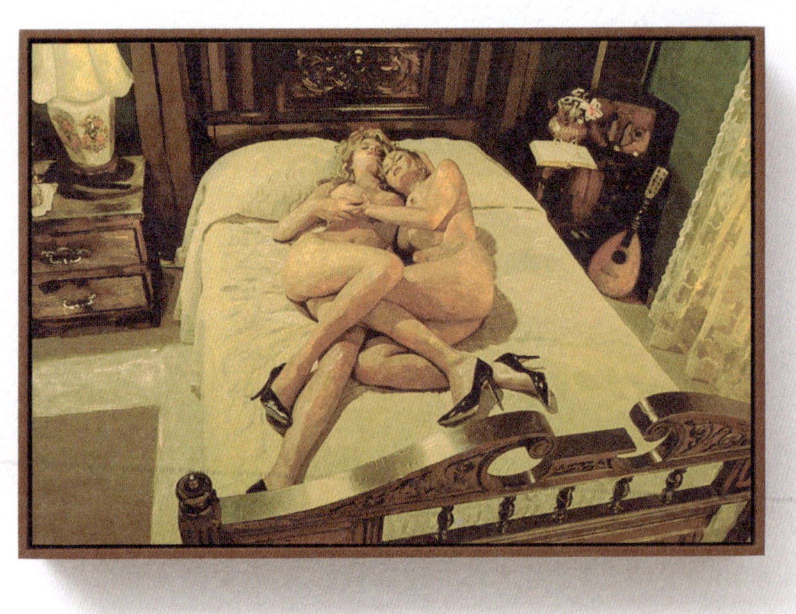

Scene #15
2014, from *Scene/Obscene*. Acrylic and inkjet print on gold metallic photo paper mounted to dibond, 6 × 10 in.

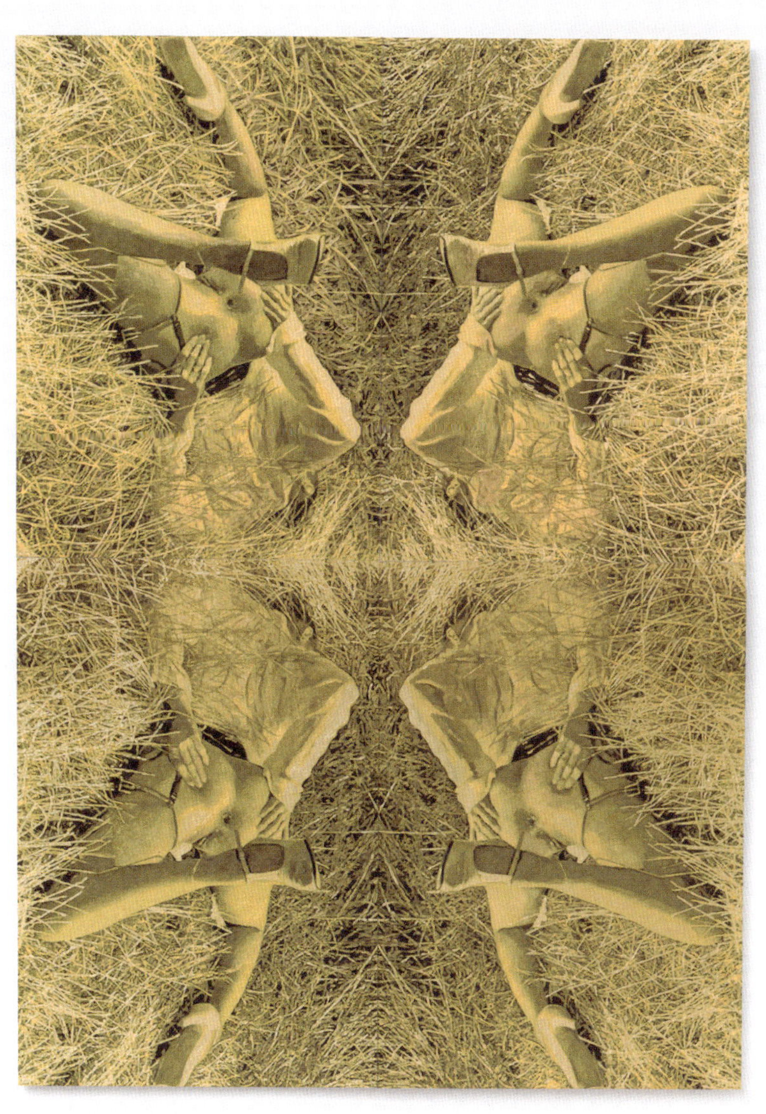

Rorschach
2014, from *The Golden Age*. Acrylic paint, inkjet print on gold metallic photo paper mounted to dibond, 34 ½ × 24 ½ in.

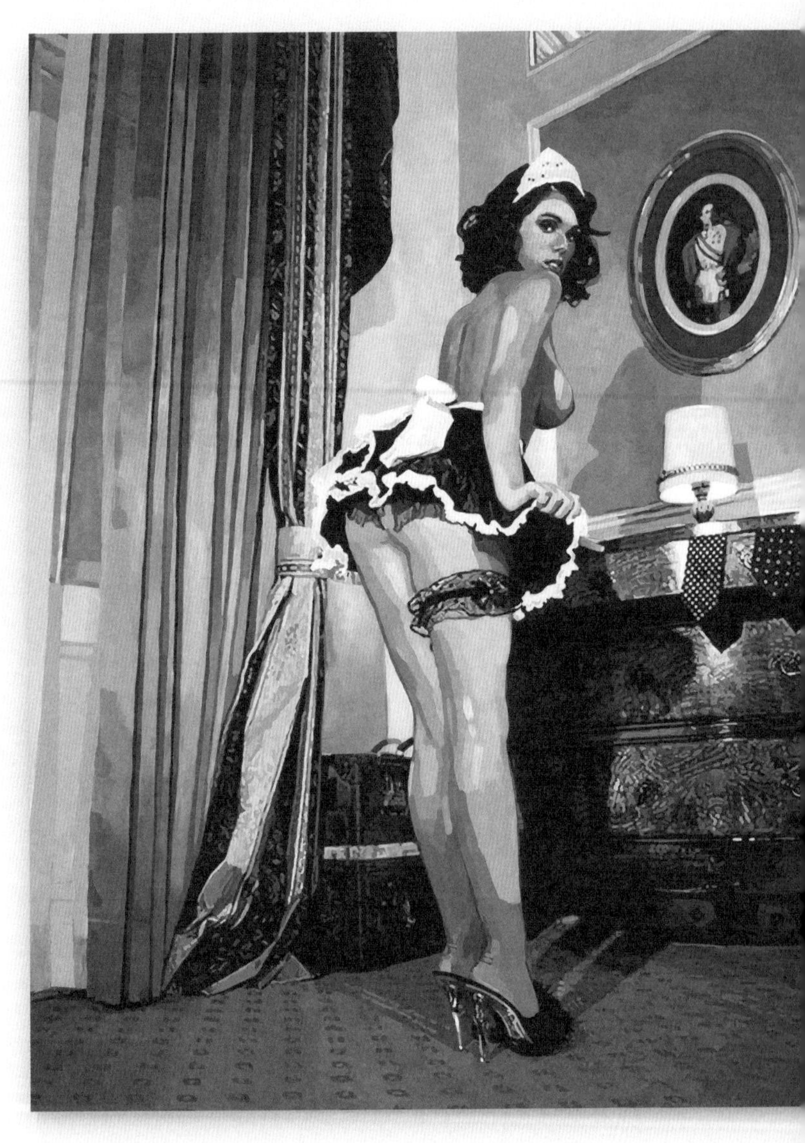

The Sexual Enlightenment of Children
2013, from *The Golden Age*. Acrylic and inkjet print on aluminum in two parts.
Each 55½ × 44 in., overall 55½ × 88 in.

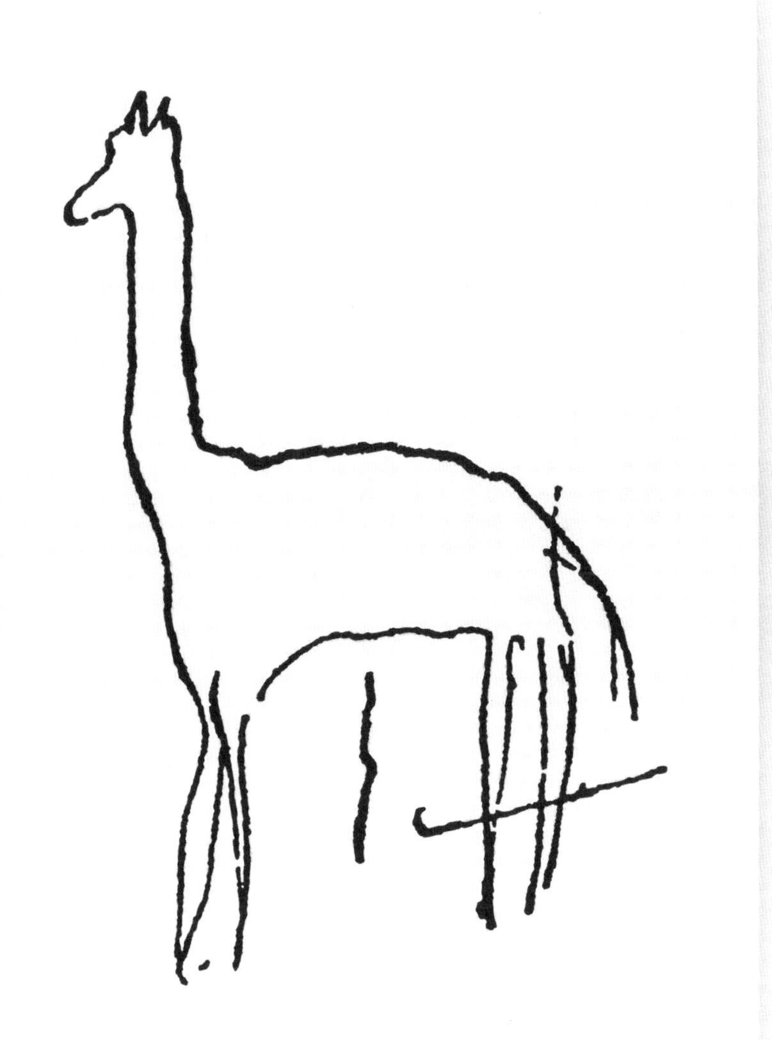

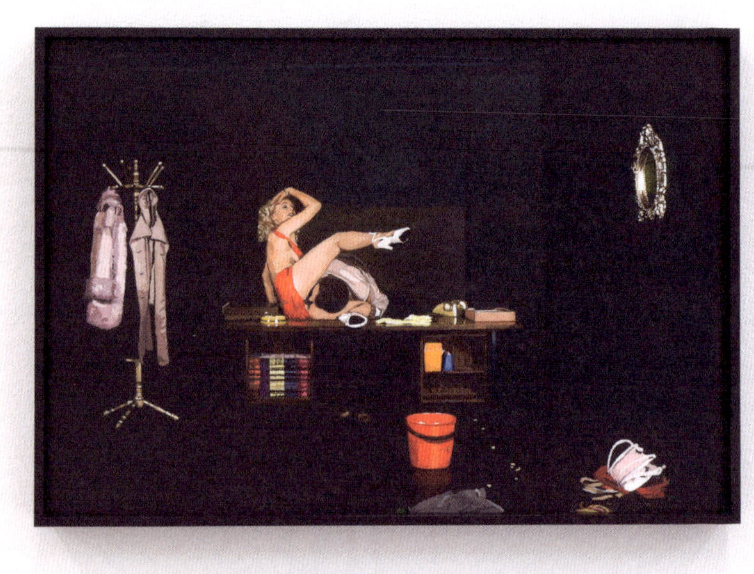

Scene: The Office
2013, from *Scene/Obscene*. Acrylic and inkjet print on aluminum, 6 × 10 in.

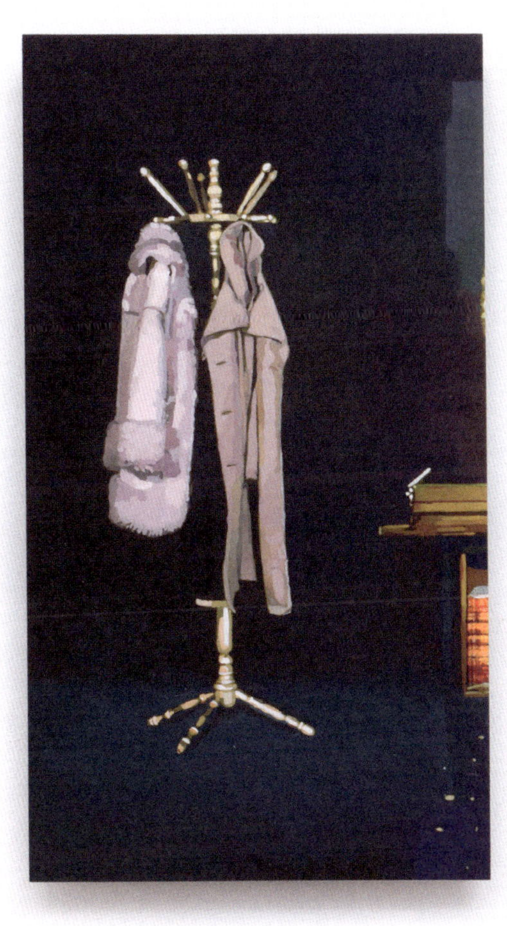

Obscene: Coatrack
2013, from *Scene/Obscene*. Acrylic and inkjet print on aluminum.

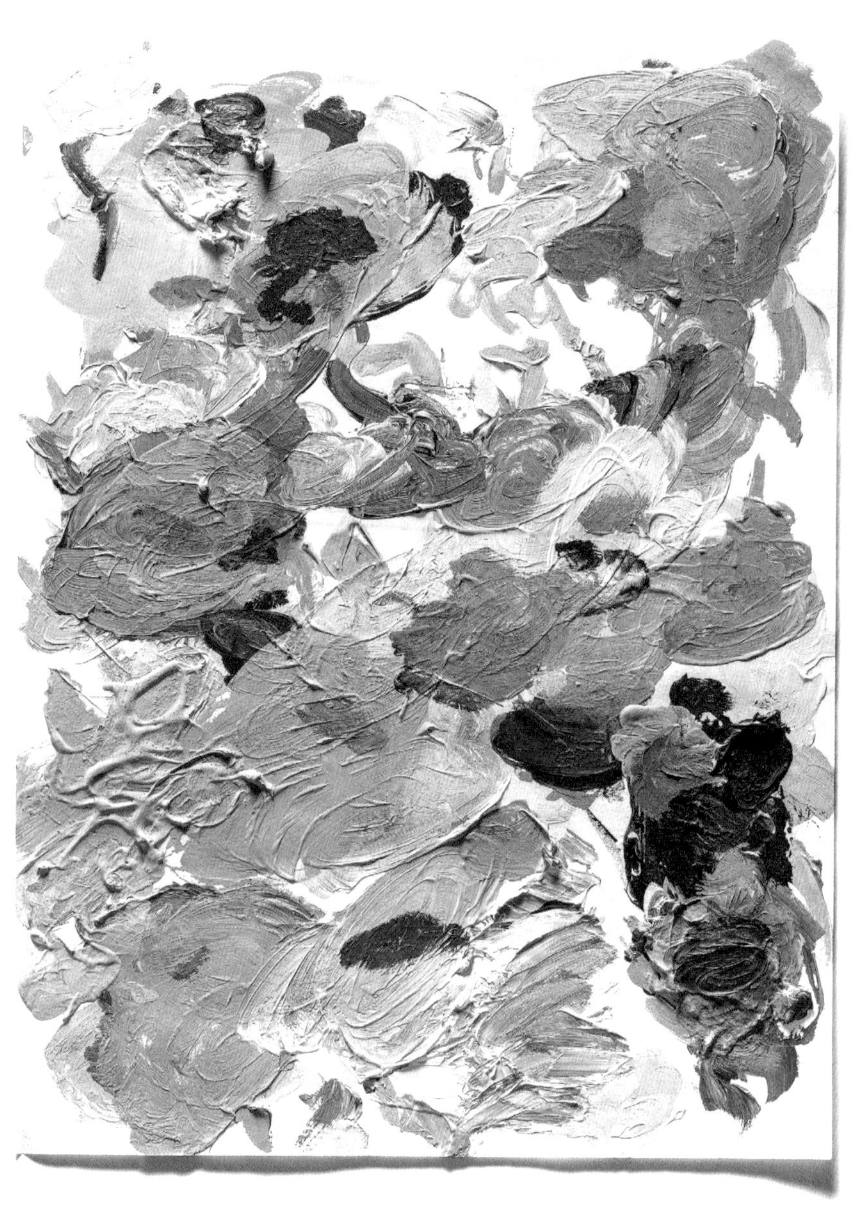

Palette (Panorama 4)
2013. Inkjet print.
18 × 12⅜ in.

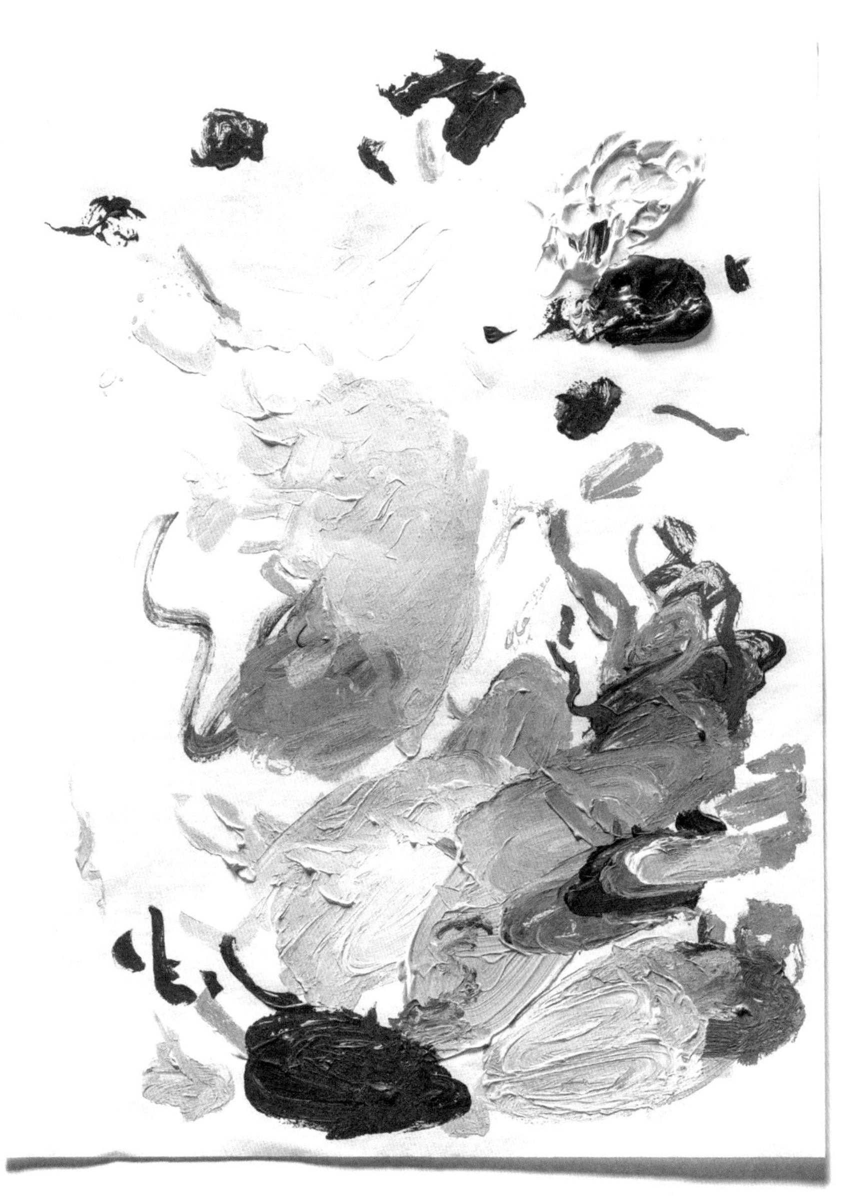

Palette (Panorama 8)
2013. Inkjet print.
18 × 12⅜ in.

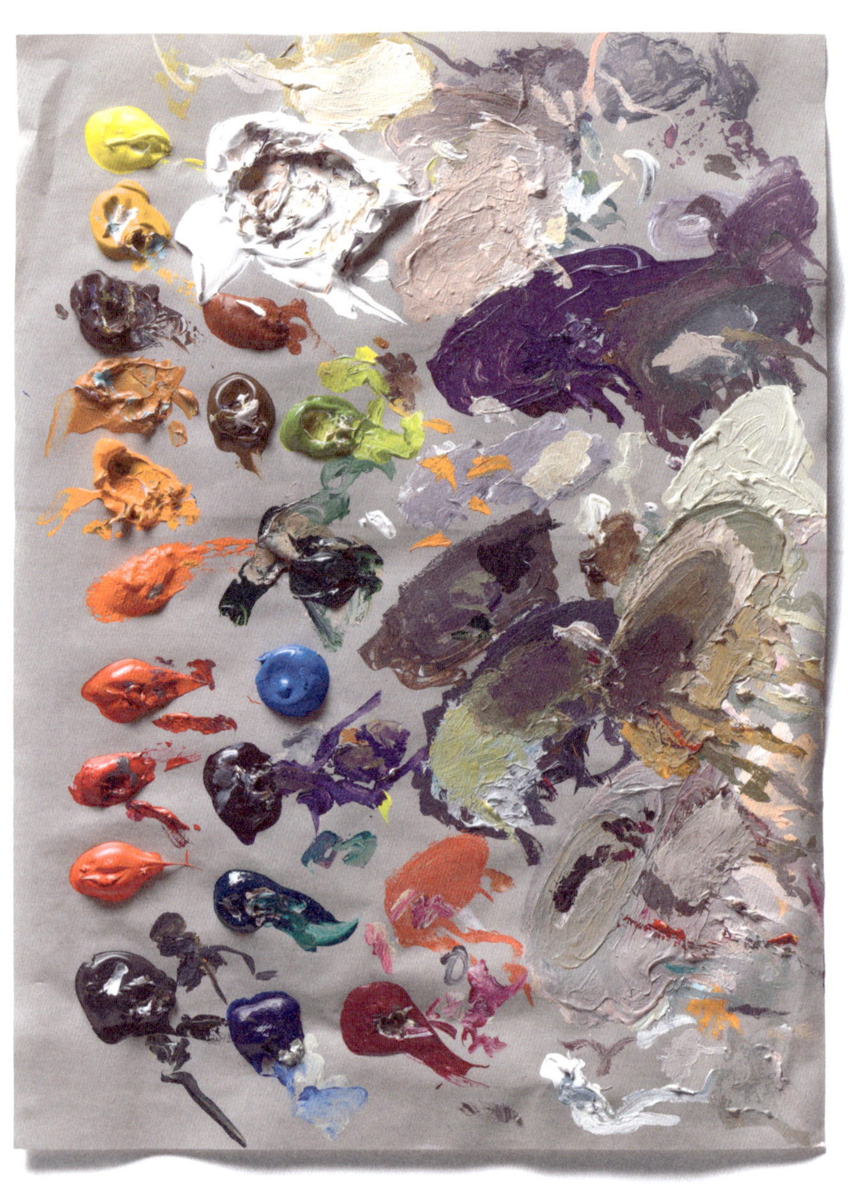

Color Palette (1)
2013. Inkjet print.
19 ½ × 17 in.

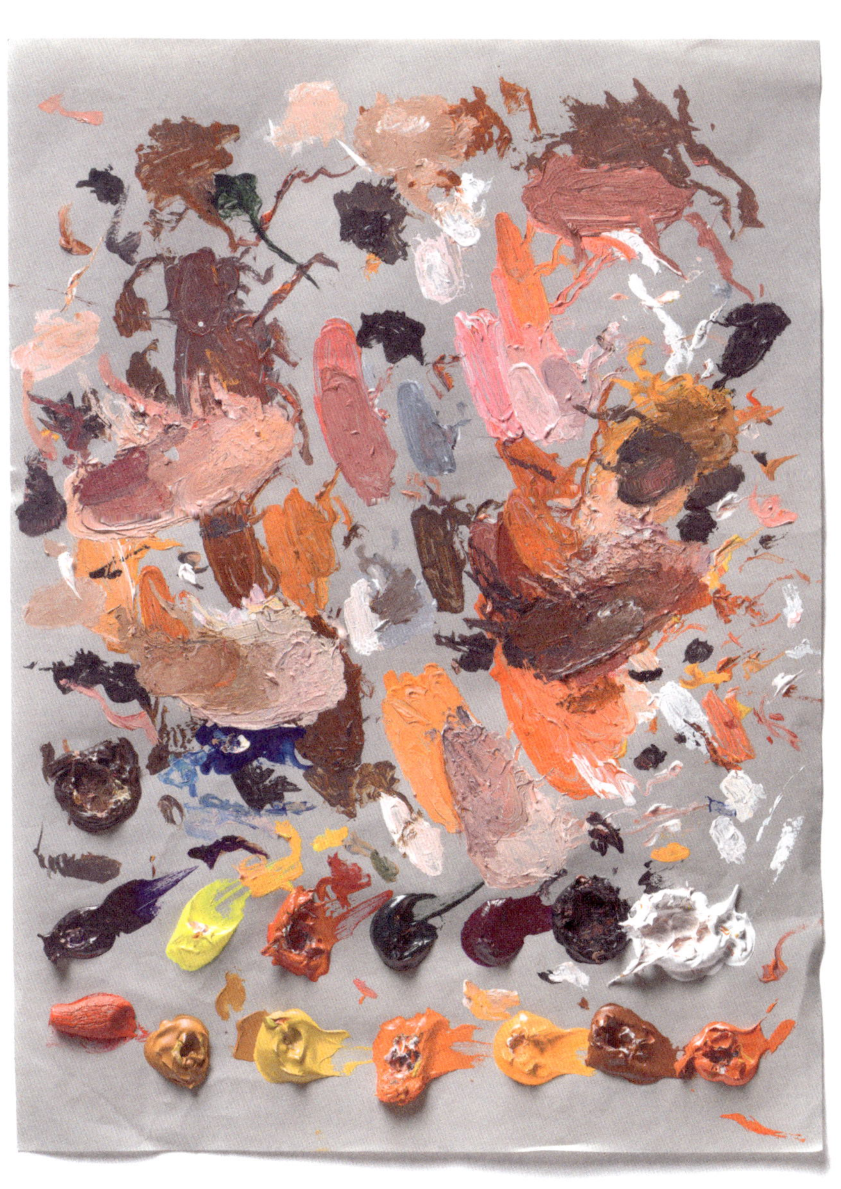

Color Palette (11)
2013. Inkjet print.
19½ × 17 in.

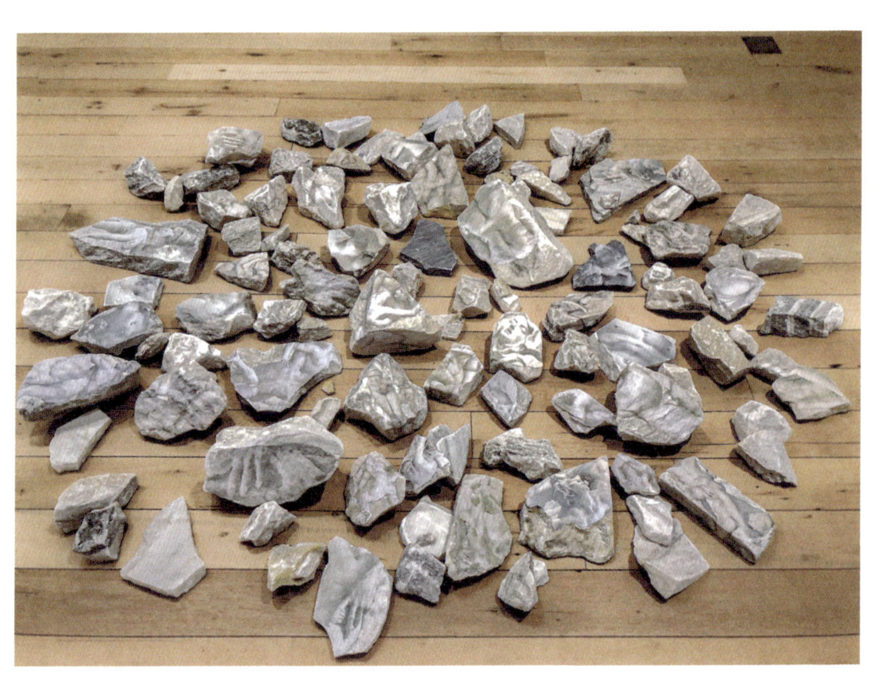

Marbles
2019, from *Statues Also Fall in Love*. Installation view, Martos Gallery, New York, 2019.

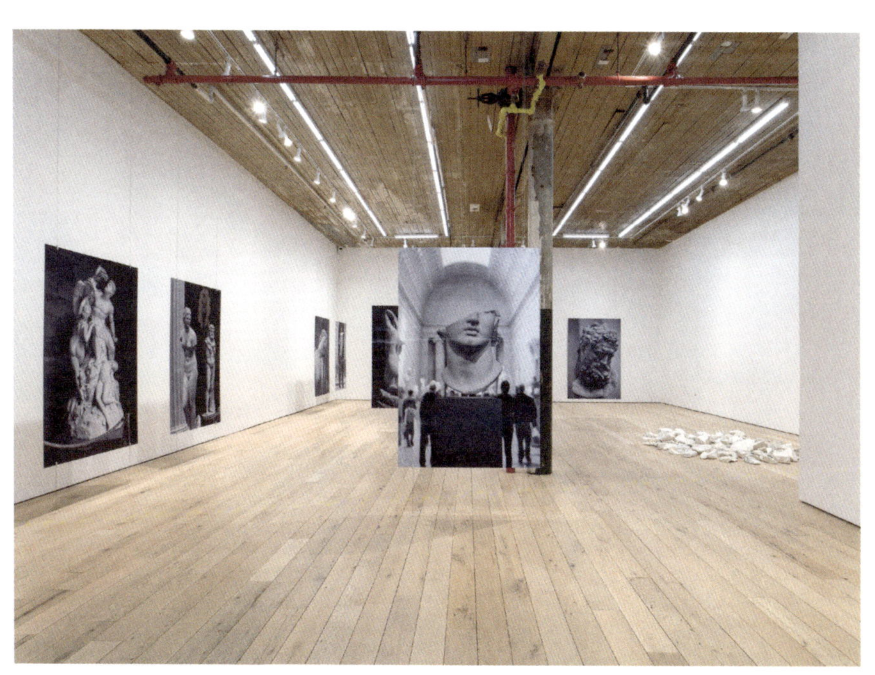

Statues Also Fall in Love
Installation view, Martos Gallery,
New York, 2019.

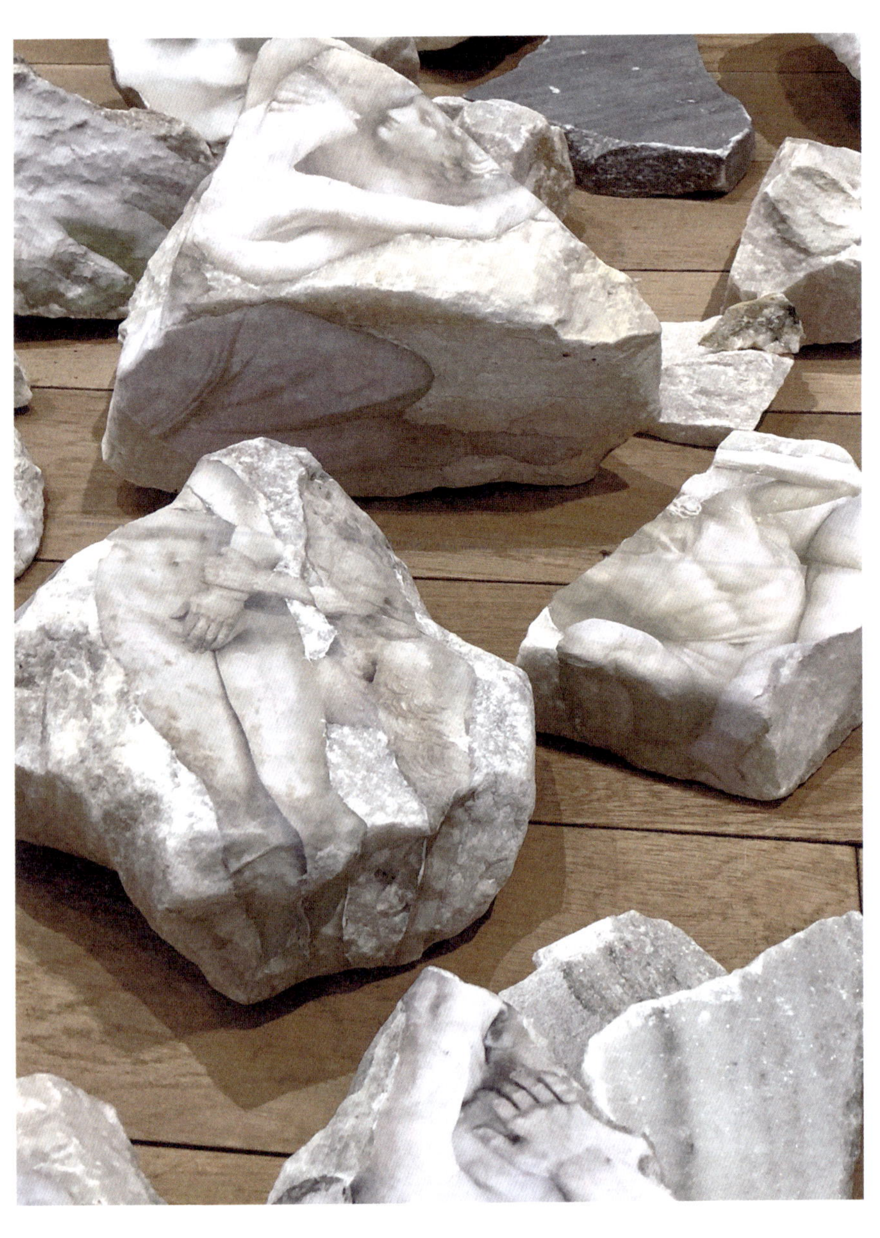

Marbles (DETAIL)
2019, from *Statues Also Fall in Love*. Installation view, Martos Gallery, New York, 2019.

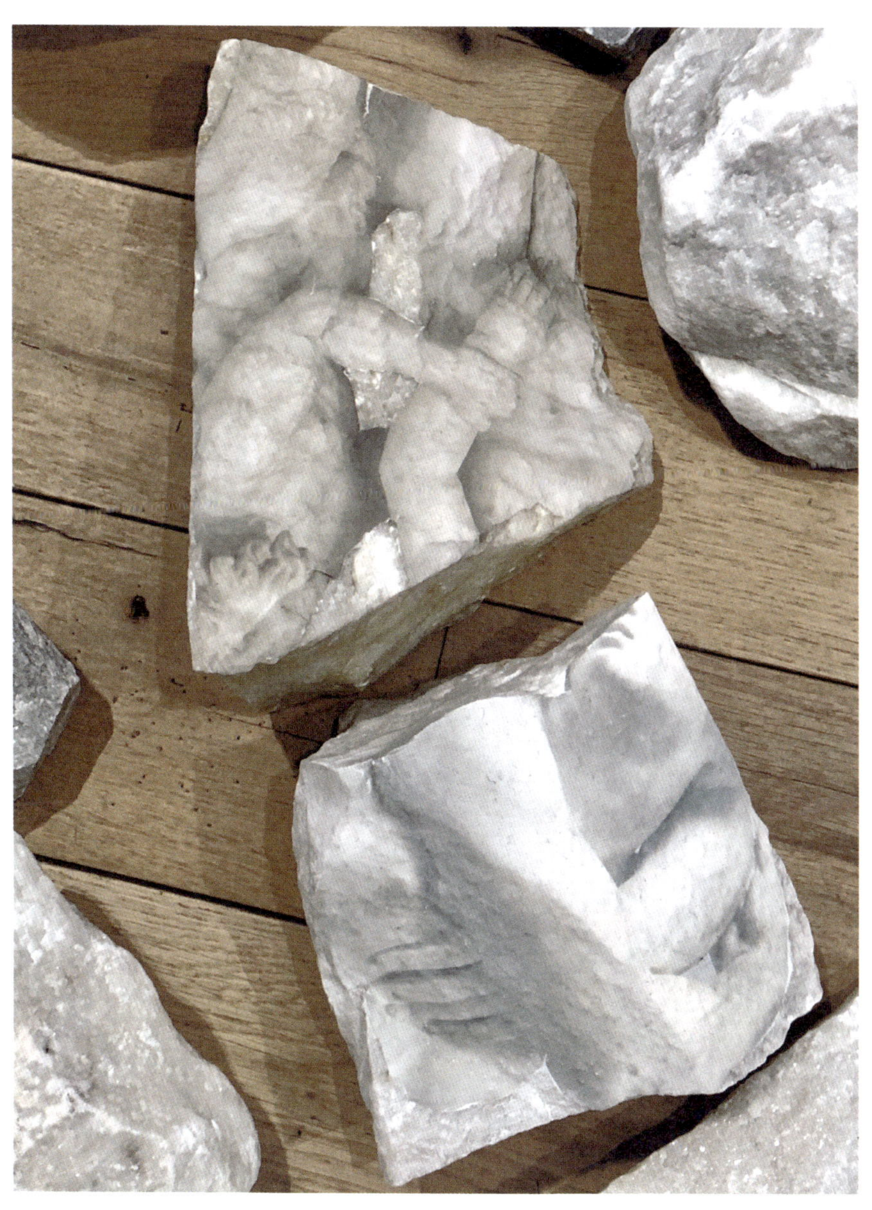

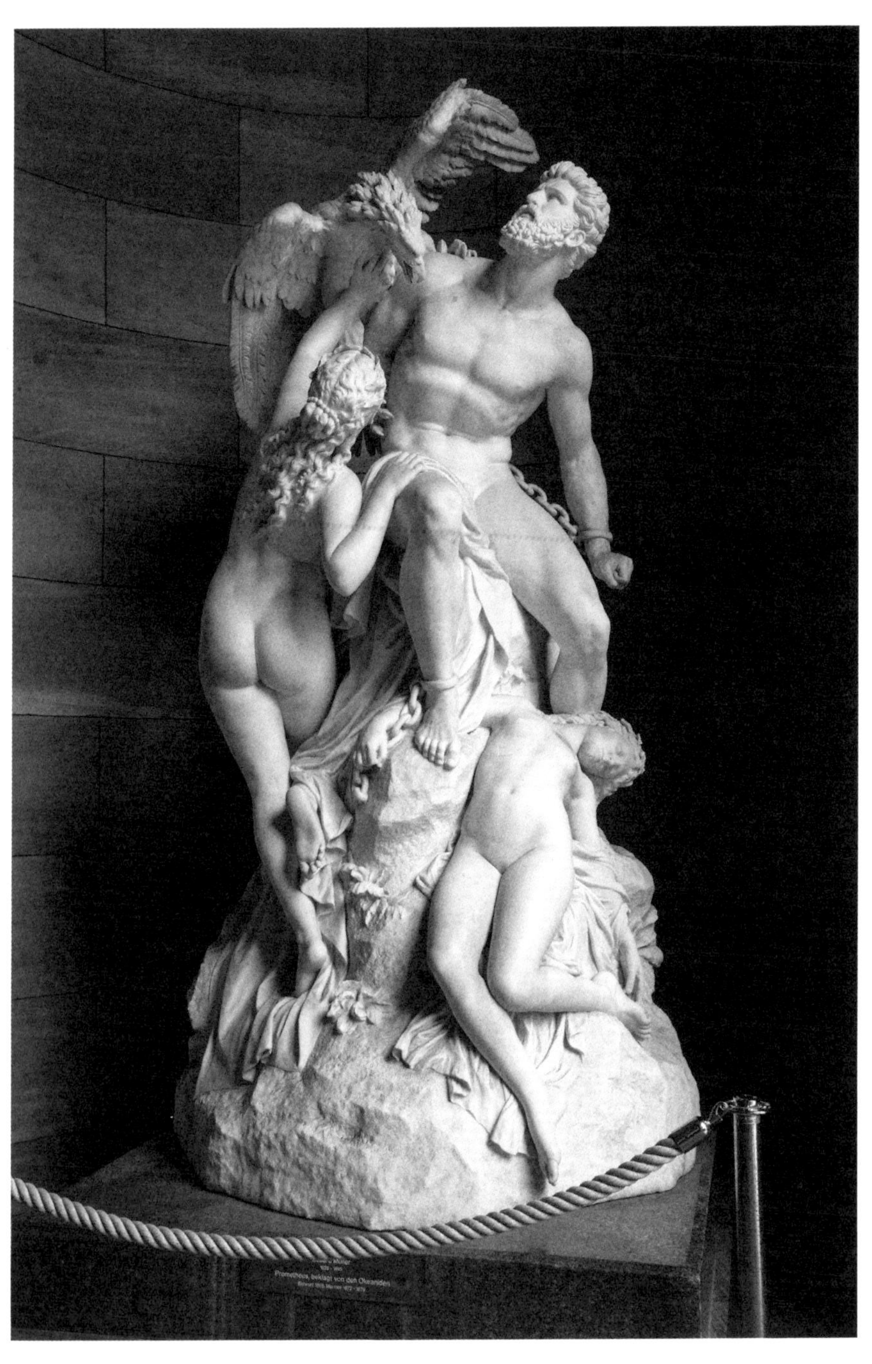

Prometheus Bound (RECTO & VERSO)
2019, from *Statues Also Fall in Love*.
Lenticular print, 71 × 47 in.

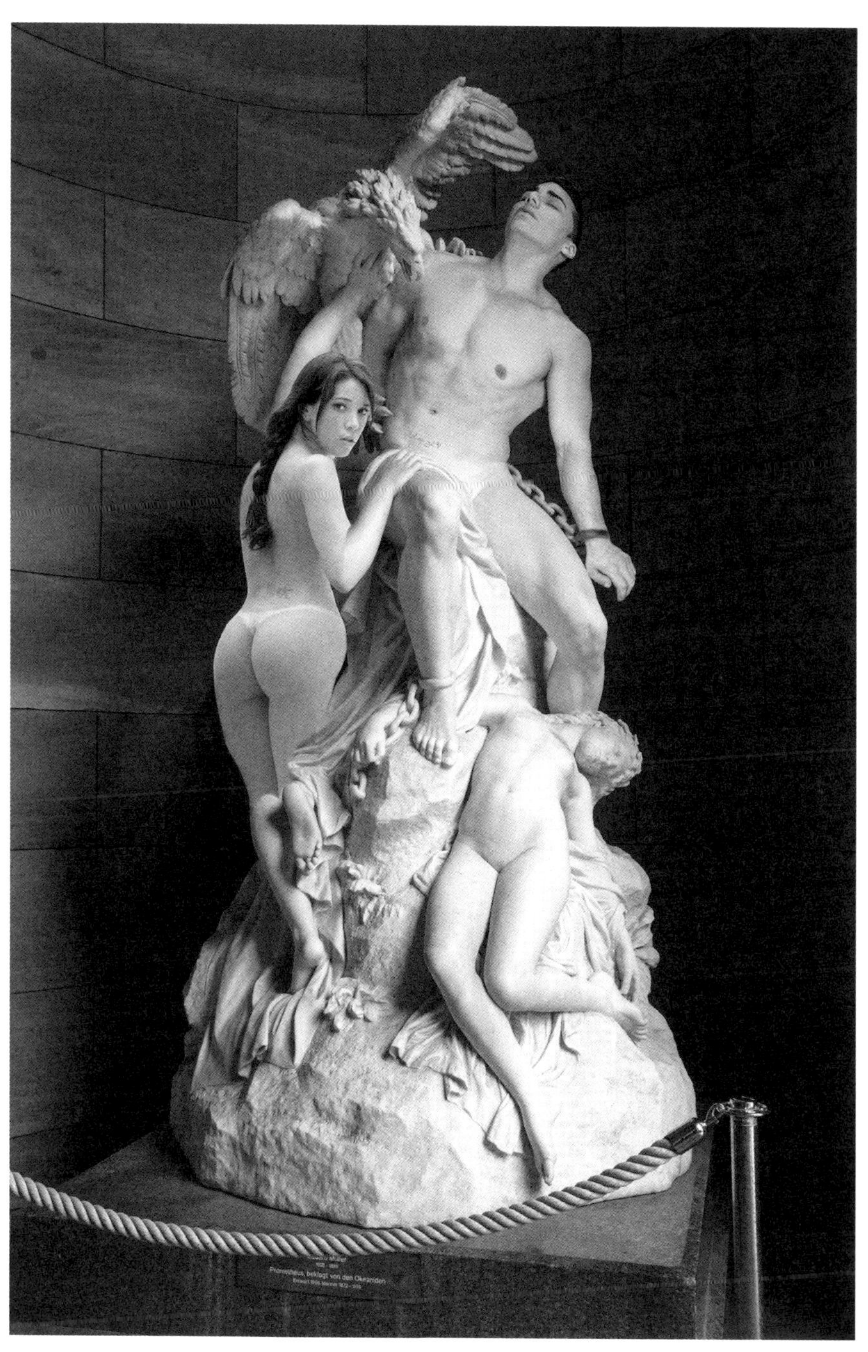
Prometheus, beklagt von den Okeaniden

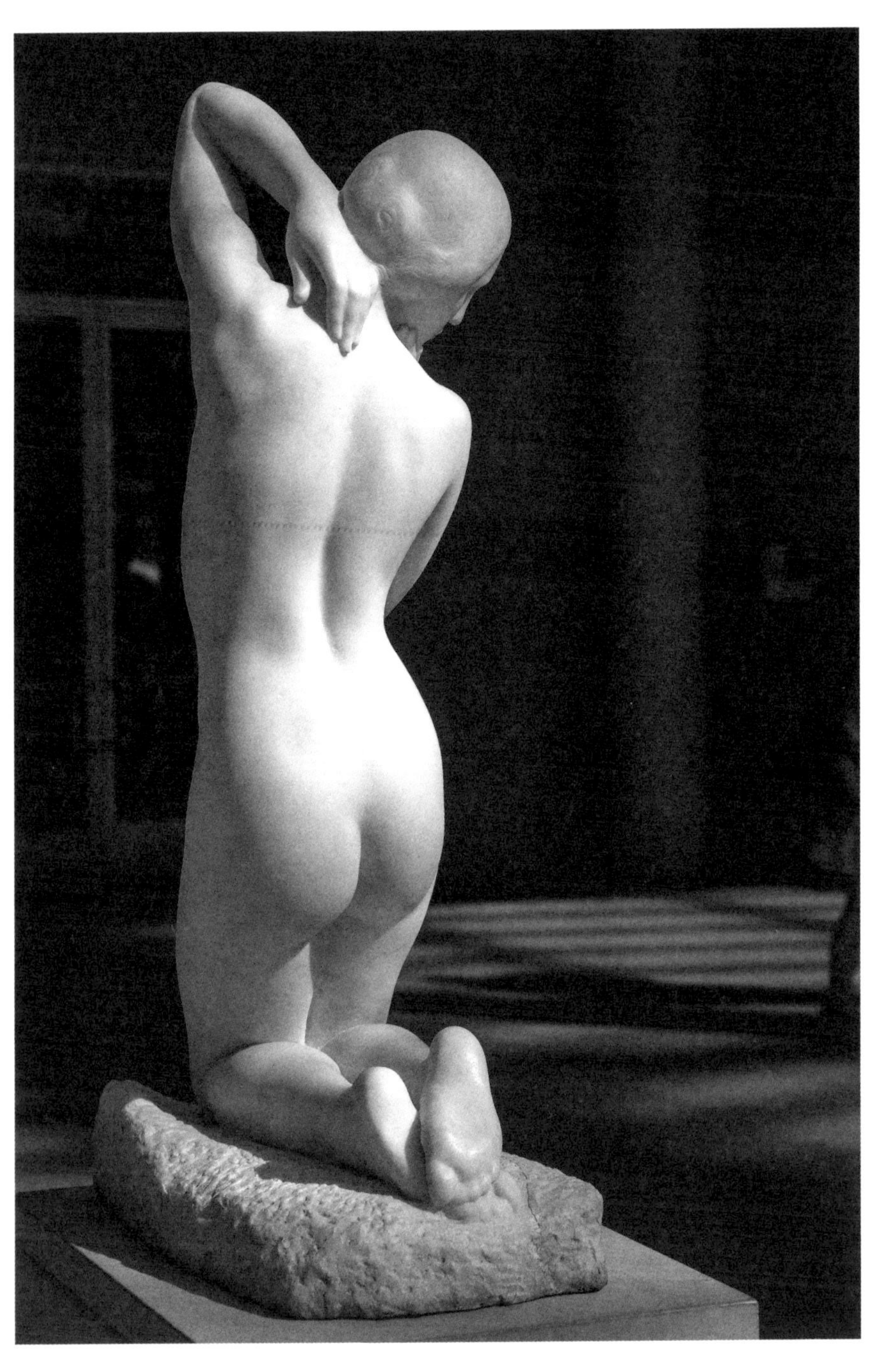

Fragilina (RECTO & VERSO)
2019, from *Statues Also Fall in Love*.
Lenticular print, 71 × 47 in.

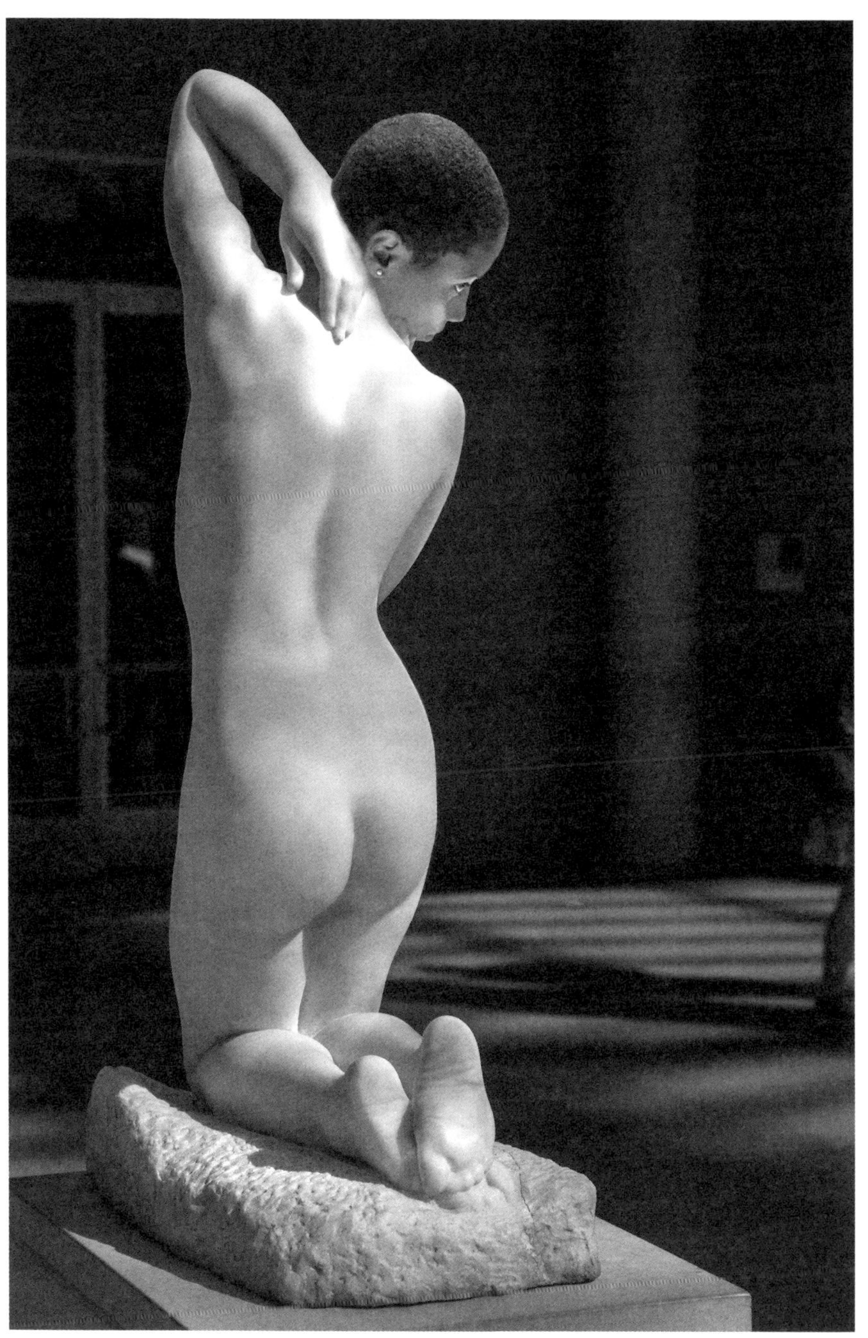

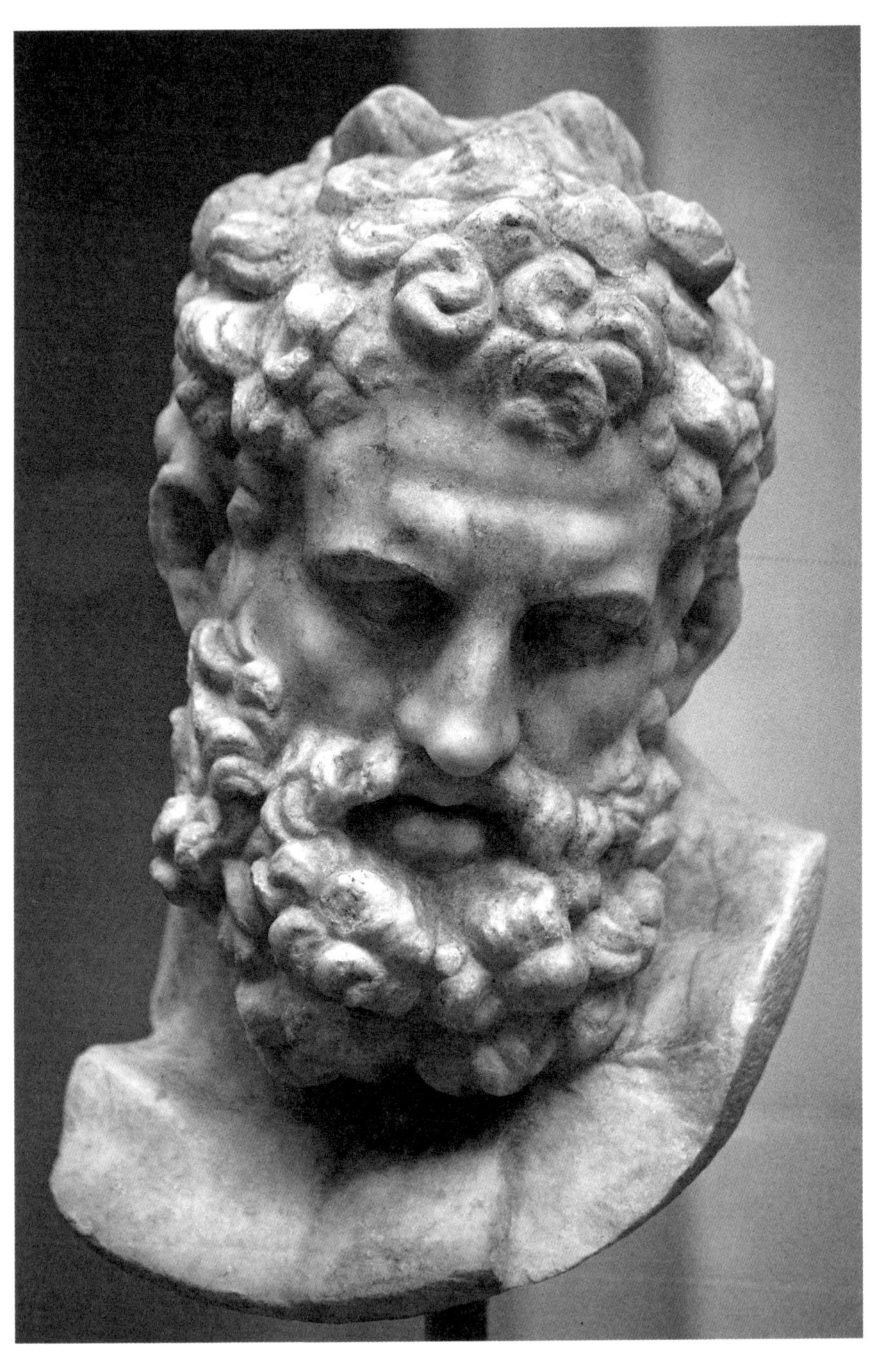

Hercules (RECTO & VERSO)
2019, from *Statues Also Fall in Love*.
Lenticular print, 71 × 47 in.

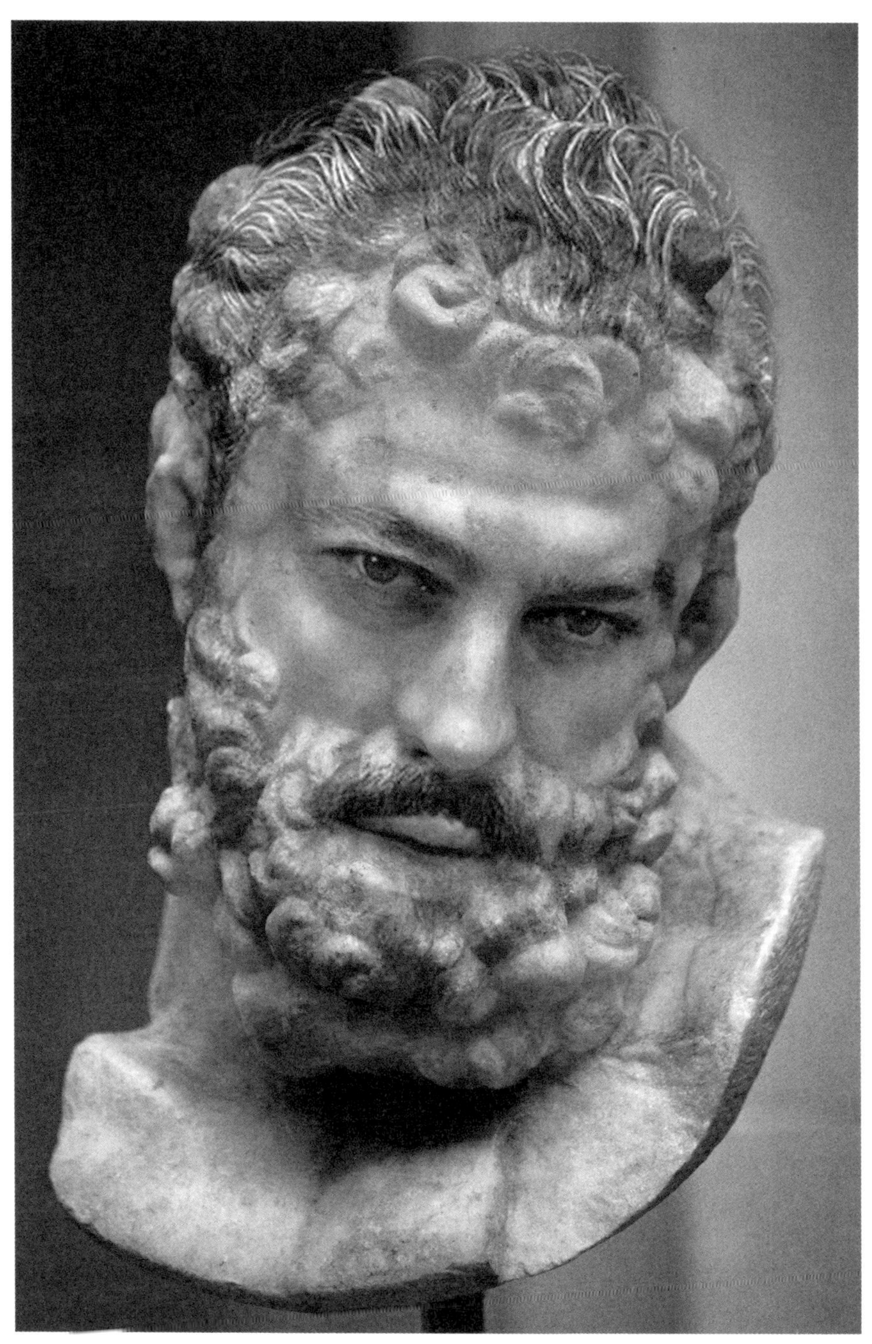

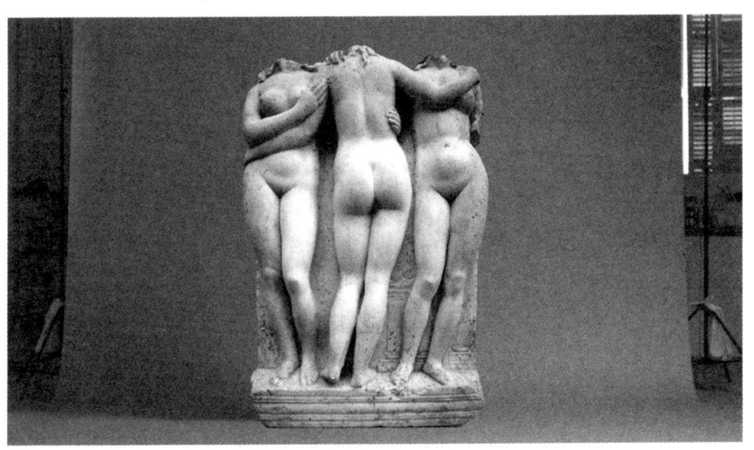

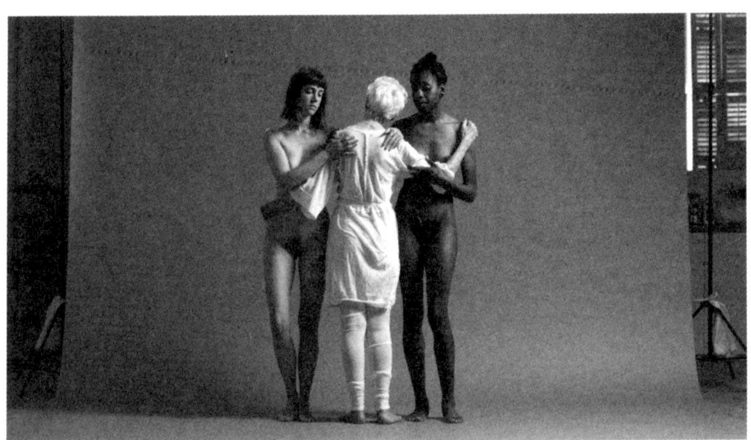

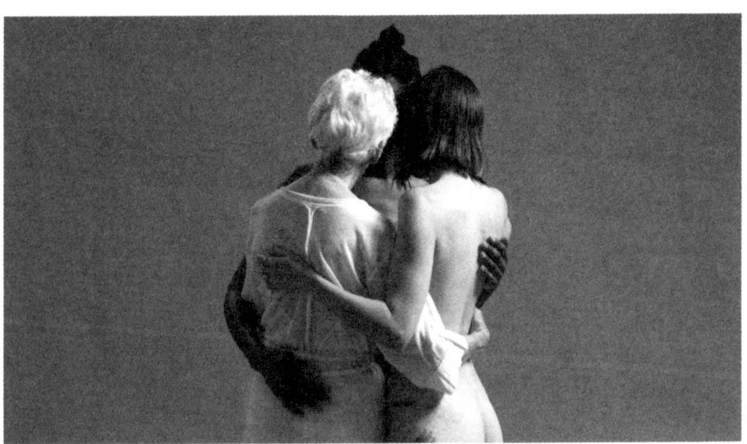

Stills from *The Three Graces*
2016, from *Statues Also Fall in Love*.
Cinematography: Dan Walworth.
Performers: Raquel Nave, Valda Setterfield, and Sharon Steven. Video, 3 min.

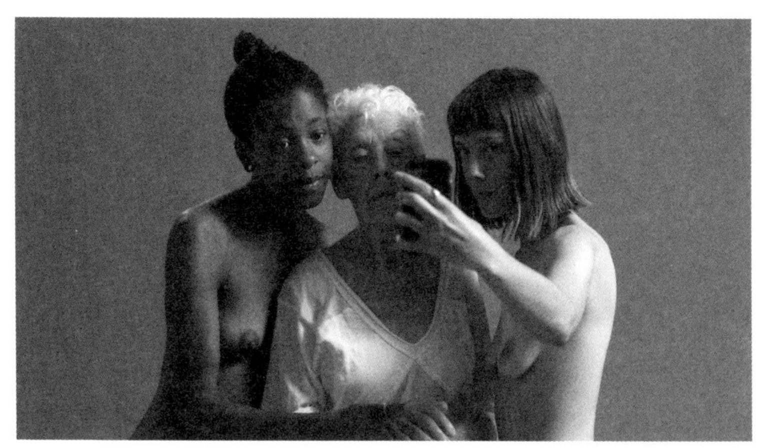

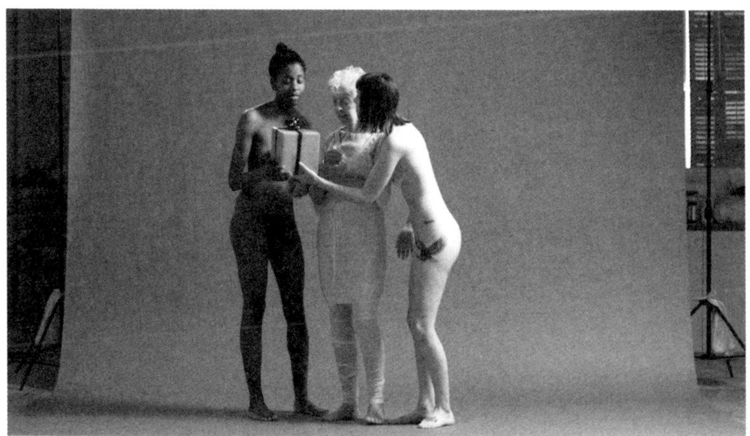

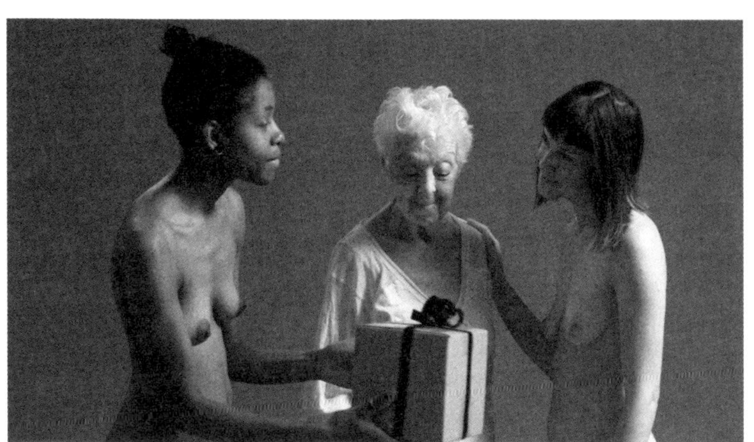

archimime

Noun
(plural archimimes)

* The chief jester or mimic who would imitate the dead person as part of ancient Roman funeral processions.

Origin
From Latin *archimimus*, from Ancient Greek *arkhimimos*

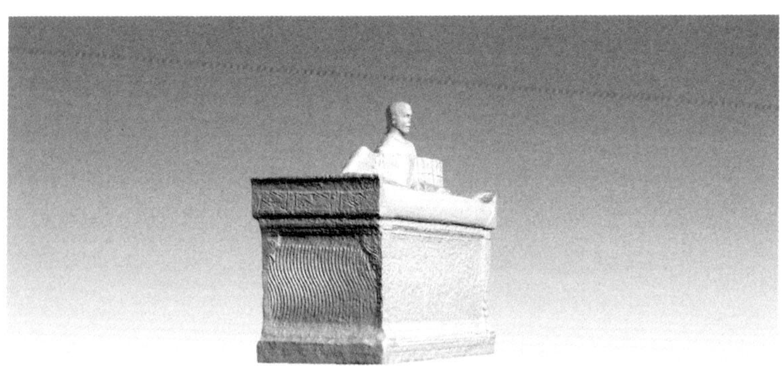

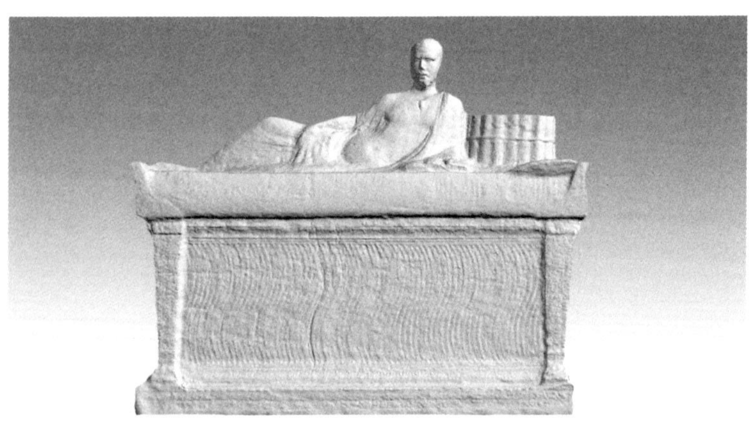

Stills from *Archemine*, by Aura Rosenberg and Tyler Coburn, 2020, from *Statues Also Fall in Love*. Video, 10 min, 37 sec.

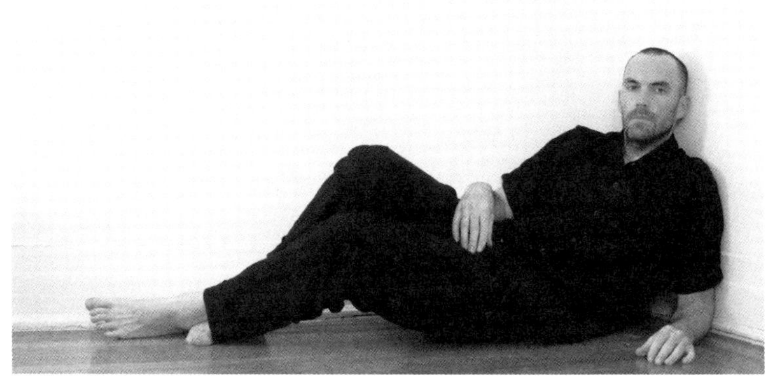

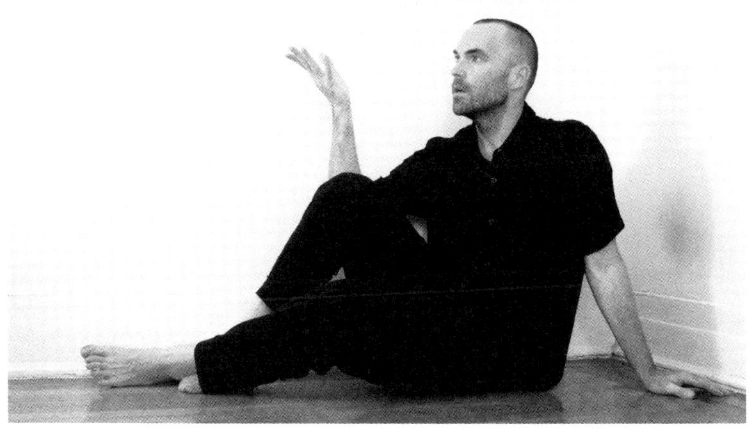

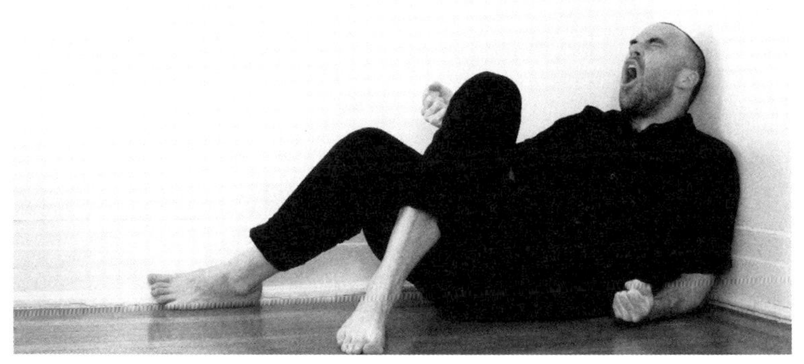

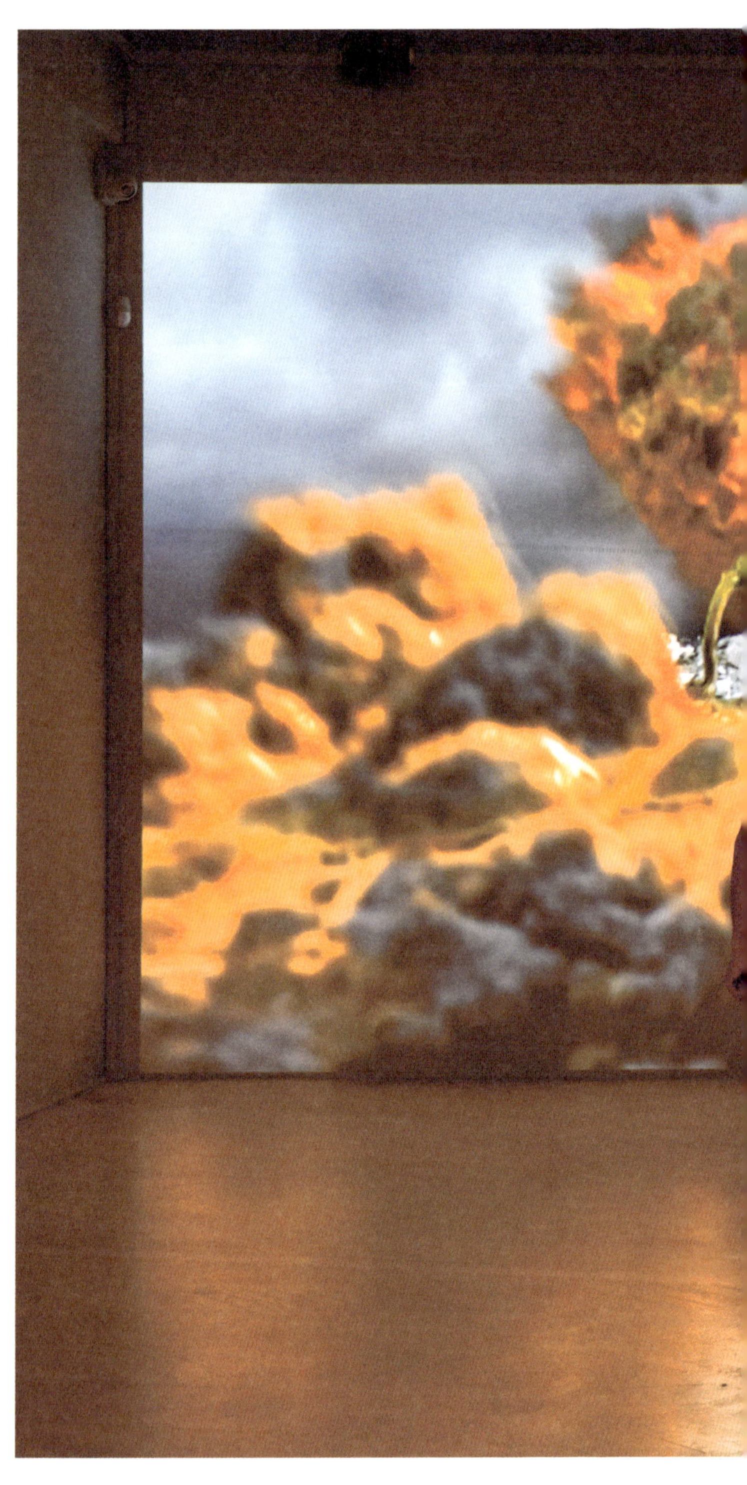

Angel of History
Installation view, Galeria Studio,
Warsaw, Poland, 2017.

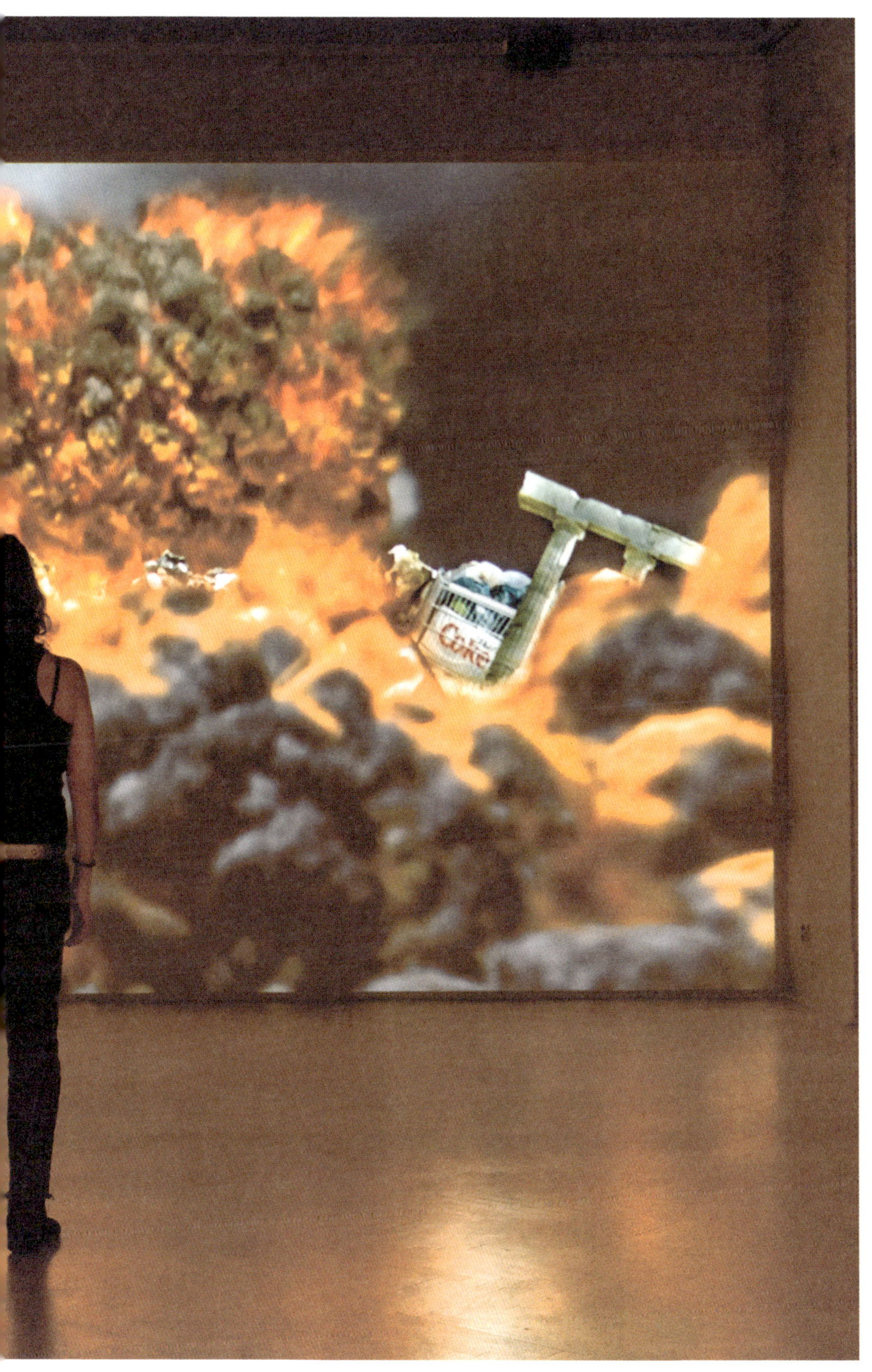
Coke

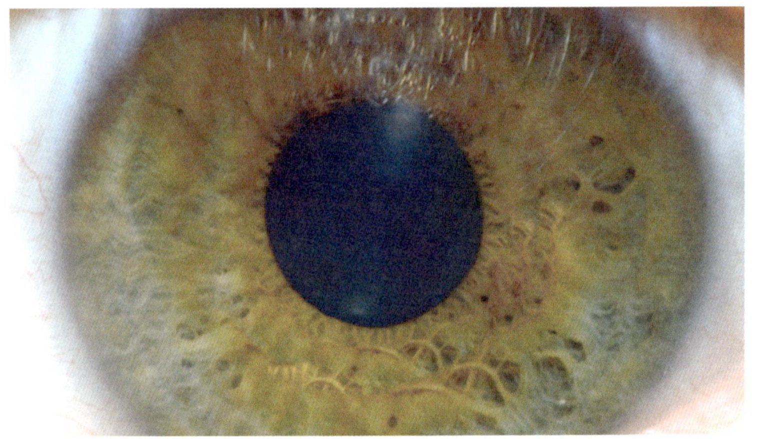

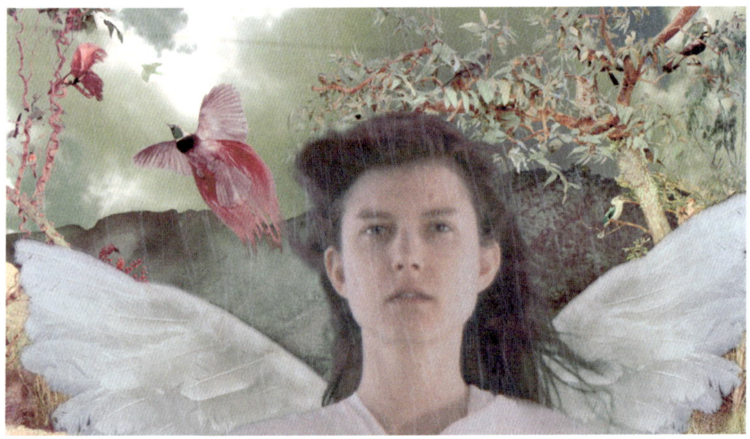

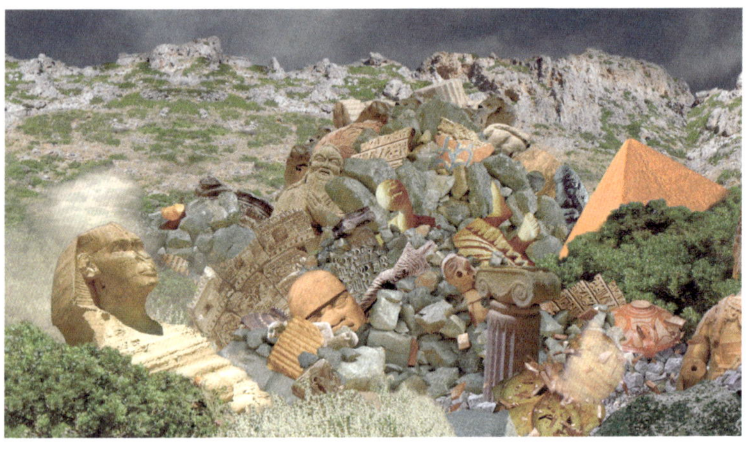

Stills from *Angel of History*
2013. Animation: Lisa Crafts. Video, 5 min, 3 sec.

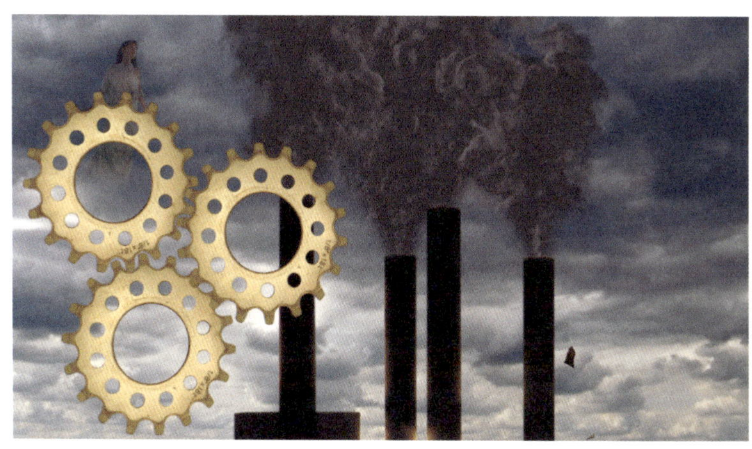

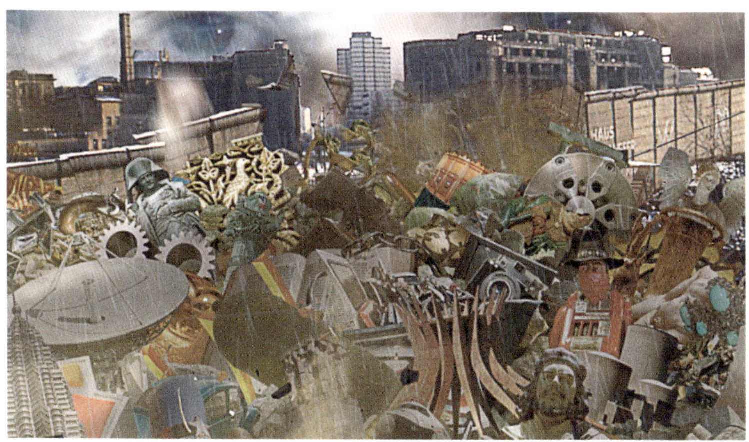

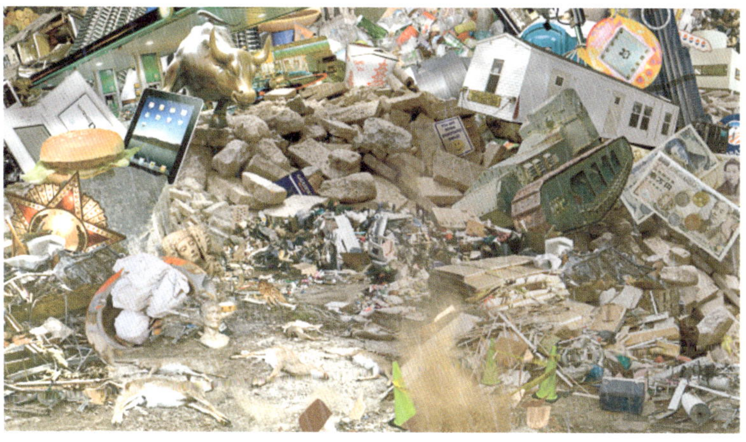

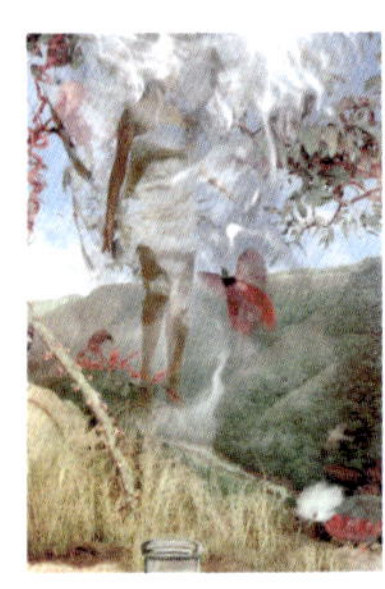
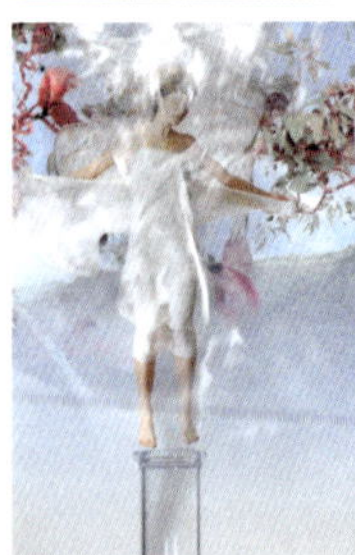
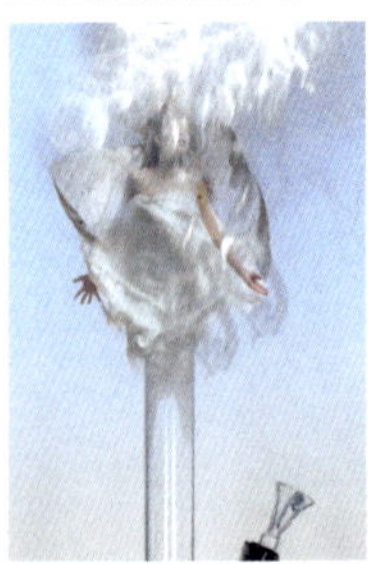
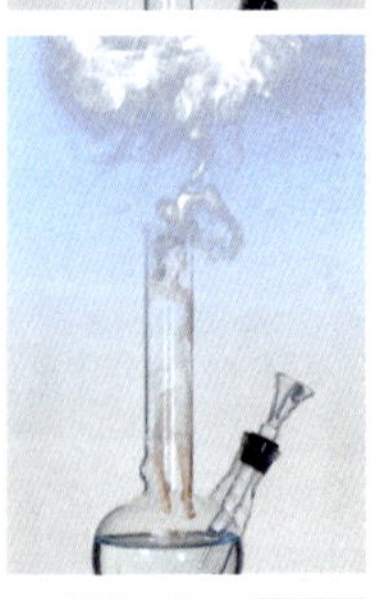
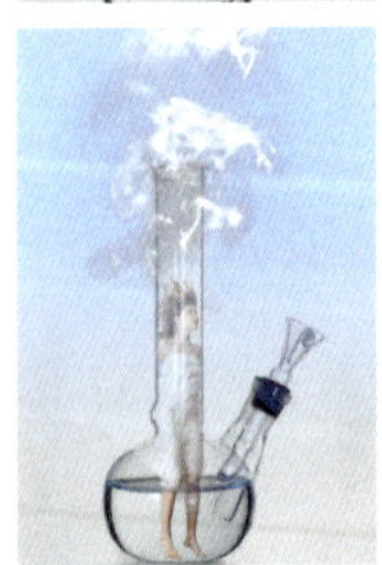

Artificial Paradise
2006. Five inkjet prints.
11 × 8½ in. each.

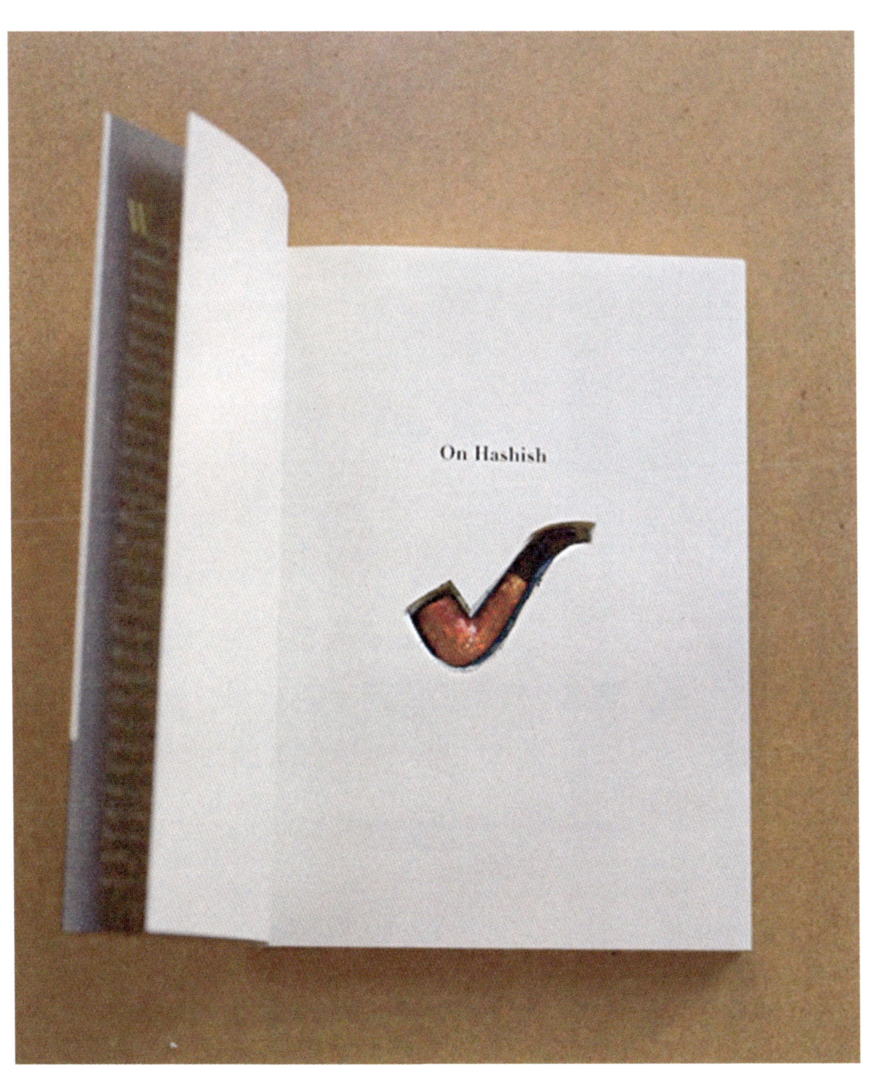

Stashbox for Benjamin
2006. Book with pipe.

Oh brownbaked Victory Column
with winter sugar from the days of childhood
2001. Installation view, *After The Fact*, Städtische Galerie im Lenbachhaus, Munich, 2017.

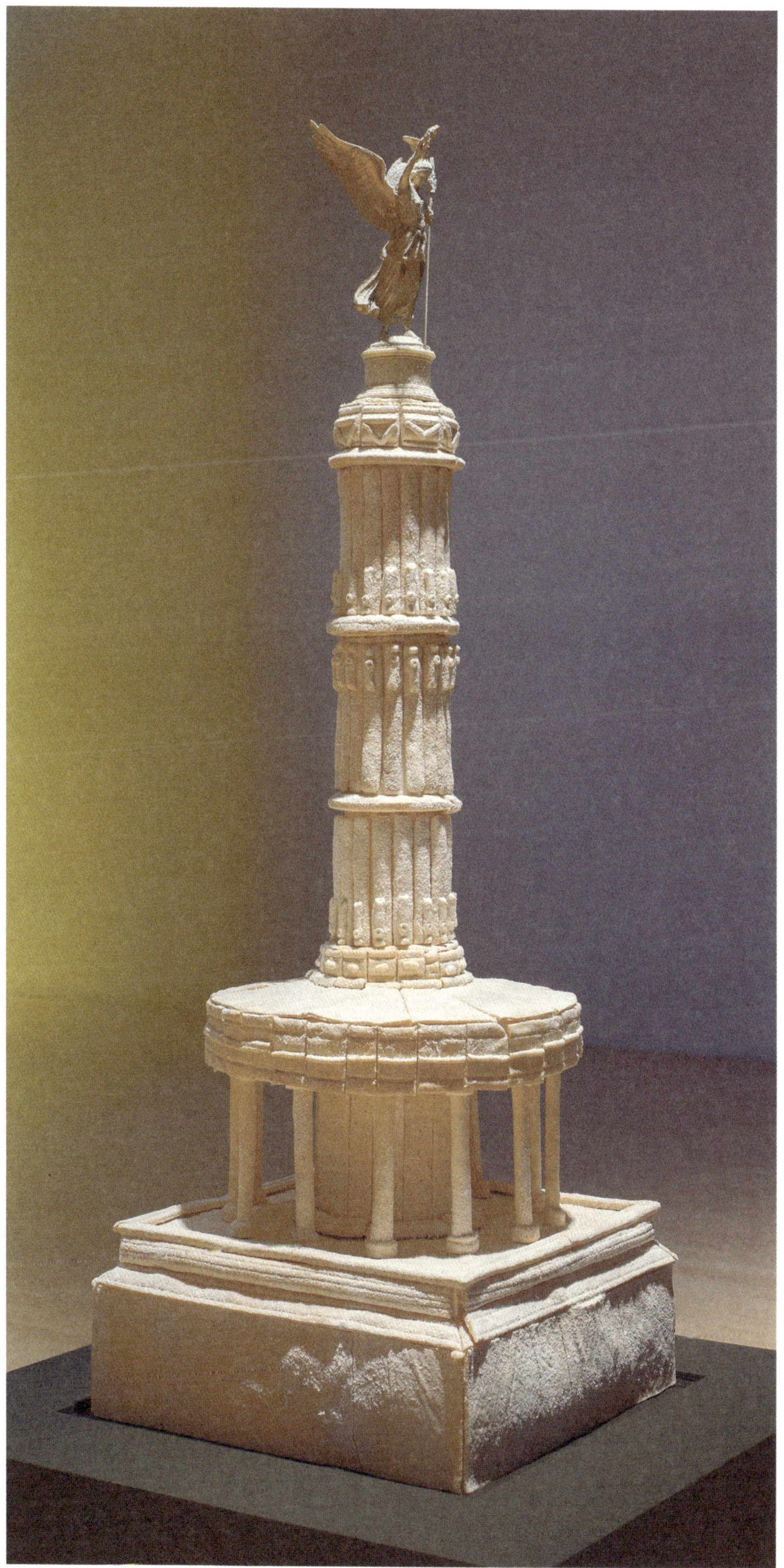

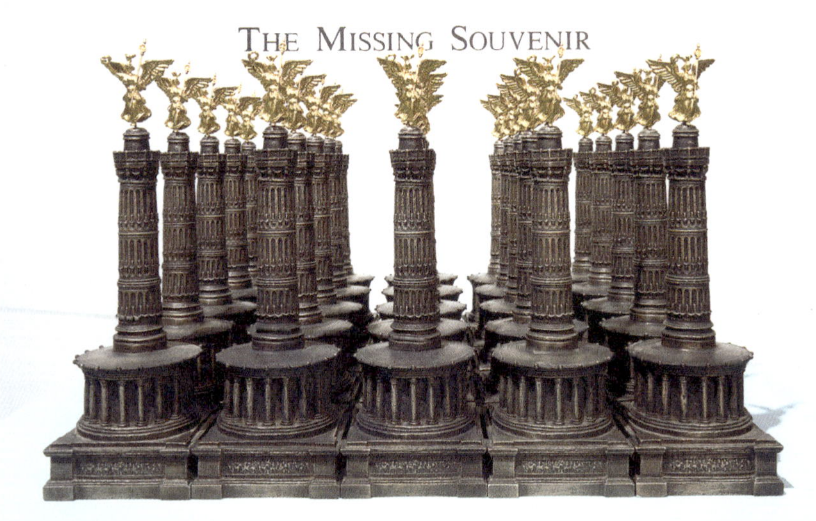

The Missing Souvenir
Installation view, Gasser and Grunert Gallery, New York, 2002.

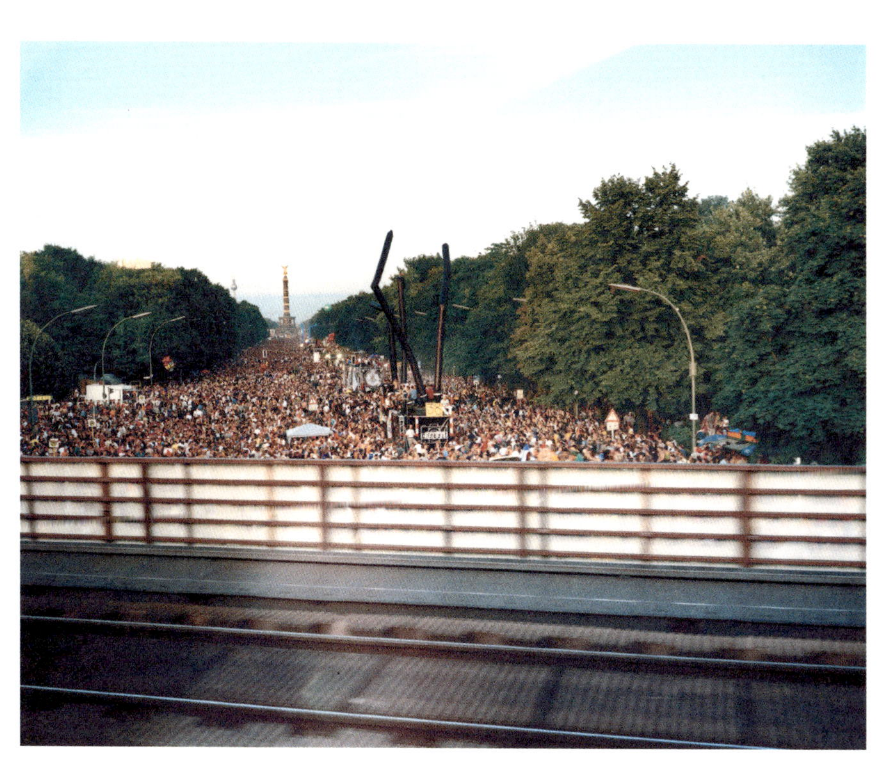

The Siegessäule (Love Parade)
2001, from *Berlin Childhood*. C-print.
30 × 40 in.

"All the News That's Fit to Print"

The New York Times

Late Edition

Today, clouds and sunshine, severe late-afternoon thunderstorms, high 78. Tonight, skies clearing, breezy, low 57. Tomorrow, partly sunny, high 74. Weather map is on Page D8.

VOL. CLXXI ... No. 425 — NEW YORK, MONDAY, MAY 16, 2022 — $3.00

GRIEF AND RAGE ROCK BUFFALO AFTER RACISM FUELS MASSACRE

NEWS ANALYSIS

Two Countries Turn to NATO In Face of ...

The Idea of Neutrality In Europe Fades ...

By ROGER COHEN

The decisions by Finland and Sweden to abandon the ... they adhered to ... and apply to join NATO ... strongest indication yet of a profound change in Europe ... face of an aggressive Russia's imperial project.

The two Scandinavian states have in effect made clear that they expect the threat from President Vladimir V. Putin's Russia to be enduring, that they will not be cowed by it, and that after the Russian butchery in Bucha, Ukraine, there is no room for bystanders. Theirs is a declaration of Western resolve.

"Military nonalignment has served Sweden well, but our conclusion is that it won't serve us equally well in the future," Sweden's prime minister, Magdalena Andersson, said on Sunday. "This is not a decision to be taken lightly."

Because the Finnish and Swedish militaries are already well integrated with NATO, one reason the application process may go quickly, the immediate impact of the countries' change of strategic course in light of Russia's invasion of Ukraine will be less practical than political.

This is a new Europe in which there is no more in-between space. Countries are either protected by NATO or they are on their own against a Russia ruled by a man determined to assert Russia's place on the world stage through force. For Sweden, and especially for Finland, with its 810-mile border with Russia, Mr.

Continued on Page A9

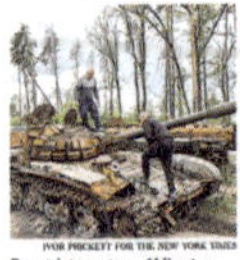

IVOR PRICKETT FOR THE NEW YORK TIMES

Russia's invasion of Ukraine has ended an era of European illusions about Moscow.

Flouting Rules Of Campaigns In Plain Sight

... Steer PACs ... Red Boxes

... takedown ... "toxic" ... Leod-Skinner — ... ing a link to a two-page, ... tion-research document about her tenure as a city manager.

The message was received.

On May 3, a super PAC that has received all its money from a secret-money group with ties to the pharmaceutical industry began running television ads that did little more than copy, paste and reorder the precise three lines of attack Mr. Schrader had outlined.

From Oregon to Texas, North Carolina to Pennsylvania, Democratic candidates nationwide are using such red boxes to pioneer new frontiers in soliciting and directing money from friendly super PACs financed by multimillionaires, billionaires and special-interest groups.

Campaign watchdogs complain that the practice further blurs the lines meant to keep big-money interests from influencing people running for office, effectively evading the strict donation limits imposed on federal candidates. And while the tactic is not new to 2022, it is becoming so widespread that a New York Times survey of candidate websites found at least 19 Democrats deploying some version of a red box in four of the states holding contested congressional primaries on Tuesday.

The practice is both brazen and breathtakingly simple. To work around the prohibition on directly coordinating with super PACs, candidates are posting their instructions to them inside the red boxes on public pages that super PACs continuously monitor.

The boxes highlight the aspects of candidates' biographies that they want amplified and the skeletons in their opponents' closets

Continued on Page A16

SCOTT OLSON/GETTY IMAGES

Friends consoling a survivor of Saturday's shooting, right, during services at True Bethel Baptist Church in Buffalo on Sunday.

Creeping Into the Mainstream, A Theory Turns Hate Into Terror

A Toxic Belief That the White Race Is at Risk Drives Violence

By NICHOLAS CONFESSORE and KAREN YOURISH

Continued on Page A20

Before Attack, Solitary Teen Caused Alarm

This article is by Ashley Southall, Chelsia Rose Marcius and Andy Newman.

Last spring, as the end of the academic year approached at Susquehanna Valley High School outside Binghamton, N.Y., students were asked for a school project about their plans after graduation.

Payton S. Gendron, a senior, said he wanted to commit a murder-suicide, according to a law enforcement official briefed on the matter.

He claimed to be joking, the official said. But the state police were summoned to investigate and took Mr. Gendron, then 17, into custody on June 8 under a state mental health law, police officials said Sunday.

He had a psychiatric evaluation in a hospital but was released within a couple of days, the officials said. Two weeks later, Mr. Gendron graduated and fell off investigators' radar.

On Saturday, he resurfaced 200 miles away in Buffalo, where the authorities say he opened fire at a supermarket in a predominantly Black area, killing 10 people and wounding three others in one of the deadliest racist massacres in recent U.S. history.

After his rampage, Mr. Gendron put his gun to his neck. But two officers persuaded him to drop his weapon and surrender.

He was charged Saturday with first-degree murder, and as he awaited his fate in jail, investigators were sifting through his past to piece together how he transformed from a quiet student to an accused killer without drawing more serious scrutiny.

New York State has what is known as a red flag law, under which people found to be a danger can be forced to surrender their guns, but no one tried to invoke it against Mr. Gendron. The state

Continued on Page A19

Victims Include Security Guard Hailed as Hero

By JESSE McKINLEY

BUFFALO — A day after one of the deadliest racist massacres in recent American history, law enforcement officials in New York descended on the home of the accused gunman and probed disturbing hints into his behavior, as Gov. Kathy Hochul promised action on hate speech that she said spreads "like a virus."

The suspect, Payton S. Gendron, 18, shot 13 people on Saturday afternoon at a Tops supermarket in east Buffalo, killing 10, officials said. Almost all the victims were Black — shoppers, grocery workers and a security guard bound together by little more than tragic happenstance.

But Mr. Gendron picked his target carefully, the police said, choosing an area known for its large Black population and even visiting the neighborhood the day before the attack in what authorities described as "reconnaissance."

And nearly a year before the mass shooting, his words had already caused alarm elsewhere.

The police said on Sunday that Mr. Gendron had been picked up at his high school last June by state police after making a threatening remark and had been taken to a hospital for a mental health evaluation.

Responding to a question for a class project about his post-graduation plans, Mr. Gendron said his involved a murder-suicide, a law enforcement official familiar with the case said.

But Mr. Gendron described the remark as a joke, the official said. And after the evaluation, which lasted about a day and a half, he was released, according to Joseph Gramaglia, the Buffalo police commissioner.

That account was confirmed by Special Agent Steven Belongia of the F.B.I., who said that Mr. Gendron was "not on the radar" of federal

Continued on Page A19

PATTERN OF RACISM In the Masten Park neighborhood, a collective anguish and anger stemming from a long history of trauma. PAGE A18

SOCIAL MEDIA Platforms again faced questions about their responsibility for allowing violent and hateful content to proliferate. PAGE A20

Why Australia's Covid Death Rate Is Only One-Tenth of U.S. Level

By DAMIEN CAVE

MELBOURNE, Australia — If the United States had the same Covid death rate as Australia, about 900,000 lives would have been saved. The Texas grandmother who made the perfect pumpkin pie might still be baking. The Red Sox-loving husband who ran marathons before Covid might still be cheering at Fenway Park.

For many Americans, imagining what might have been will be painful. But especially now, at the milestone of one million deaths in the United States, the nations that did a better job of keeping people alive show what Americans could have done differently and what might still need to change.

Many places provide insight. Japan. Kenya. Norway. But Australia offers perhaps the sharpest comparisons with the American experience. Both countries are English-speaking democracies with similar demographic profiles. In Australia and in the United States, the median age is 38. Roughly 86 percent of Australians live in urban areas, compared with 83 percent of Americans.

Yet Australia's Covid death rate sits at one-tenth of America's, putting the nation of 25 million people (with around 7,500 deaths) near the top of global rankings in the protection of life.

Australia's location in the distant Pacific is often cited as the cause of its relative Covid success. That, however, does not fully explain the difference in outcomes between the two countries, since Australia has long been, like the United States, highly connected to the world through trade, tourism

Continued on Page A6

18 YEARS AND OVER MUST BE FULLY VACCINATED FOR ENTRY

ASANKA BRENDON RATNAYAKE FOR THE NEW YORK TIMES

People showing vaccination certificates before entering the Melbourne Cricket Ground in March.

INTERNATIONAL A4-14

Preventing 'Ghost Surgeries'

After scandals in which doctors let unsupervised assistants operate on patients, South Korea is requiring cameras in operating rooms. PAGE A4

Somber Election in Somalia

The militants of Al Shabab collect taxes, decide court cases and control the streets. Somalis ask whether a new government will even matter. PAGE A8

London's High-Tech Trains

The Elizabeth line, a transit project 13 years in the making, features cathedral-like stations and roomy cars. PAGE A10

NATIONAL A15-21

Houses Lost to the Sea

A group of vacation homes off the coast of North Carolina has become a symbol of the effects of rising oceans. PAGE A15

Special Counsel Gets Started

The prosecutor assigned by the Trump administration to scour the Russia inquiry is opening a trial. PAGE A15

SPORTS D1-7

Rangers Complete a Comeback

With an overtime goal in Game 7, they ousted the Penguins and capped a rally from a 3-1 series deficit. PAGE D1

Celtics and Mavericks Survive

Boston and Dallas won in Game 7 routs, ousting the defending champion Bucks and the No. 1-seeded Suns. PAGE D6

BUSINESS B1-4

Everything Going Electric

Beyond electric cars, there is a growing market for battery-powered scooters, bicycles, snowmobiles and watercraft. Buyers are converting for fuel savings and other practical advantages. PAGE B1

Chasing Savings at the Grocery

As shoppers feel the pinch of rising prices, they're keeping their food bills down by store-hopping, cutting back on expensive items and using coupons more — anything for a bargain. PAGE B1

OPINION A22-23

Pamela Paul PAGE A22

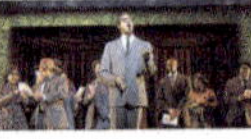

ARTS C1-6

Singing to the Future

An opera about Malcolm X, with Davóne Tines, above, has stretches of incantation that are akin to a sacred rite, Zachary Woolfe writes. PAGE C1

Angel of History (New York Times, May 16, 2022)
2022. Inkjet print, 24 × 13 in.

"All the News That's Fit to Print"

The New York Times

Late Edition
Today, clouds and sunshine, windy, chilly for late April, high 55. **Tonight,** partly cloudy, brisk, chilly, low 38. **Tomorrow,** partly sunny, chilly wind, high 54. Weather map, Page B12.

VOL. CLXXI .... No. 59,406 © 2022 The New York Times Company NEW YORK, WEDNESDAY, APRIL 27, 2022 $3.00

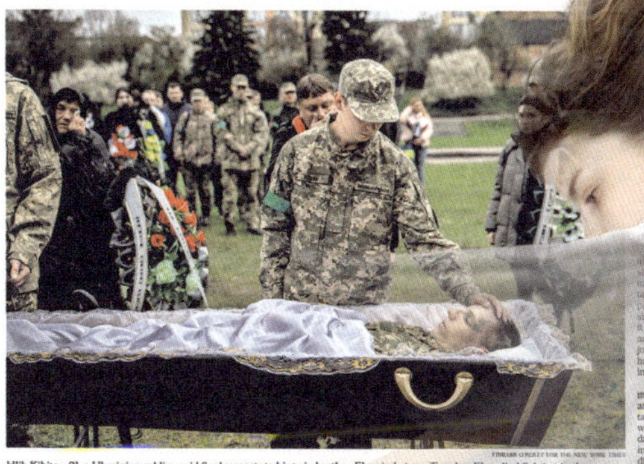

Hlib Kihitov, 21, a Ukrainian soldier, paid final respects to his twin brother, Ehor, in Lviv on Tuesday. Ehor died fighting in the east.

U.S. PUSHES ALLIES FOR UKRAINE ARMS AS WAR ESCALATES

In Critical Shift, Germany Offers Armor — Hopes for Diplomacy Dim

This article is by John Ismay, Christopher F. Schuetze and Michael Levenson.

RAMSTEIN AIR BASE, Germany — The United States marshaled 40 allies on Tuesday to furnish Ukraine with long-term military aid for what could become a protracted battle against the Russian invasion, and Germany said it would send dozens of armored antiaircraft vehicles. It was a major policy shift for a country that had wavered over fear of provoking Russia.

The announcement by Germany, Europe's biggest economy and one of Russia's most important Western trading partners, was among many signals on Tuesday pointing to further escalation in the war and disappointment for diplomacy.

Germany's shift on weapons also was seen as a strong affirmation of a toughened message by the Biden administration, which has said it wants to see Russia not only defeated in Ukraine but seriously weakened from the conflict that President Vladimir V. Putin began two months ago.

The increasing flow of Western weapons into Ukraine — including howitzers, armed drones, tanks and ammunition — also amounted to another sign that a war Mr. Putin had expected would divide his Western adversaries had instead drawn them much closer together.

"Putin never imagined that the world would rally behind Ukraine so swiftly and surely," the American defense secretary, Lloyd J. Austin III, said on Tuesday to uniformed and civilian officials at the U.S. air base in Ramstein, Germany, where he convened defense officials from 40 allied countries.

"Nobody is fooled" by Mr. Putin's "phony claims on Donbas," Mr. Austin said, referring to the eastern region of Ukraine, where Russia recently refocused its assaults. "Russia's invasion is indefensible and so are Russian atrocities," he said.

Russia's foreign minister, Sergey V. Lavrov, said on Tuesday that the influx of heavy weapons from Western countries was effectively pushing Ukraine to sabotage peace talks with Moscow, which have shown no concrete signs of progress.

"They will continue that line by filling Ukraine with weapons," Mr. Lavrov said after meeting in Moscow with the United Nations secretary general, António Guterres, who was undertaking his most active effort yet at diplomacy to halt the war. "If that continues, negotiations won't yield any result."

On Monday, Mr. Lavrov resurrected the specter of nuclear war, as Mr. Putin has done at least twice before. Mr. Lavrov said that while such a possibility would be "unacceptable" to Russia, the

Continued on Page A11

60% of Nation Has Had Virus, C.D.C. Reports

By APOORVA MANDAVILLI

Sixty percent of Americans, including 75 percent of children, had been infected with the coronavirus by February, federal health officials reported on Tuesday — another remarkable milestone in a pandemic that continues to confound expectations.

The highly contagious Omicron variant was responsible for much of the toll. In December 2021, as the variant began spreading, only half as many people had antibodies indicating prior infection, according to new research from the Centers for Disease Control and Prevention.

While the numbers came as a shock to many Americans, some scientists said they had expected the figures to be even higher, given the contagious variants that have marched through the nation over the past two years.

There may be good news in the data, some experts said. A gain in population-wide immunity may offer at least a partial bulwark against future waves. And the trend may explain why the surge that is now roaring through China and many countries in Europe has been muted in the United States.

A high percentage of previous infections may also mean that there are now fewer cases of life-threatening illness or death relative to infections. "We will see less and less severe disease, and more and more a shift toward clinically mild disease," said Florian Krammer, an immunologist at the Icahn School of Medicine at Mount Sinai in New York.

"It will be more and more difficult for the virus to do serious damage," he added.

Administration officials, too, believe that the data augur a new

Continued on Page A19

Terror in Frontline Villages Under Constant Fire

By MICHAEL SCHWIRTZ

ORIKHIV, Ukraine — Squeezed between the Ukrainian and Russian front lines in an increasingly volatile battlefield in southeastern Ukraine, the small town of Orikhiv is constantly under fire, and Tamara Mikheenko, one of the few residents who remain, rarely leaves her basement.

"All the time in the basements, at night, under fire," Ms. Mikheenko, 70, said as yet another explosion thumped outside. "It's very scary, like a lightning bolt, everything is falling apart, the house is falling apart."

Struggling to communicate through tremendous sobs on Tuesday, Ms. Mikheenko begged

In Russian Army's Path, a Pledge 'to Resist Until the Last'

world leaders, including the presidents of the United States, Russia and Ukraine, to do whatever was necessary to stop the savagery, even as Russian forces appeared to be preparing a large offensive that officials said could steamroll Orikhiv in the coming days.

"Let them agree to stop this madness," she said.

The night before, an explosion had ripped into the unoccupied house next door, violently jolting the dark cellar Ms. Mikheenko was hiding in.

Orikhiv lies among a small constellation of tidy farming villages standing right in the path of Russian troops advancing from the south and east. Ukrainian officials believe Russian forces are preparing to make a major push forward in an attempt to expand a stretch of territory they seized in the opening days of the war.

Shelling along this front has intensified in recent days, and all over the region Ukrainian forces are digging new trenches and fortifying positions.

It is in and around these villages, still home to goats, cows and chickens, but to fewer and

Continued on Page A10

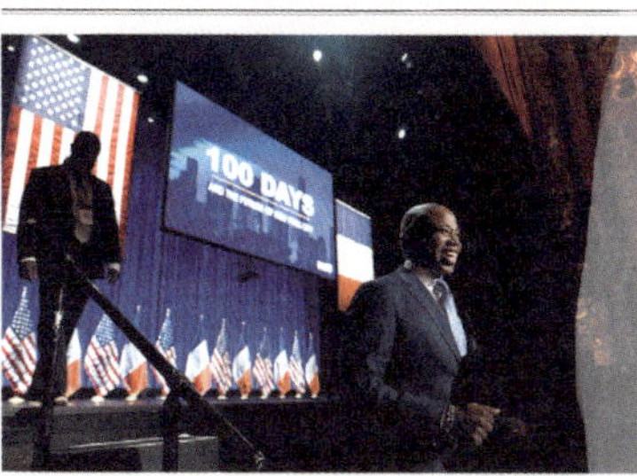

TODD HEISLER/THE NEW YORK TIMES

A Hopeful Vision for New York

In his State of the City speech on Tuesday, Mayor Eric Adams vowed to invest in safety. Page A21.

Oil Companies, Awash in Profit, Fear Opening Spigot for Europe

By CLIFFORD KRAUSS

HOUSTON — Oil and gasoline prices are climbing. Energy company profits are surging. President Biden, who came into office promising to reduce the use of fossil fuels, has effectively joined the "drill, baby, drill" chorus. Europe would love to end its dependence on Russia.

Yet most U.S. oil businesses are not eager to capitalize on this moment by pumping more oil.

Production of oil by U.S. energy companies is essentially flat and unlikely to increase substantially for at least another year or two. If Europe stops buying Russian oil and natural gas as some of its leaders have promised, they will not be able to replace that energy with fuels from the United States anytime soon.

U.S. oil production is up less than 2 percent, to 11.8 million barrels a day, since December and remains well below the record 13.1 million barrels a day set in March 2020 just before the pandemic paralyzed the global economy. Government forecasters predict that American oil production will average just 12 million barrels a day in 2022, and increase by roughly another million in 2023. That would be well short of the nearly four

BRANDON THIBODEAUX FOR THE NEW YORK TIMES

Investors worry that raising production will drop prices.

Continued on Page A11

G.O.P. Lawmakers Bolstered Plans to Keep Trump in Office

By LUKE BROADWATER and ALAN FEUER

WASHINGTON — It was less than two weeks before President Donald J. Trump's staunchest allies in Congress would have what they saw as their last chance to overturn the 2020 election, and Representative Scott Perry, Republican of Pennsylvania, was growing anxious.

"Time continues to count down," he wrote in a text message to Mark Meadows, then the White House chief of staff, adding: "11 days to 1/6 and 25 days to inauguration. We gotta get going!"

It has been clear for more than a year that ultraconservative members of Congress were deeply involved in attempts to keep Mr. Trump in power: They joined baseless lawsuits, spread the lie of widespread election fraud and were among the 147 Republicans who voted on Jan. 6, 2021, against certifying President Biden's victory in at least one state.

But in a court filing and in text messages obtained by CNN, new pieces of evidence have emerged in recent days fleshing out the degree of their involvement with the Trump White House in strategy sessions, at least one of which in-

Continued on Page A16

Shanghai Residents Bend Lockdown Rules to Help One Another

*This article is by **Alexandra Stevenson, Amy Chang Chien** and **Isabelle Qian**.*

Four days into a coronavirus lockdown in her Shanghai neighborhood, Ding Tingting began to worry about the old man who lived alone in the apartment below her. She knocked on his door and found that his food supply was dwindling and that he didn't know how to go online to buy more.

Ms. Ding helped him buy food, but also got to thinking about the many older people who lived alone in her neighborhood. Using the Chinese messaging app WeChat, she and her friends created groups to connect people in need with nearby volunteers who could get them food and medicine.

When a woman's father-in-law fainted, the network of volunteers found a neighbor with a blood pressure monitor and made sure it

Doing What Authorities Can't or Won't

was delivered quickly.

"Life cannot be suspended because of the lockdown," said Ms. Ding, a 25-year-old art curator.

In its relentless effort to stamp out the virus, China has relied on hundreds of thousands of low-level party officials in neighborhood committees to arrange mass testing and coordinate transport to hospitals and isolation facilities. The officials have doled out special passes for the sick to seek medicine and other necessities during lockdown.

In Beijing on Monday, the government ordered about three-quarters of the city's 22 million residents to undergo three man-

Continued on Page A6

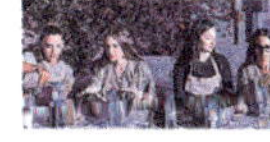

INTERNATIONAL A4-11

Baking Challah in Dubai

Jewish life is opening up in the Persian Gulf emirate, another sign of a new reality in the Middle East. PAGE A4

Macron's Political Challenges

France's runoff election was marked by record abstention, and many voted only to keep the far right out. PAGE A3

NATIONAL A14-21

Harvard Addresses Slavery Ties

The university is committing $100 million to a fund, joining other schools that are grappling with their complicity in the trade of humans. PAGE A20

Busing of Migrants Backfires

The Texas governor's program to pressure President Biden by sending busloads of migrants to Washington hasn't caused the intended chaos. PAGE A14

The End of Incandescence

New efficiency standards will phase out the sale of most classic light bulbs in favor of LEDs, reducing electricity use and, ultimately, electric bills. PAGE A20

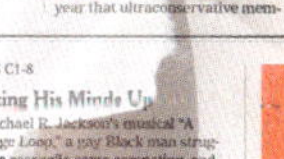

SPORTS B7-9

N.B.A. Juggernauts Fall Short

Kevin Durant and the Nets, supposedly a superteam, lost early in the playoffs. The Lakers didn't get that far. PAGE B7

N.C.A.A. Chief to Step Down

With collegiate sports changing rapidly, Mark Emmert's tumultuous reign will come to an end next year. PAGE B9

ARTS C1-8

Making His Minds Up

In Michael R. Jackson's musical "A Strange Loop," a gay Black man struggles to reconcile some competing, and very lifelike, thoughts. PAGE C1

BUSINESS B1-6

How U.S. Covid Aid Stacks Up

The United States spent more on its policy response than other advanced economies. Now economists are revisiting how that worked. PAGE B1

OPINION A22-23

Thomas L. Friedman PAGE A22

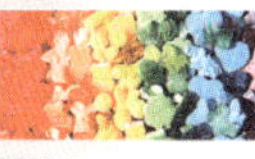

FOOD D1-8

A Hunger for Gummy Bears

A century after the colorful, squishy candies were first made, their universe is expanding into some unexpected (and some very obvious) ways. PAGE D1

U(D54GID)y+#(!%&?

Angel of History (New York Times, April 27, 2022)
2022. Inkjet print, 24 × 13 in.

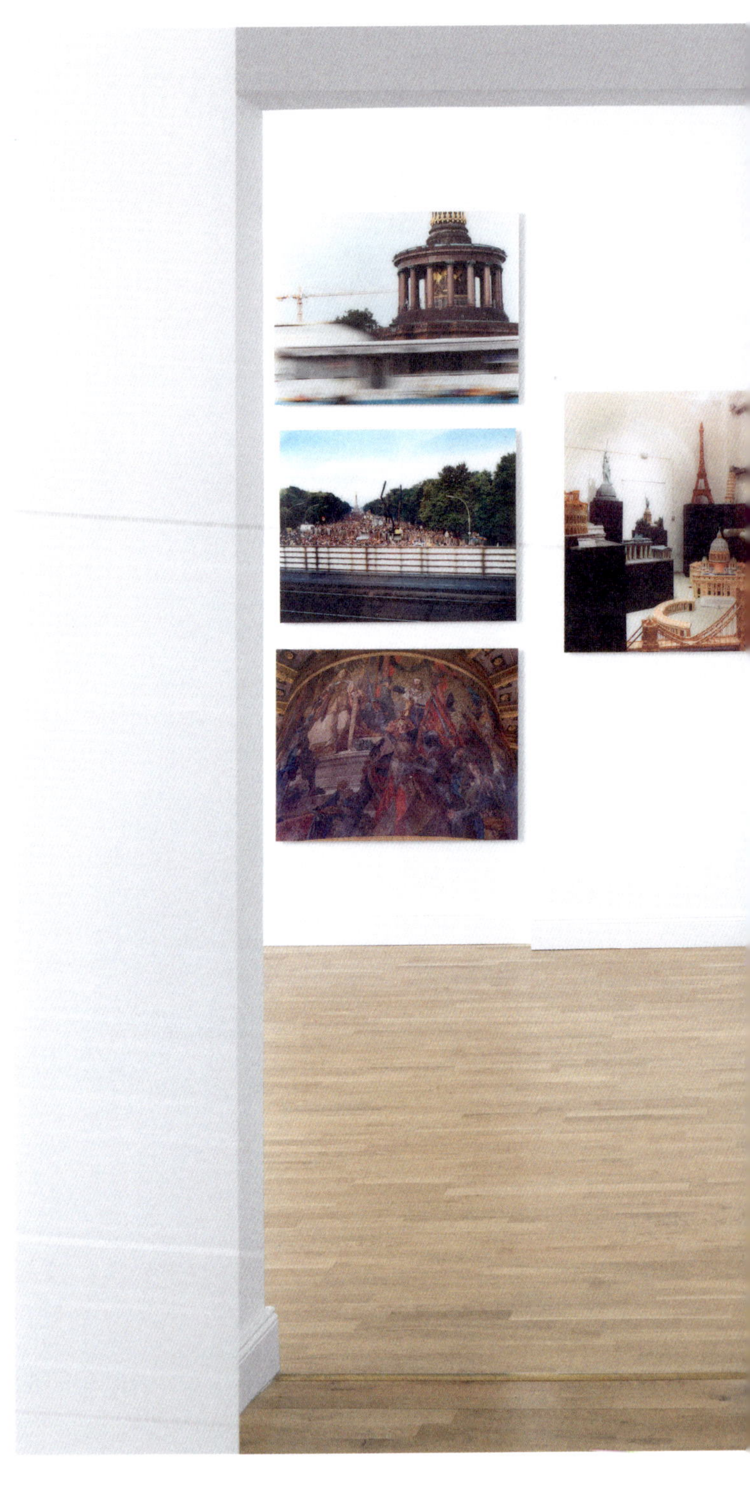

Berlin Childhood and The Angel of History
Installation view, RL16 Gallery, Berlin, 2022.

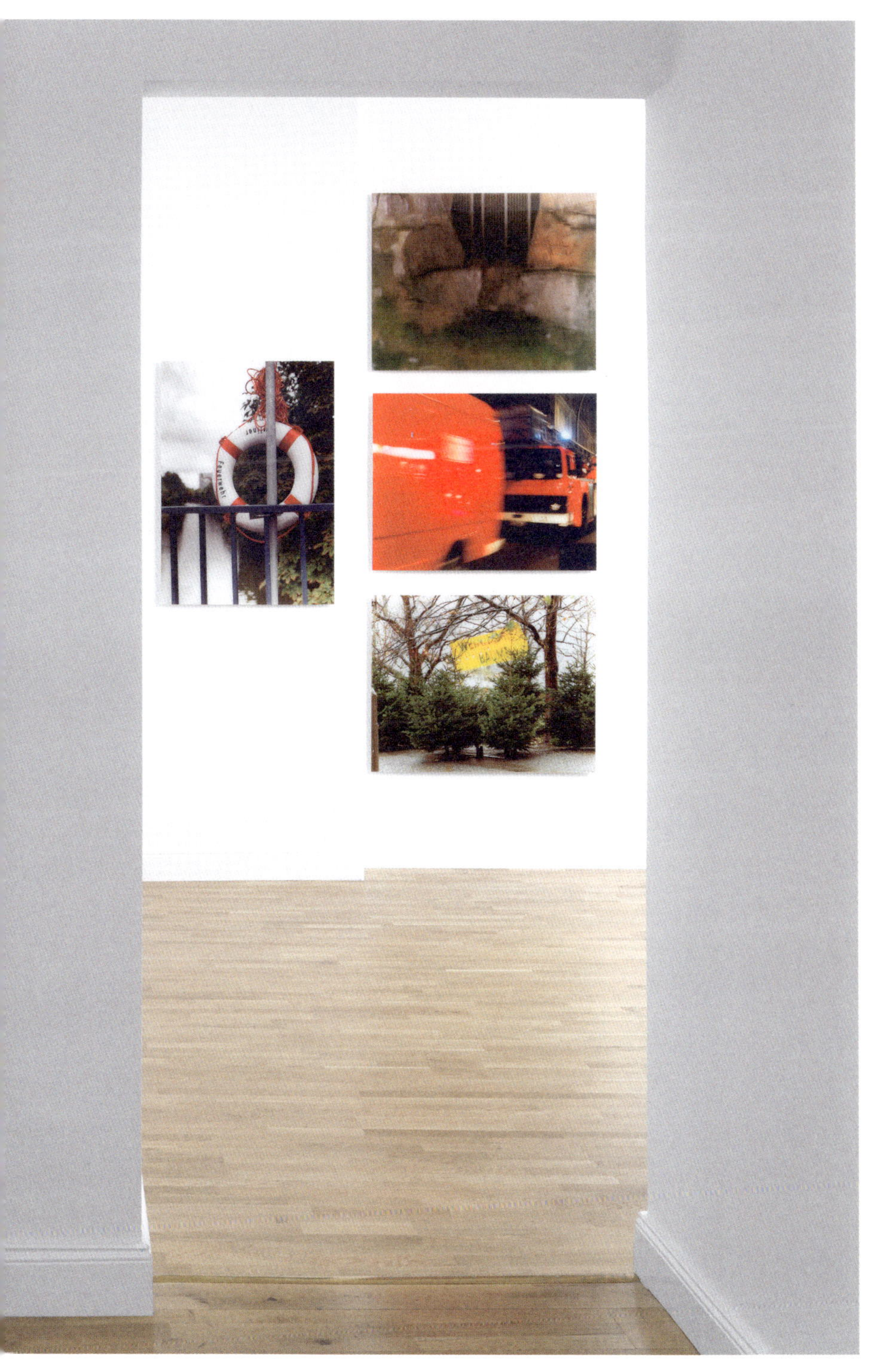

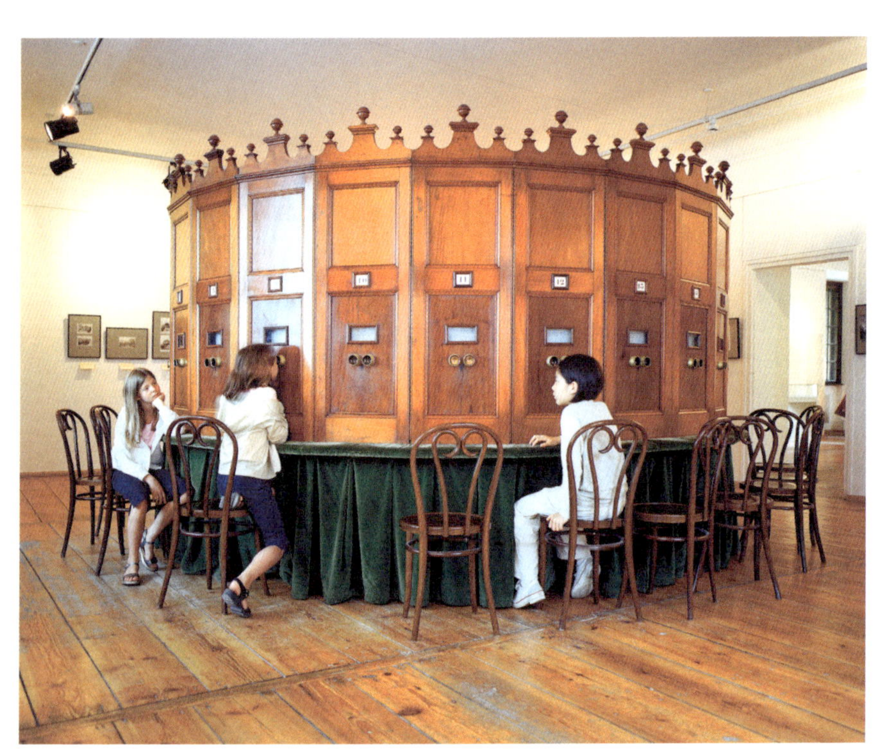

Kaiserpanorama
2000, from *Berlin Childhood*. C-print.
30 × 40 in.

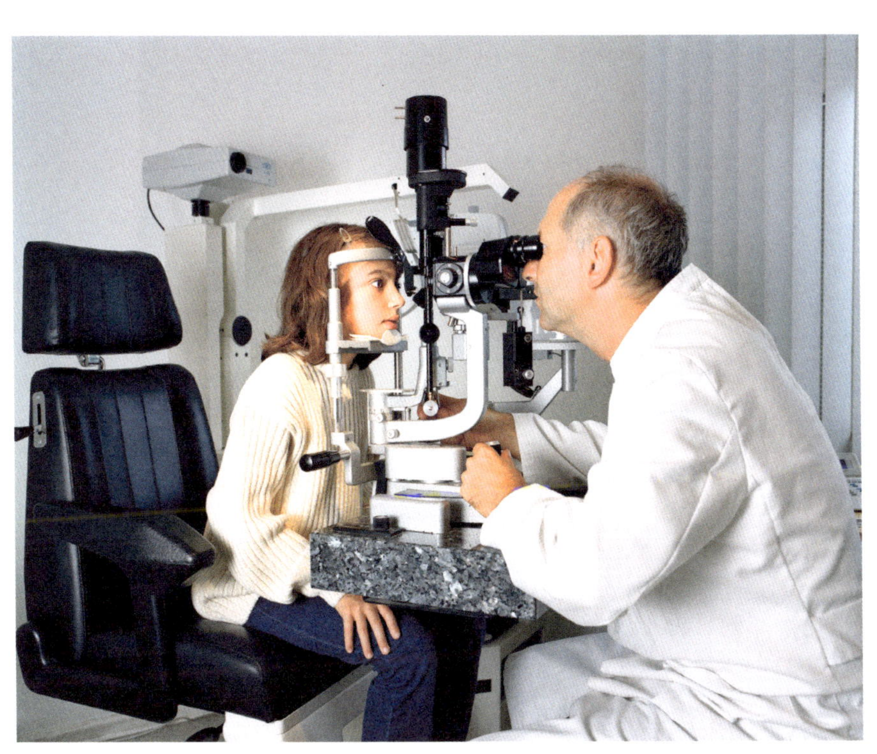

The Reading Desk (Eye Exam)
1999, from *Berlin Childhood*. C-print.
30 × 40 in.

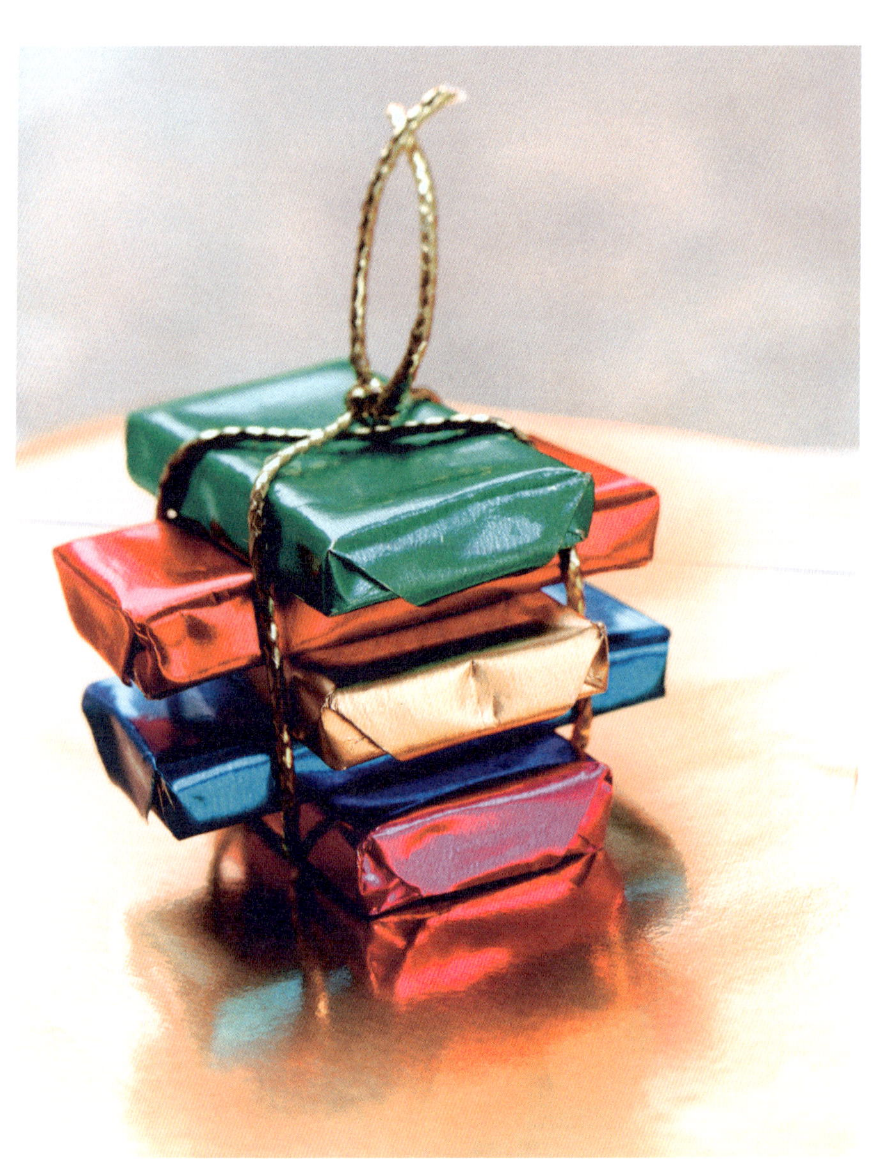

The Colors
1999, from *Berlin Childhood*. C-print.
40 × 30 in.

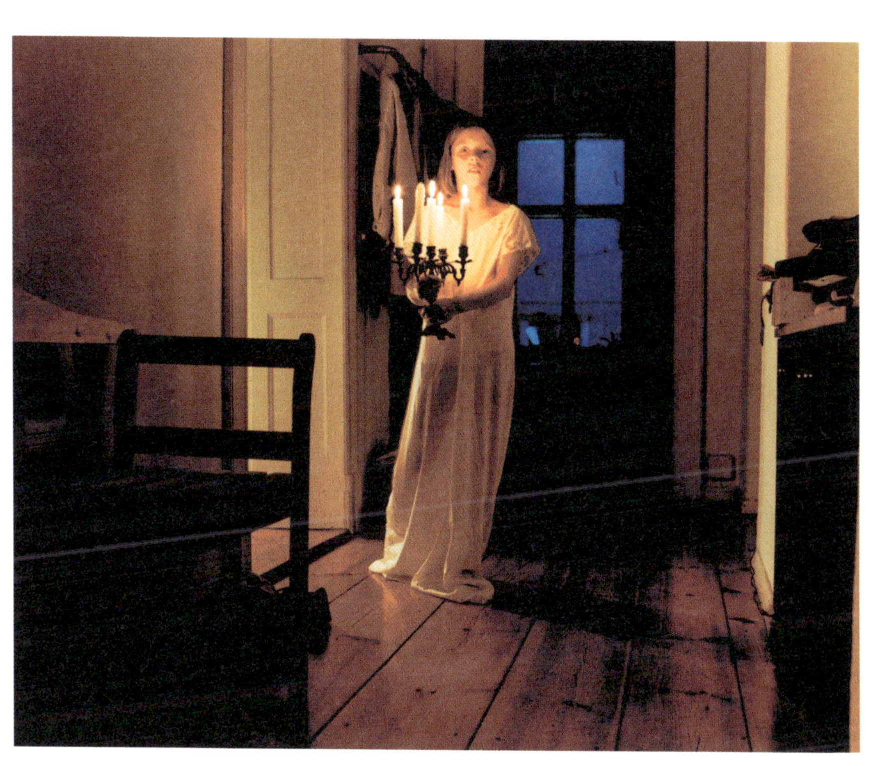

Student Library (The Sleepwalker)
2000, from *Berlin Childhood*. C-print.
30 × 40 in.

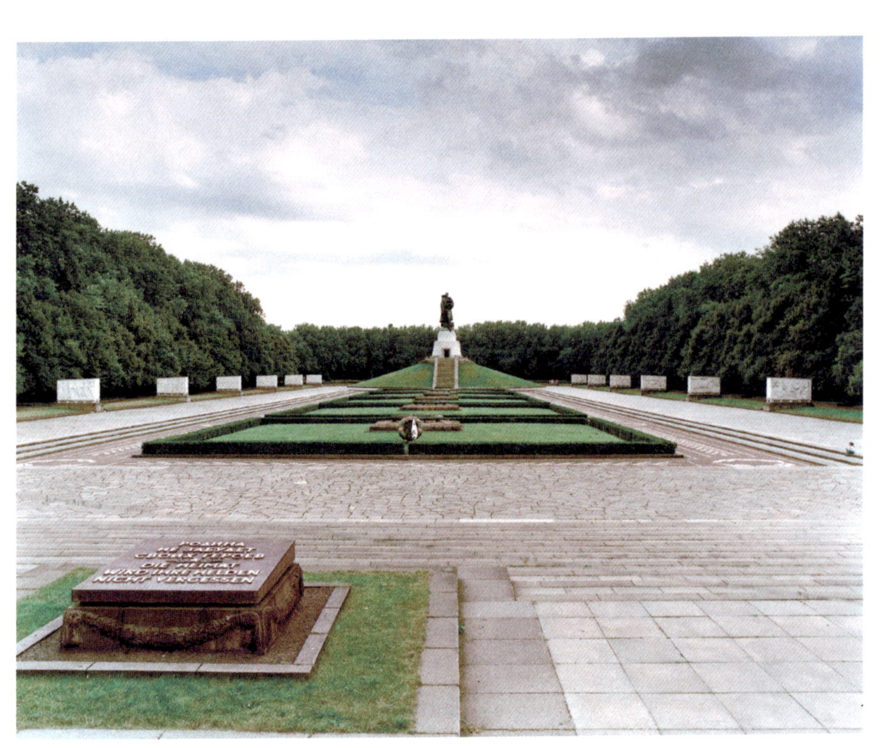

Two Puzzle Pictures
(Soviet War Memorial, Treptower Park)
1998, from *Berlin Childhood*. C-print.
30 × 40 in.

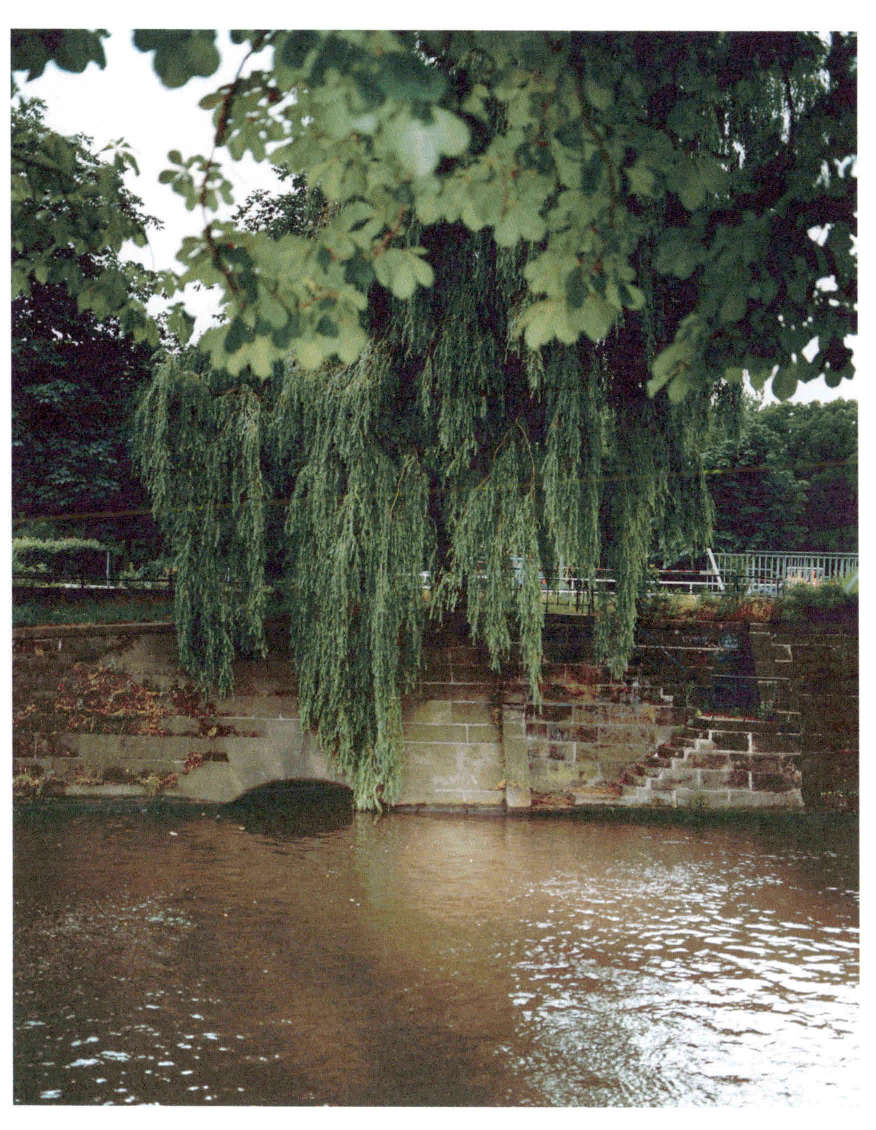

Two Puzzle Pictures (Landwehr Canal)
1998, from *Berlin Childhood*. C-print.
40 × 30 in.

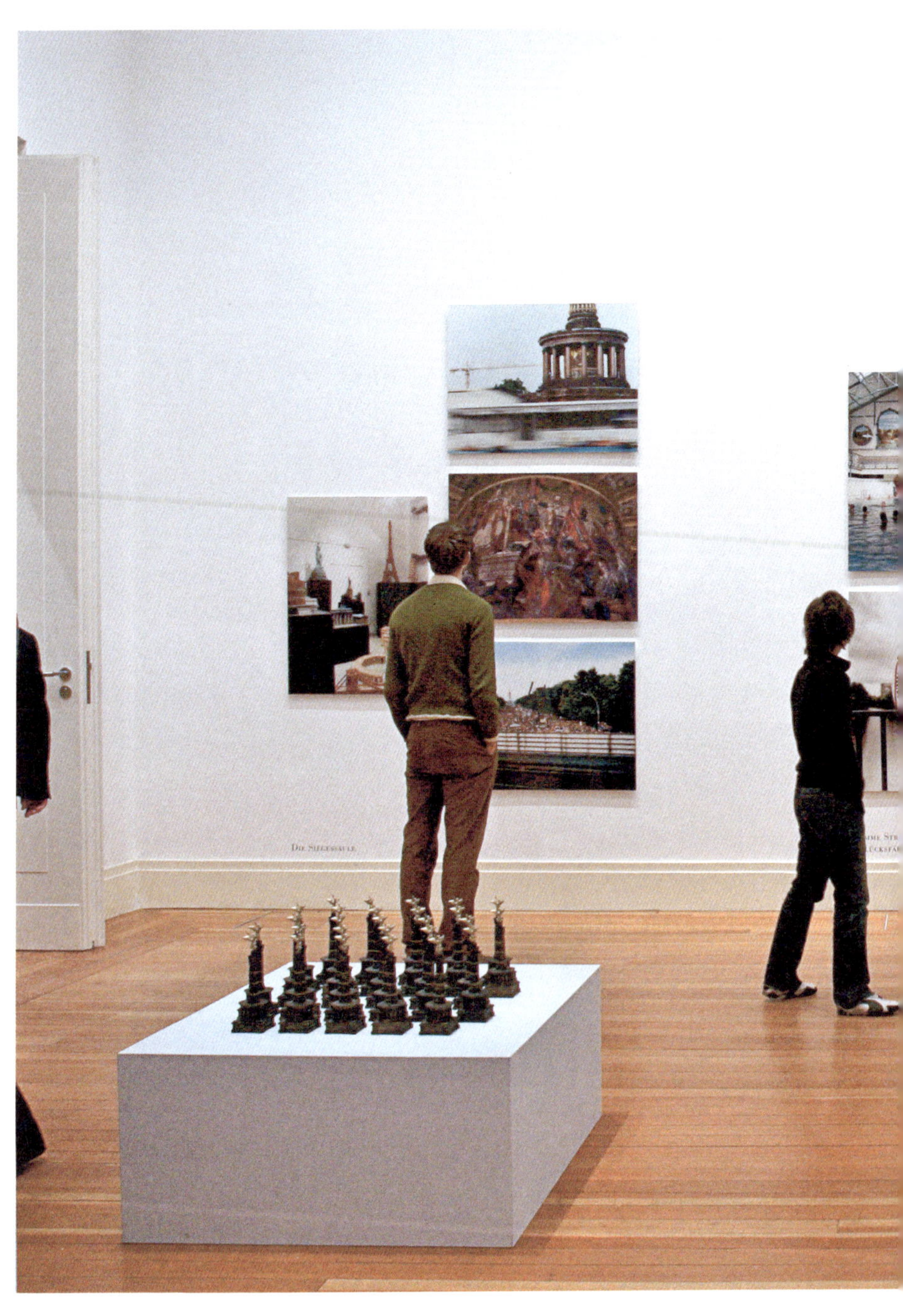

Berlin Childhood
Installation view, 3rd Berlin Biennale,
Martin Gropius Bau, Berlin, 2004.

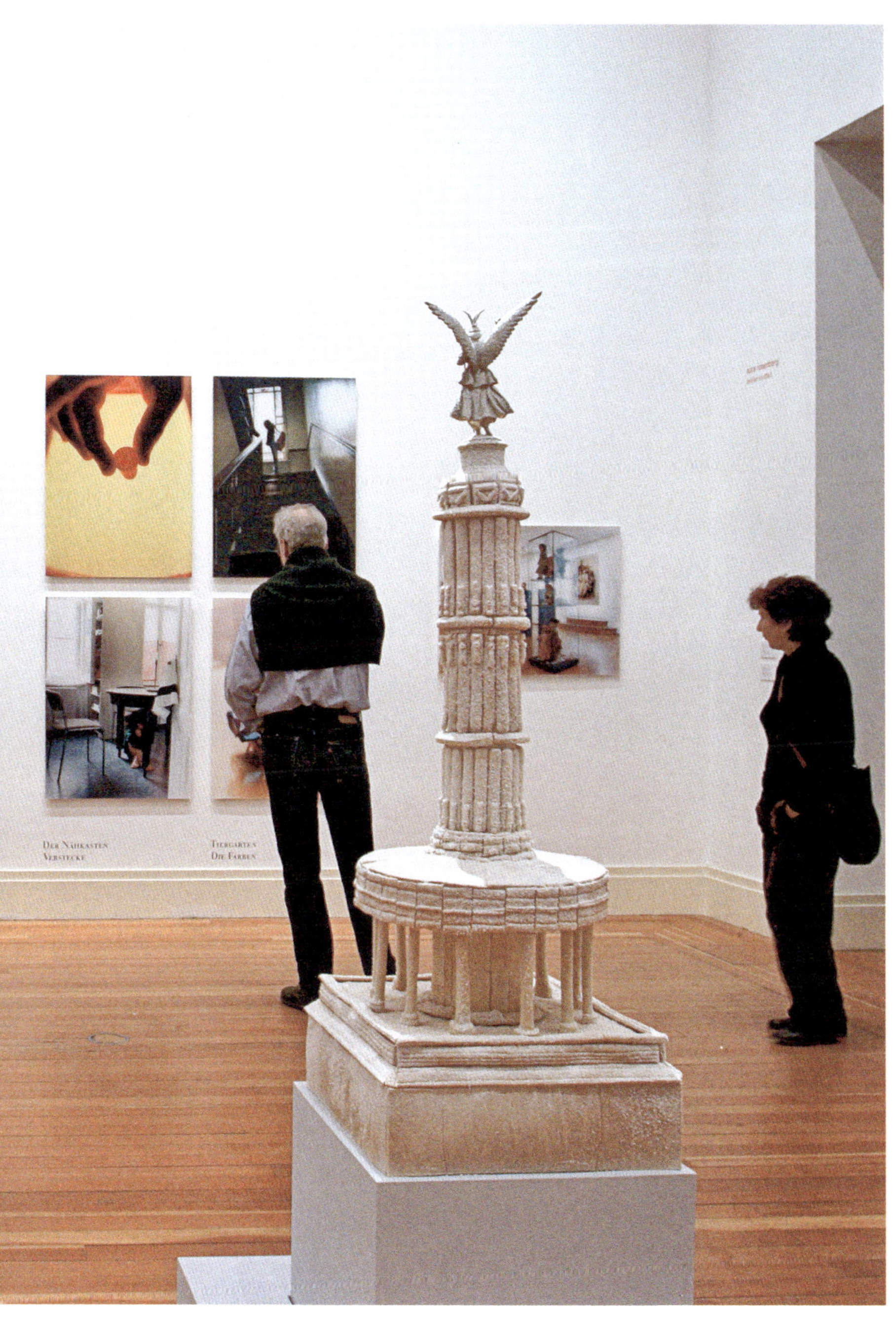
Der Nähkasten
Verstecke
Tiergarten
Die Farben

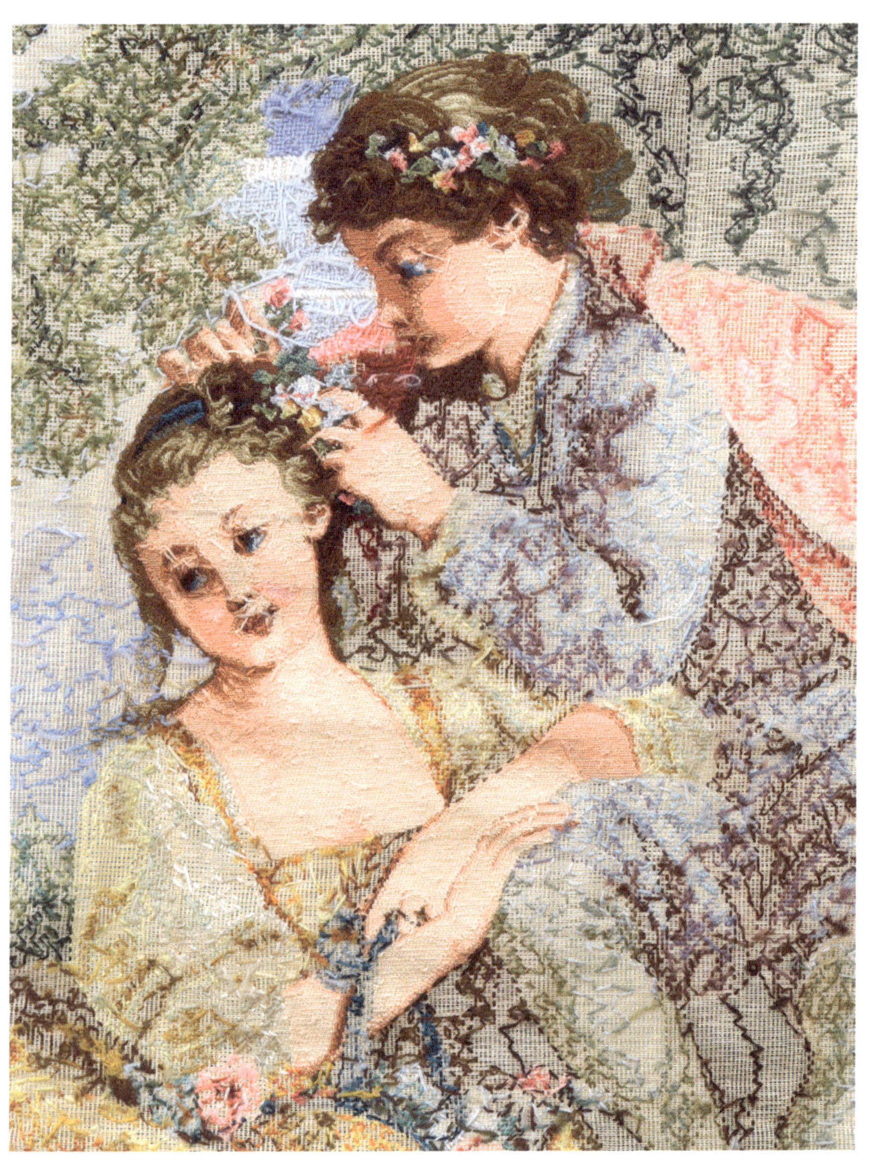

The Sewing Basket (DETAIL)
2002. Installation view, RL16, Berlin, 2022.

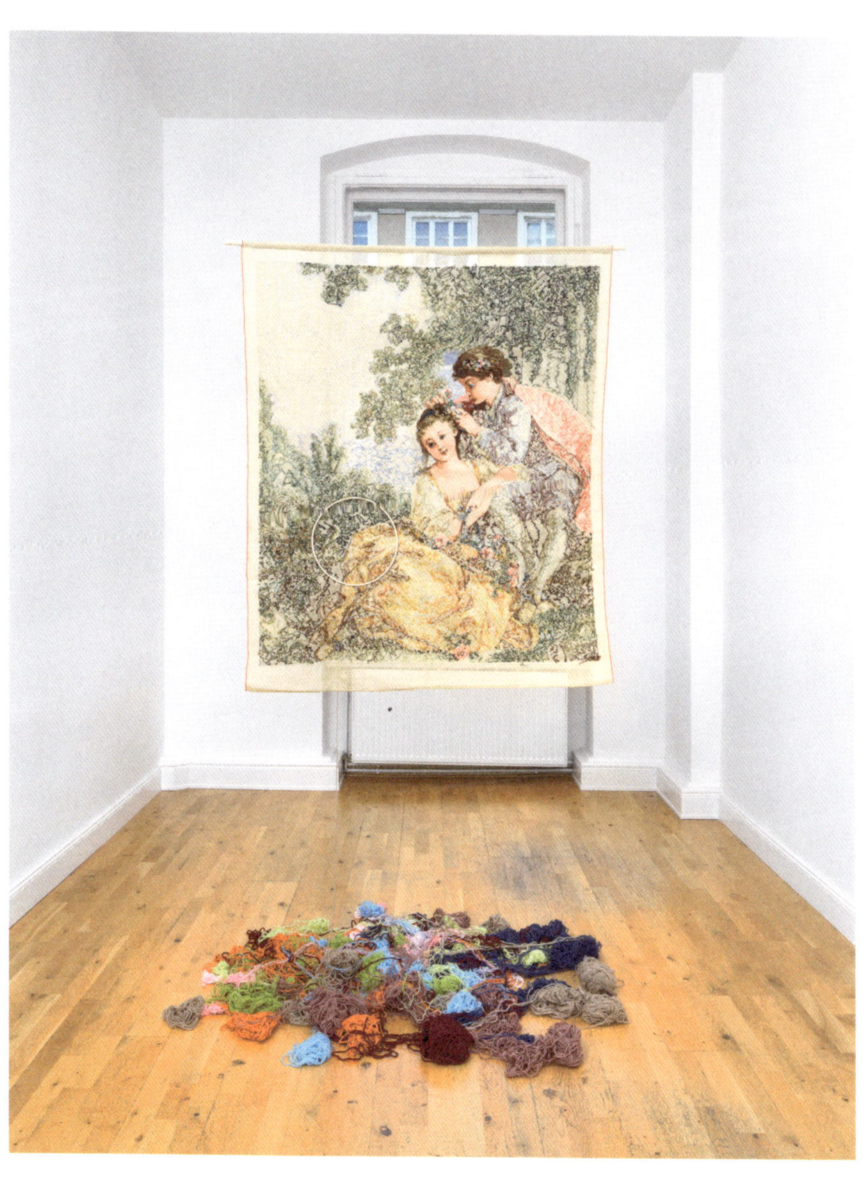

The Sewing Basket
2002. Installation view, RL16, Berlin, 2022.

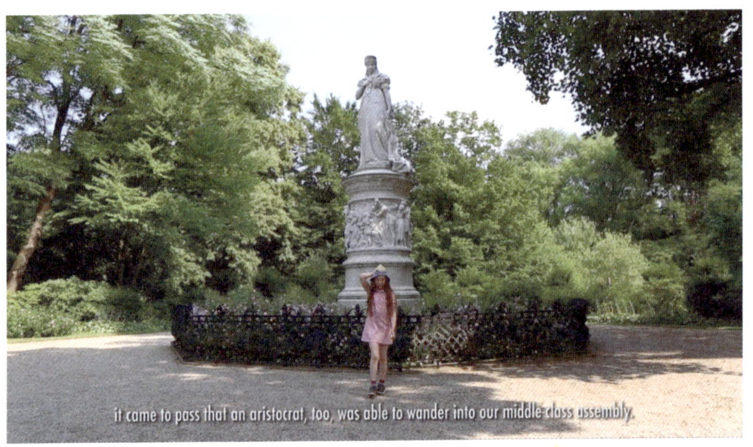

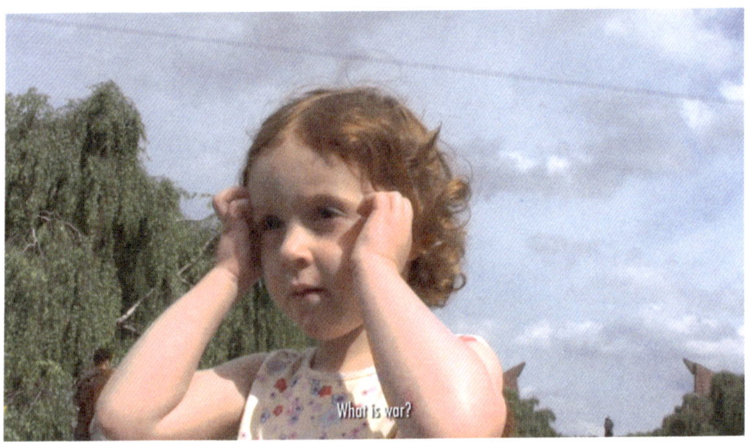

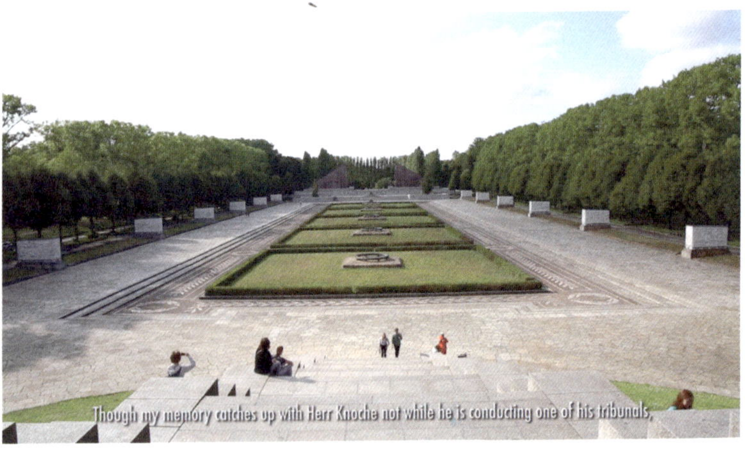

Stills from *Two Riddles*
2010–15, from *Berlin Childhood*.
Video, 6 min, 58 sec.

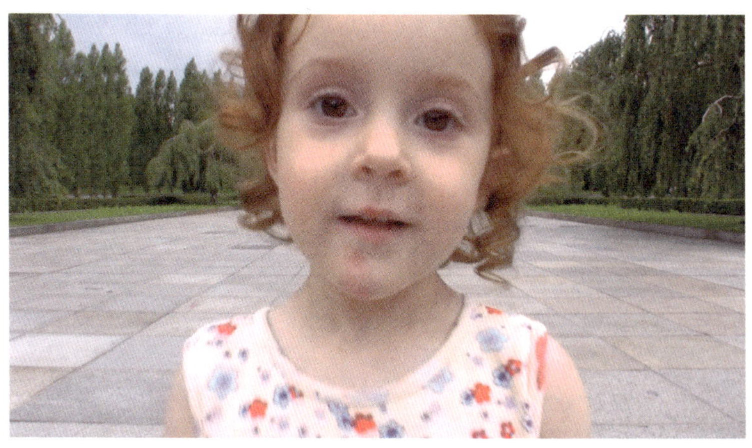

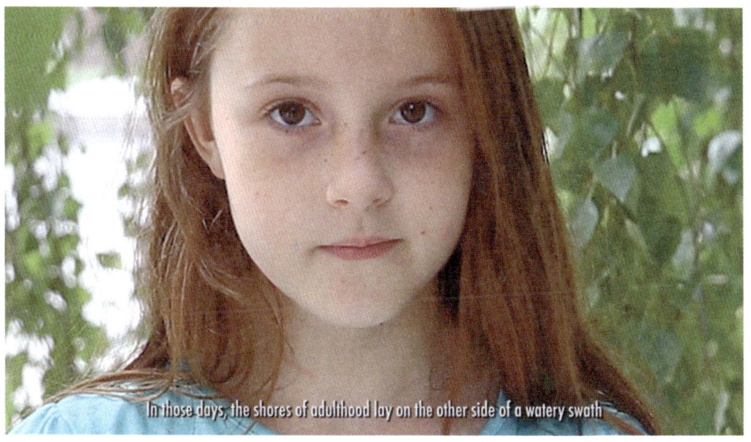
In those days, the shores of adulthood lay on the other side of a watery swath

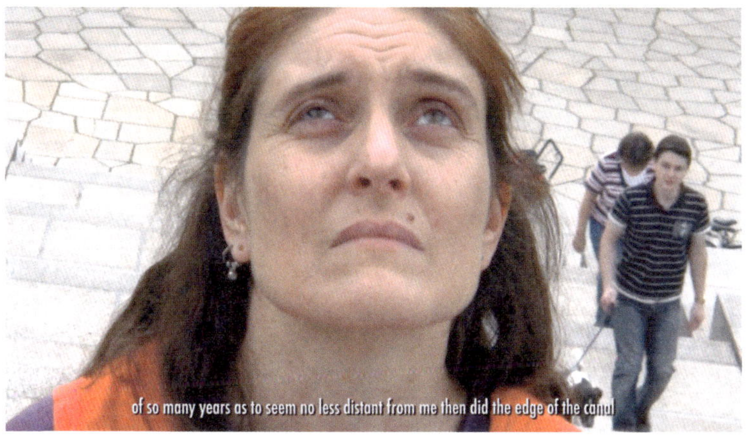
of so many years as to seem no less distant from me then did the edge of the canal

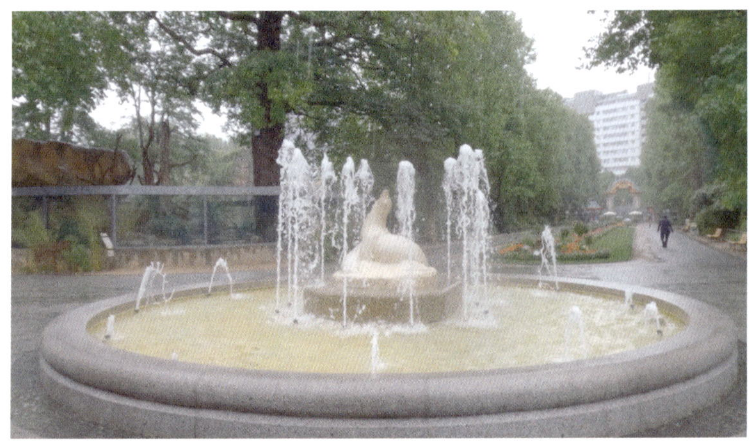

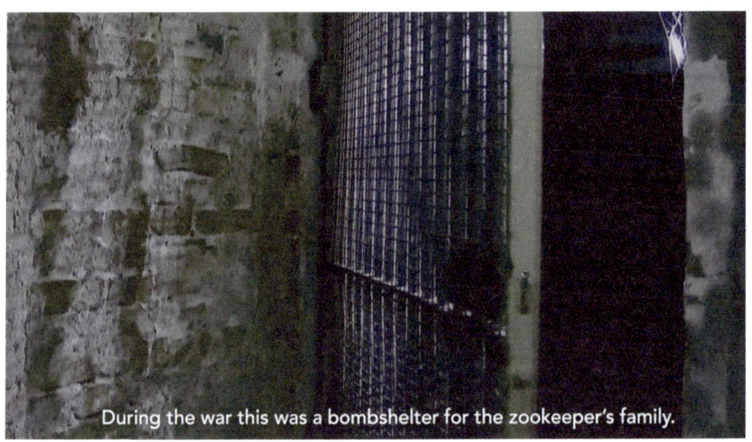

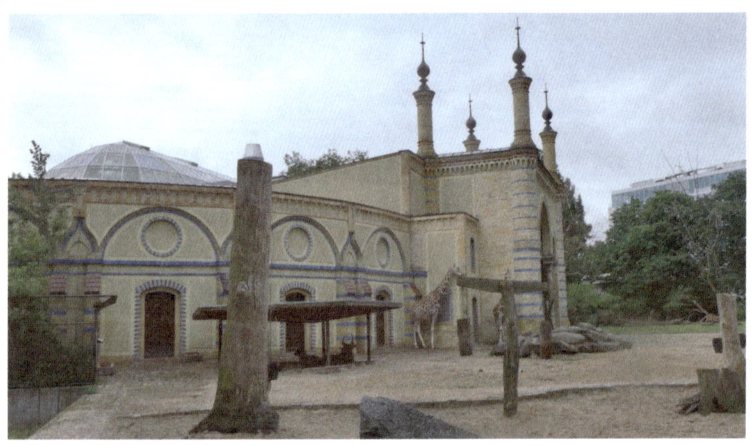

Stills from *The Fish Otter*
2022, from *Berlin Childhood*.
Video, approx. 12 min.

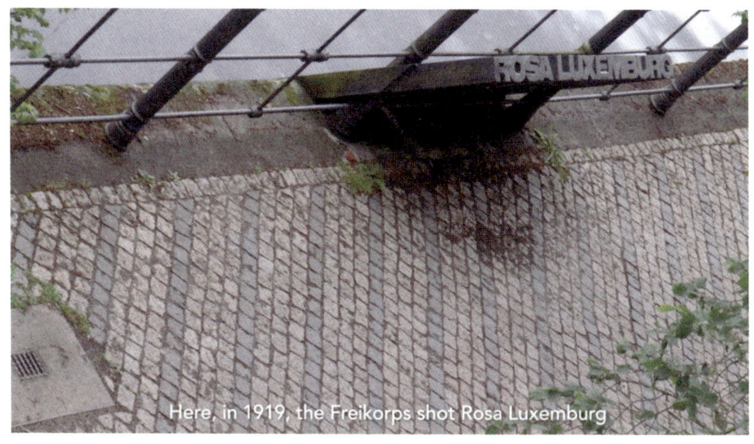
ROSA LUXEMBURG
Here, in 1919, the Freikorps shot Rosa Luxemburg

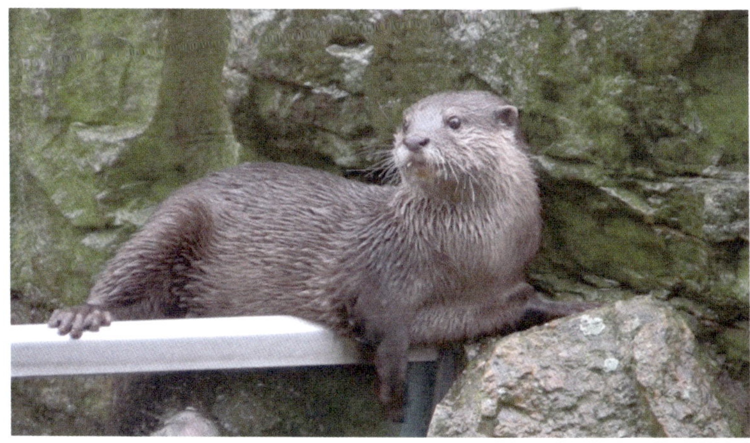

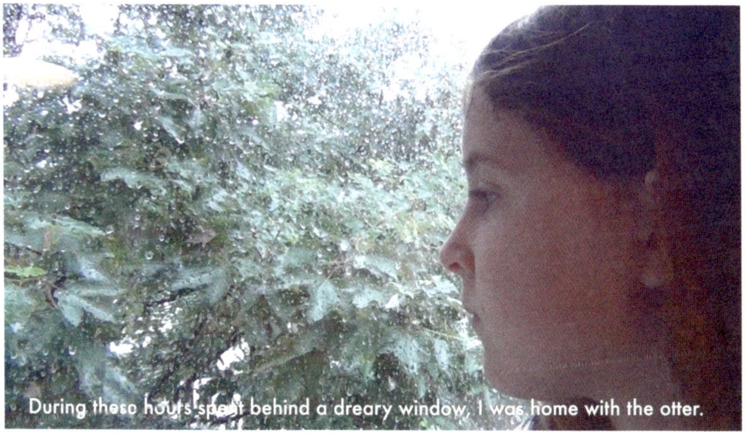
During these hours spent behind a dreary window, I was home with the otter.

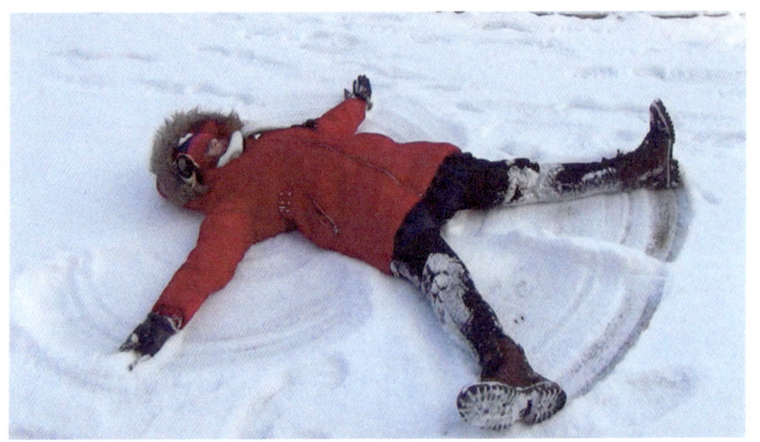

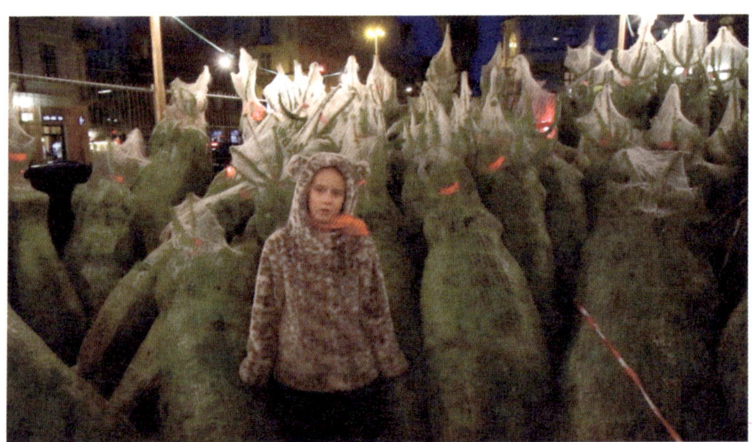

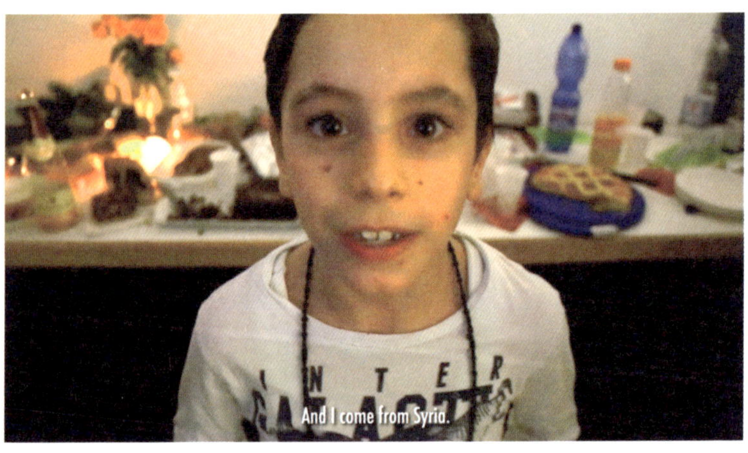

Stills from *A Christmas Angel*
2015, from *Berlin Childhood*.
Video, 12 min, 8 sec.

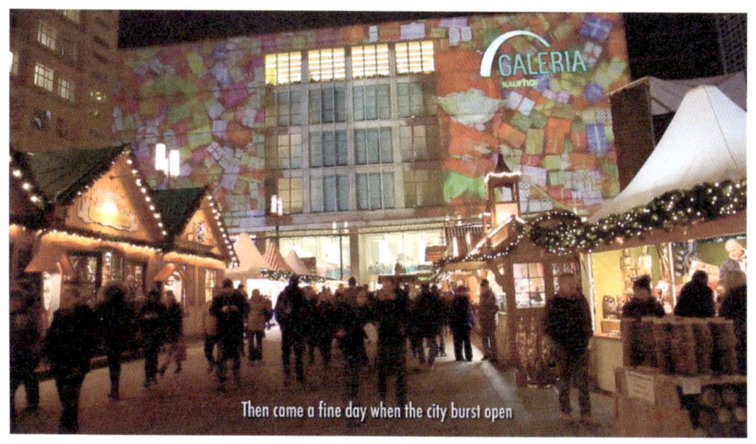
GALERIA
Then came a fine day when the city burst open

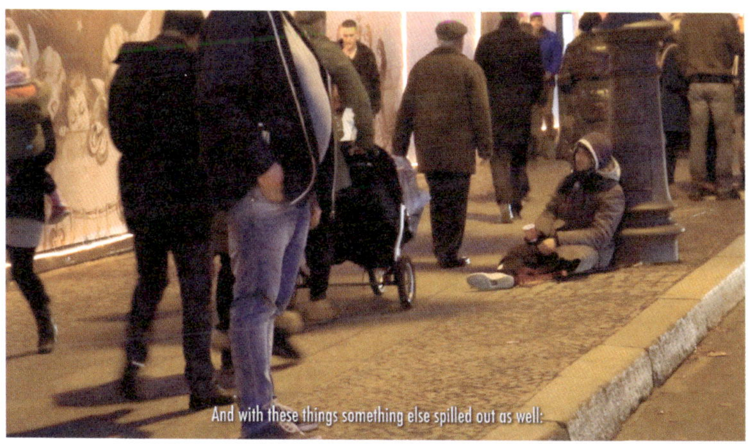
And with these things something else spilled out as well:

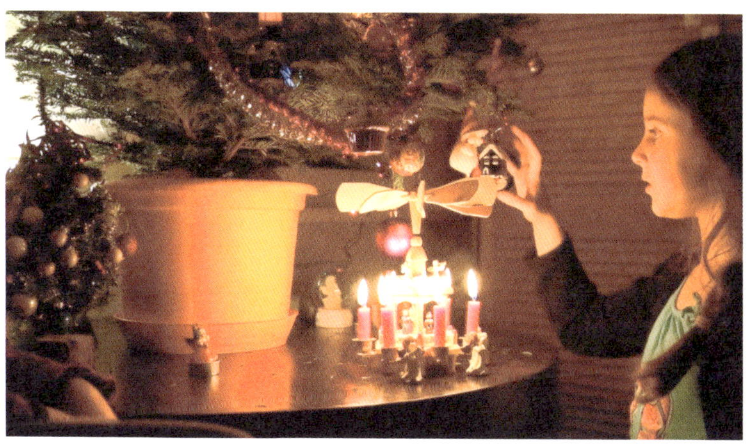

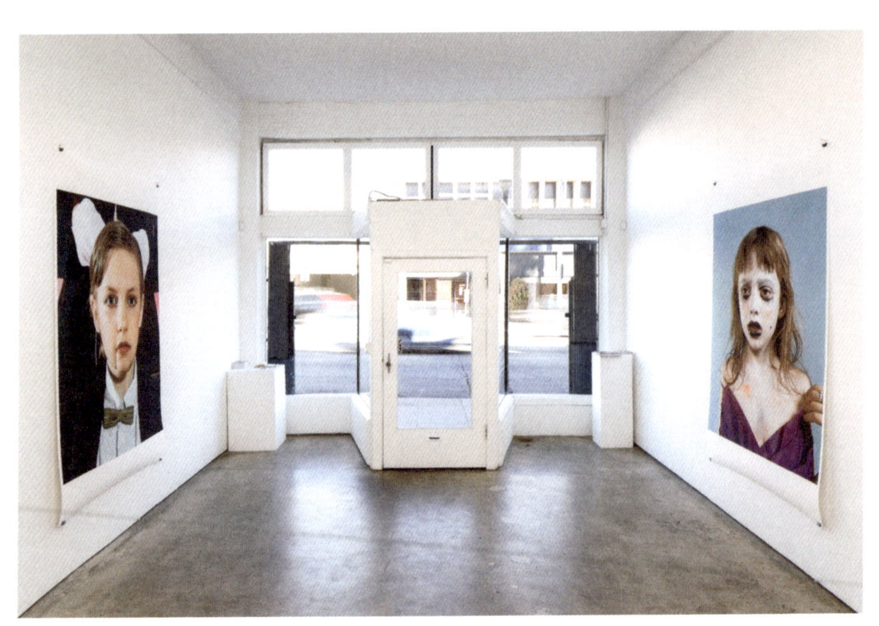

Who Am I? What Am I? Where Am I?
Installation view, Meliksetian | Briggs Gallery,
Los Angeles, 2015.

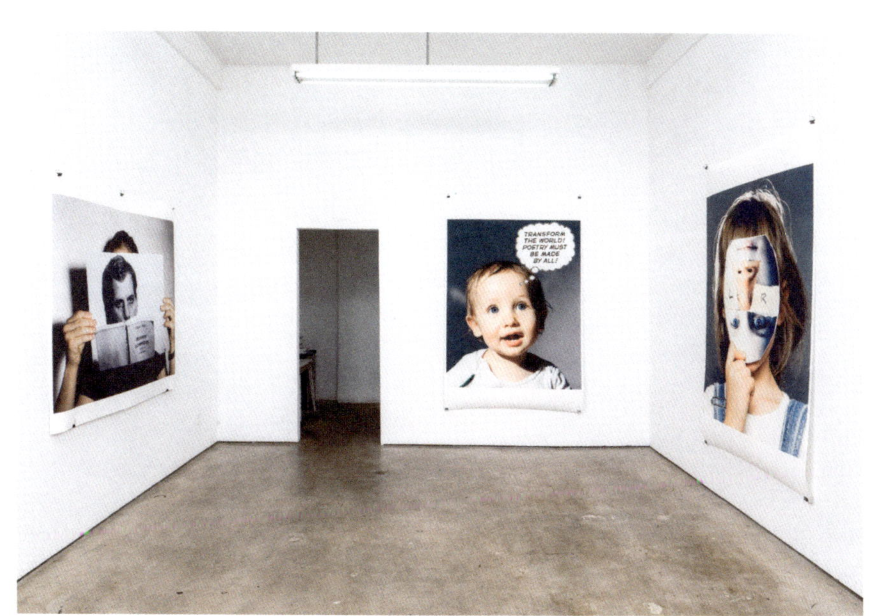
TRANSFORM THE WORLD! POETRY MUST BE MADE BY ALL!

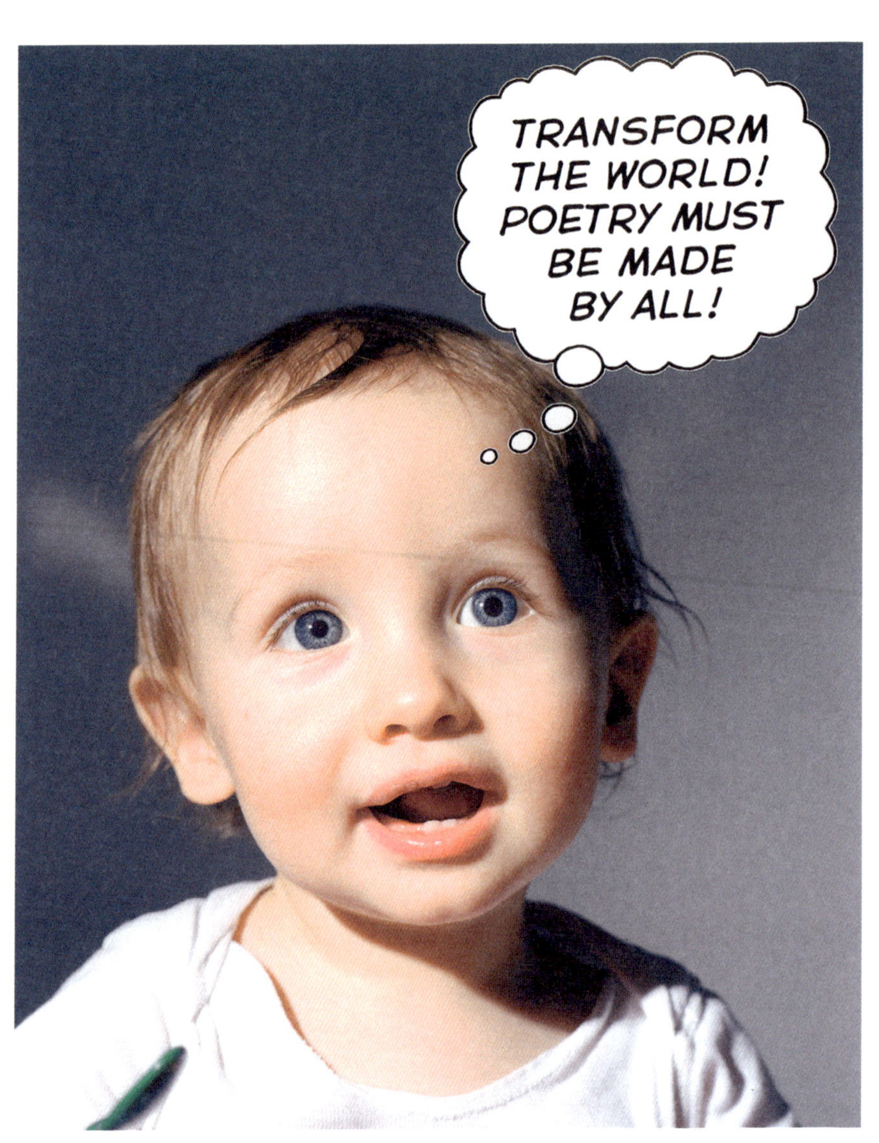

Christopher Williams/Bram
1996–98, from *Who Am I? What Am I? Where Am I?*
Inkjet print, 46 × 36 in.

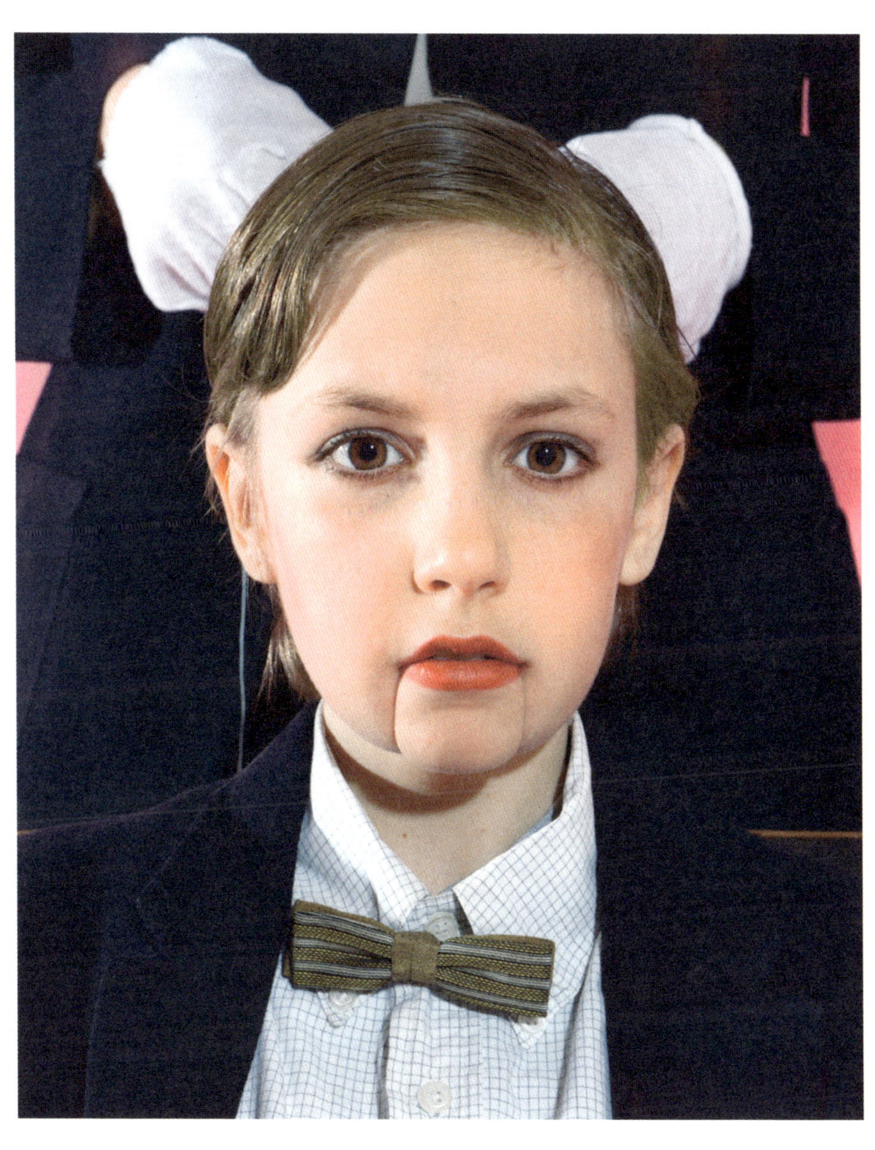

Laurie Simmons/Lena
1996–98, from *Who Am I? What Am I? Where Am I?*
Inkjet print, 46 × 36 in.

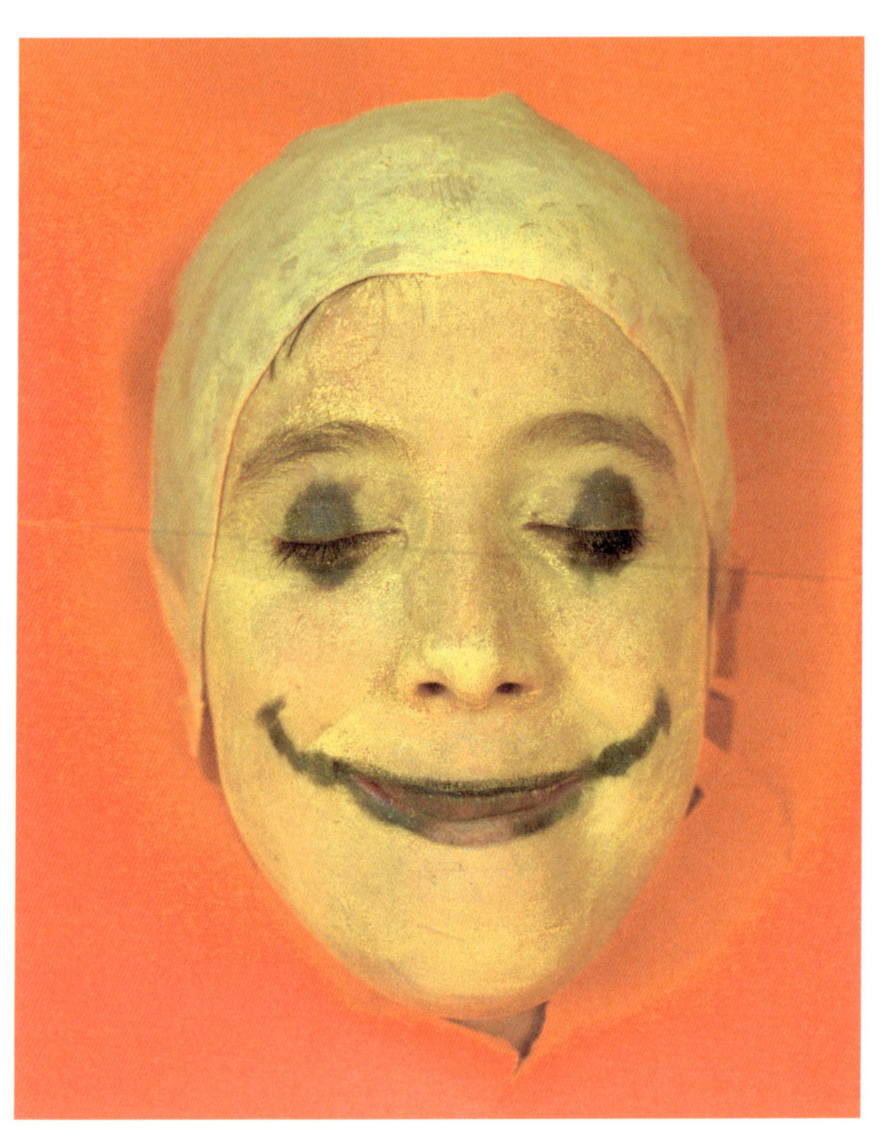

Louise Lawler/Felix
1996–98, from *Who Am I? What Am I? Where Am I?*
Inkjet print, 46 × 36 in.

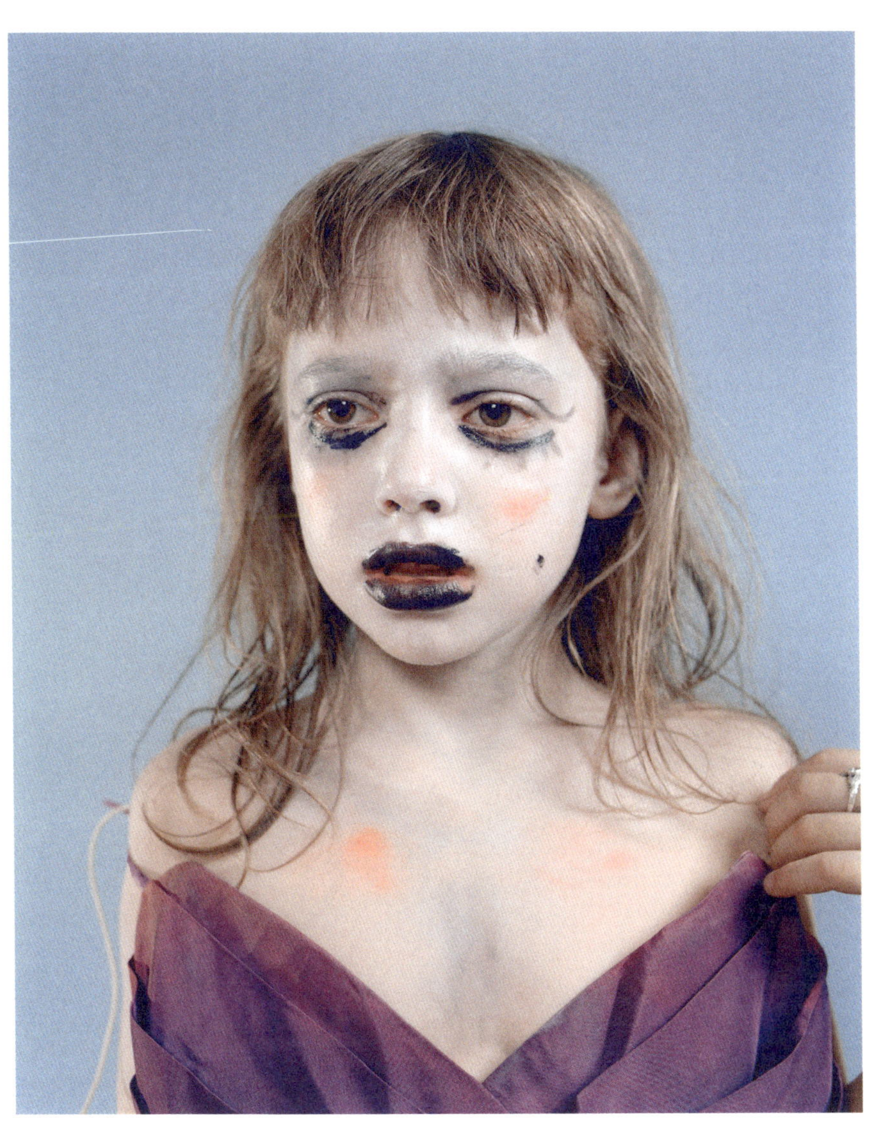

Mike Kelley/Carmen
1996–98, from *Who Am I? What Am I? Where Am I?*
Inkjet print, 46 × 36 in.

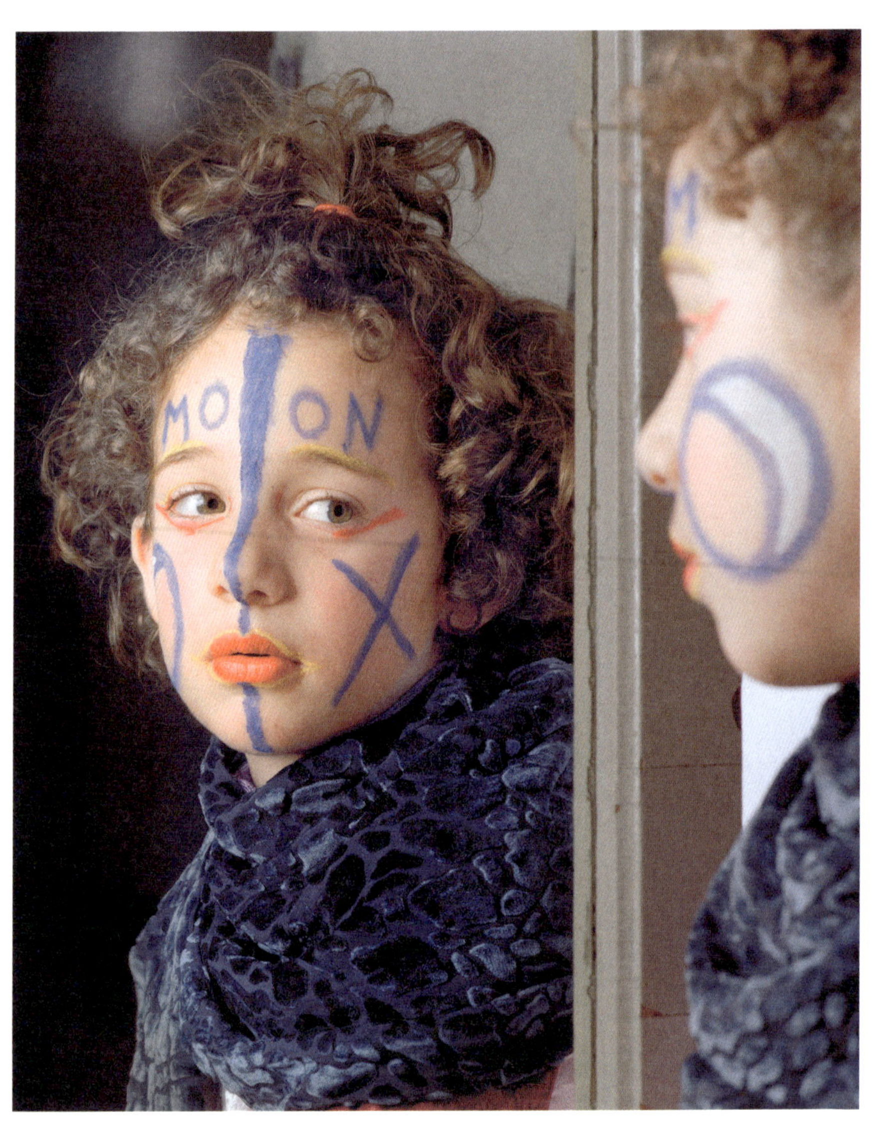

Joan Jonas/Davida
1996–98, from *Who Am I? What Am I? Where Am I?*
Inkjet print, 46 × 36 in.

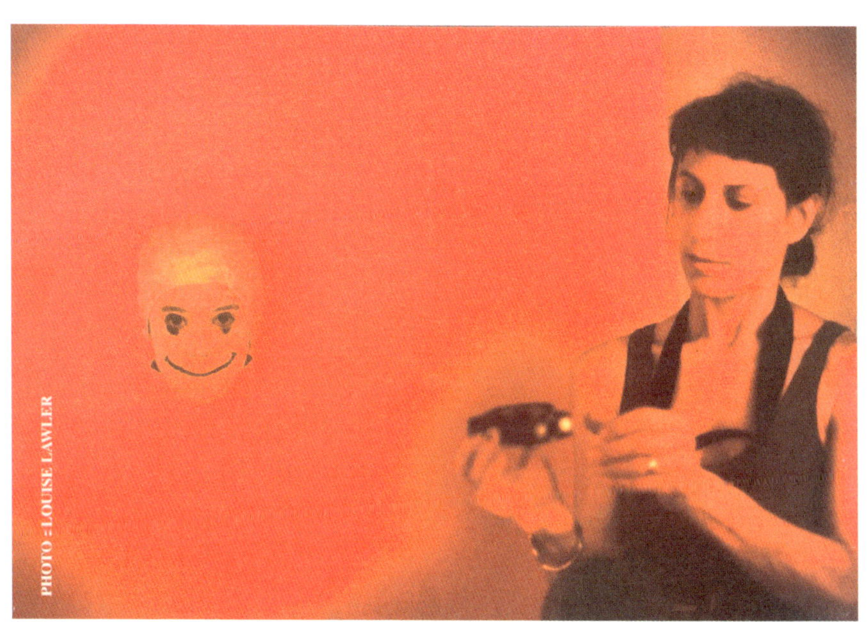

Announcement for *Who Am I? What Am I? Where Am I?* at Windows, Brussels, Belgium, 1998.

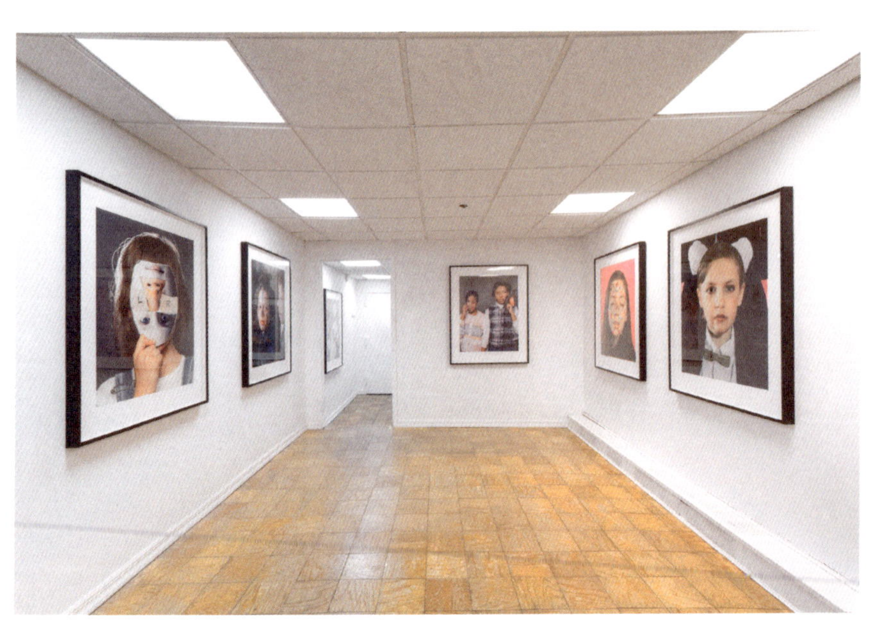

Who Am I? What Am I? Where Am I?
Installation view, Meredith Rosen Gallery,
New York, 2022.

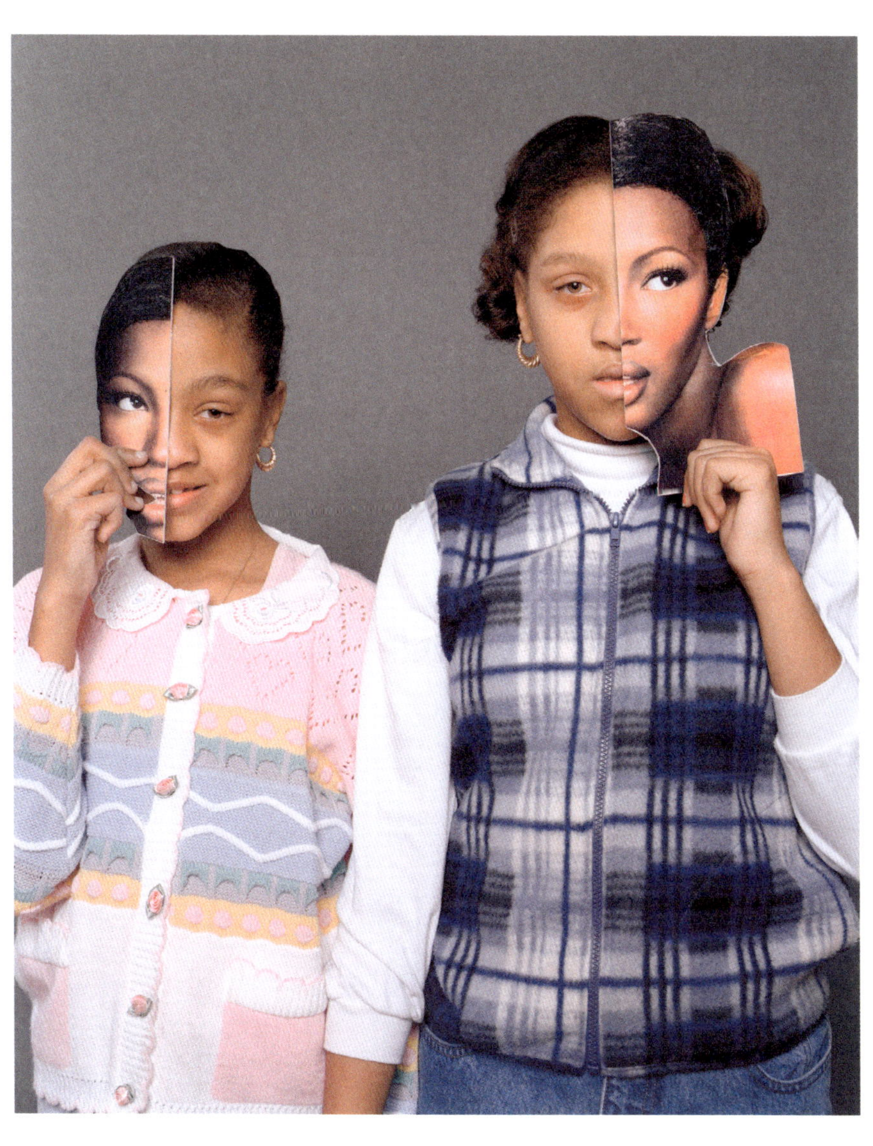

Gerald Jackson/Toni and Ti
1996–98, from *Who Am I? What Am I? Where Am I?*
Inkjet print, 46 × 36 in.

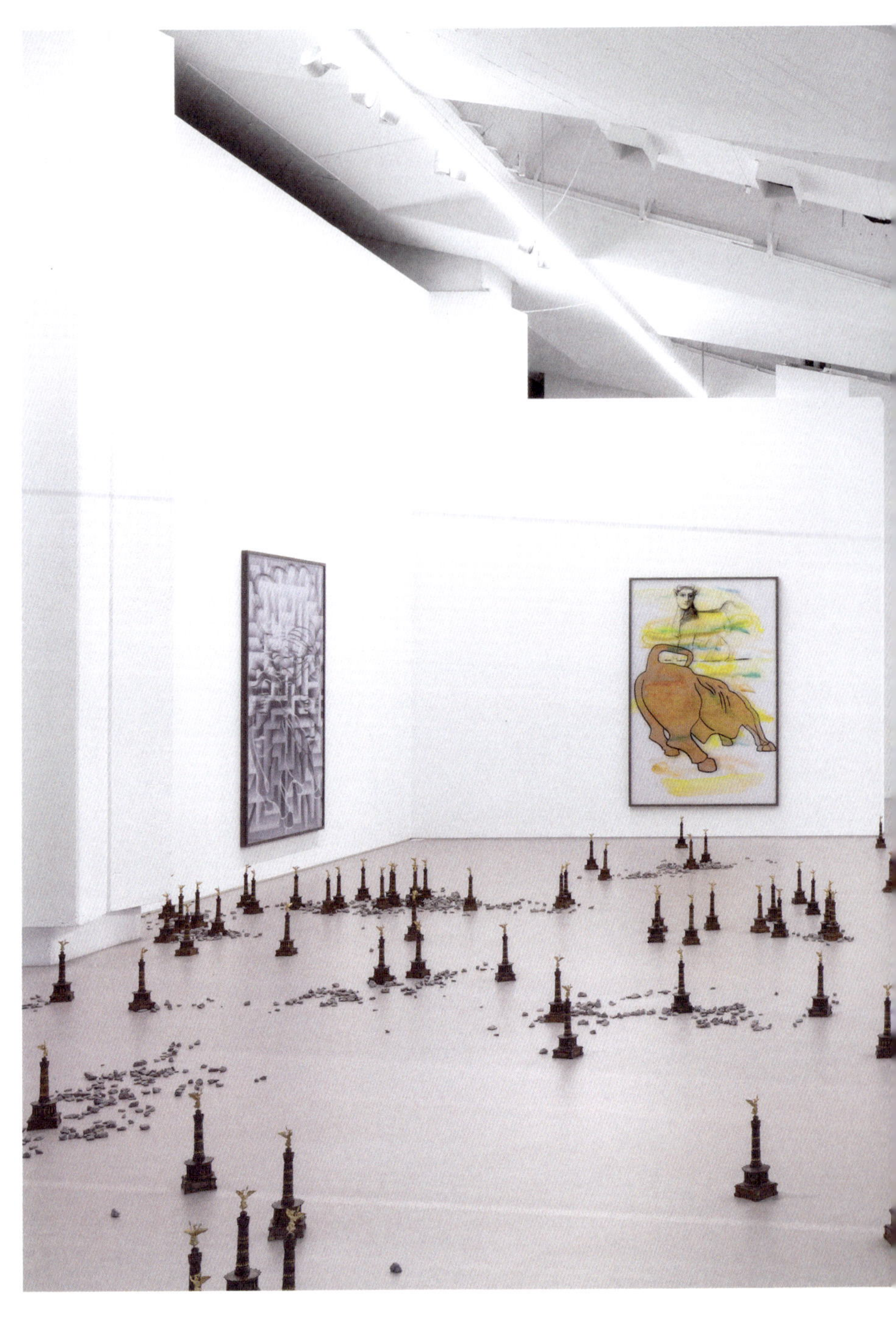

The Bull, The Girl and the Siegessäule
Installation view, Efremidis Gallery, Berlin, 2021.

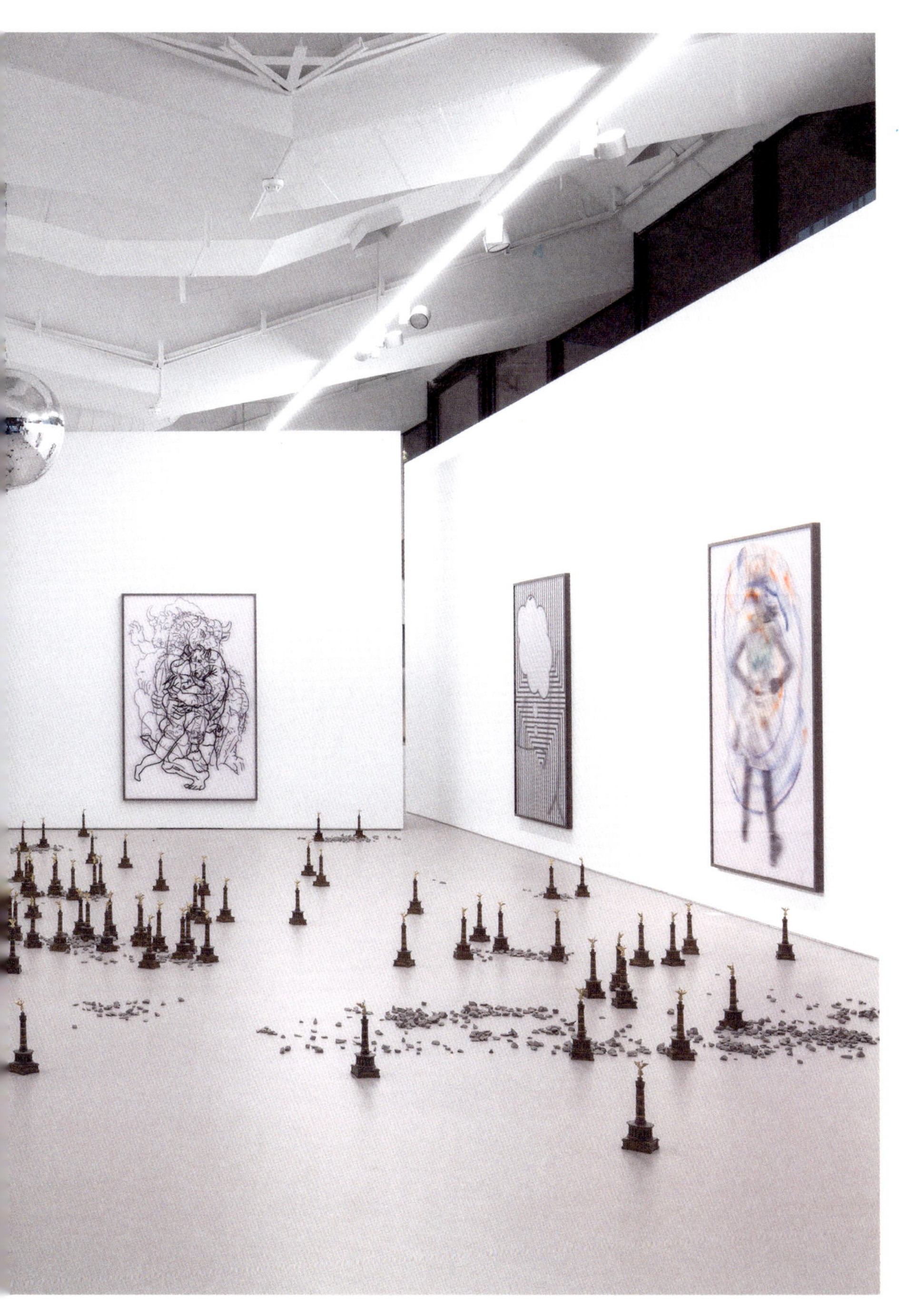

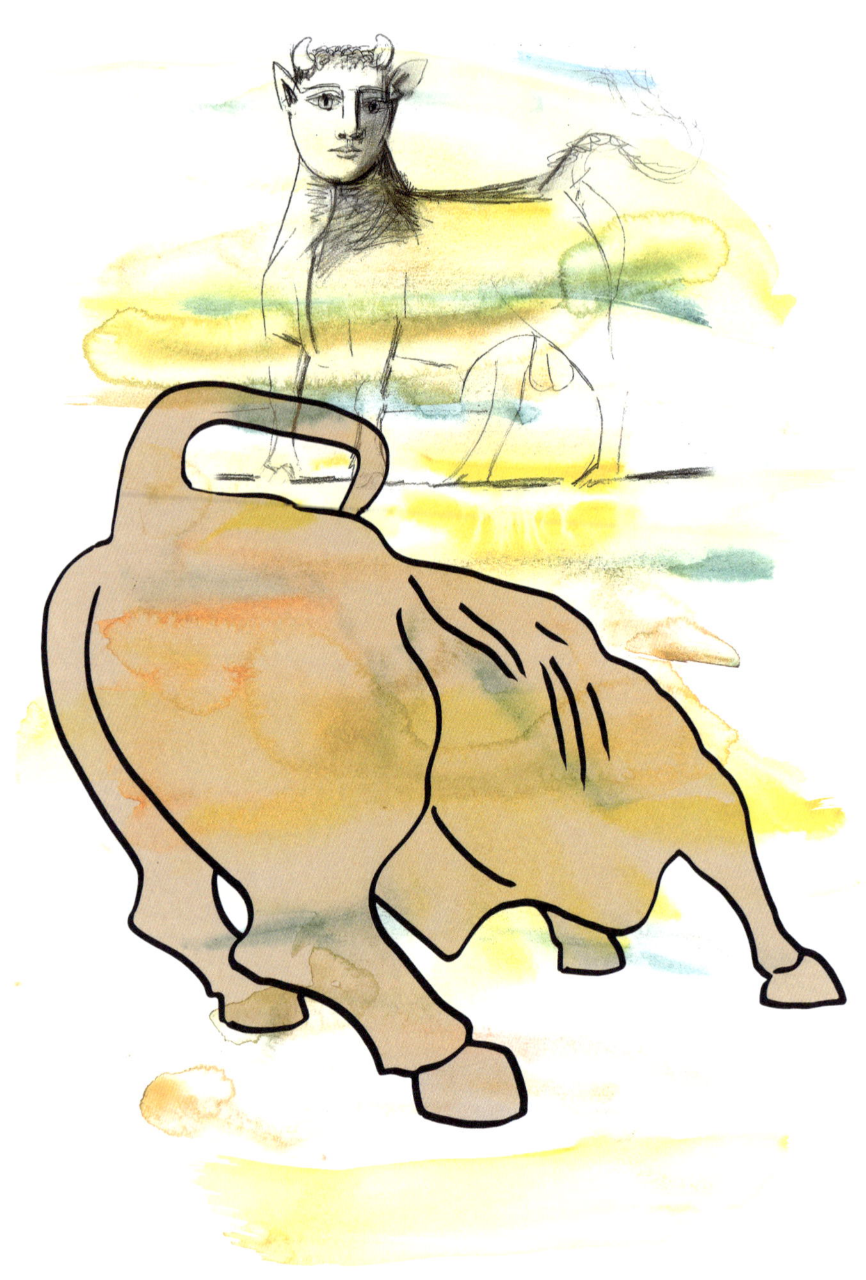

You Are Afraid of the Echo
2021. 3D Lenticular print, 71 × 47 in.

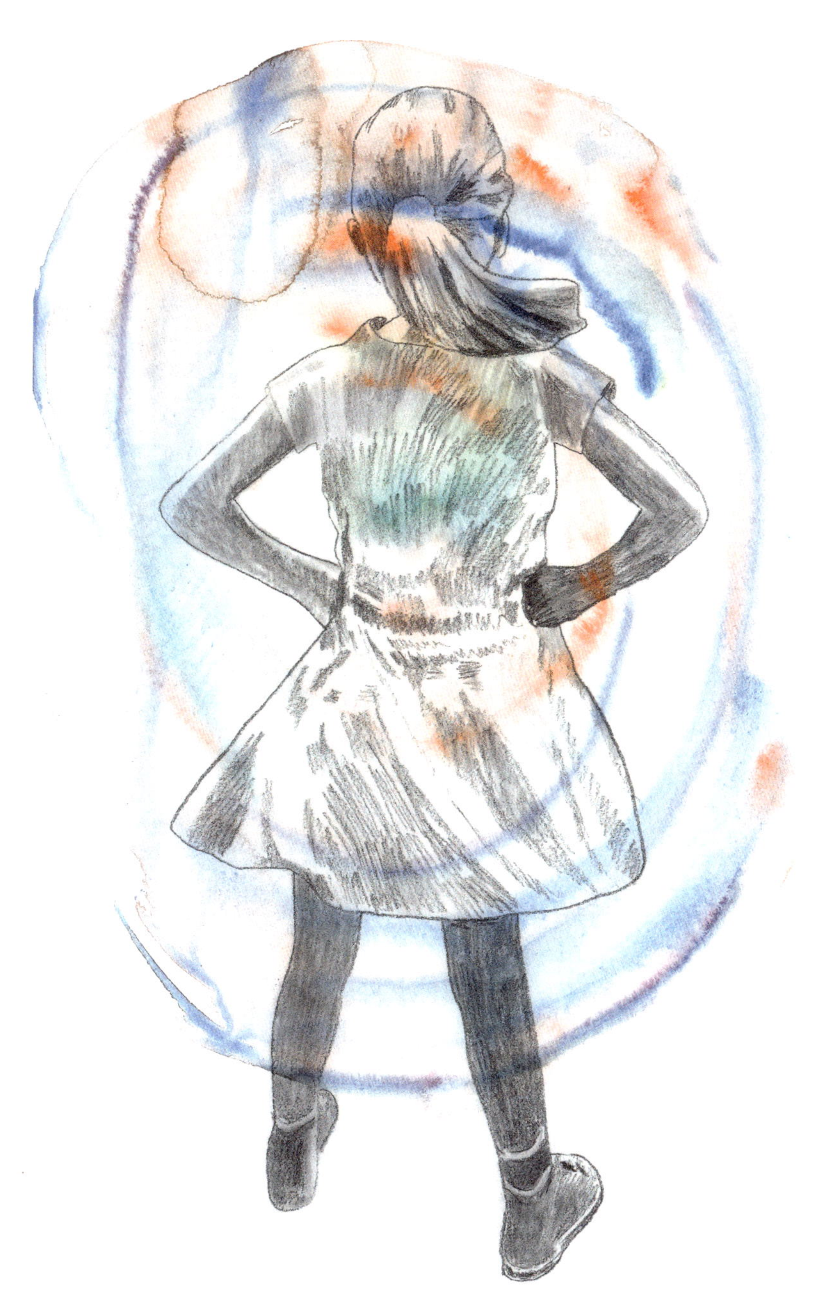

I Want to Penetrate Men's Dreams, Their Secret Heavens and Remote Stars, Those Called Upon When Dawn and Destiny Are at Play
2021. 3D Lenticular print, 71 × 47 in.

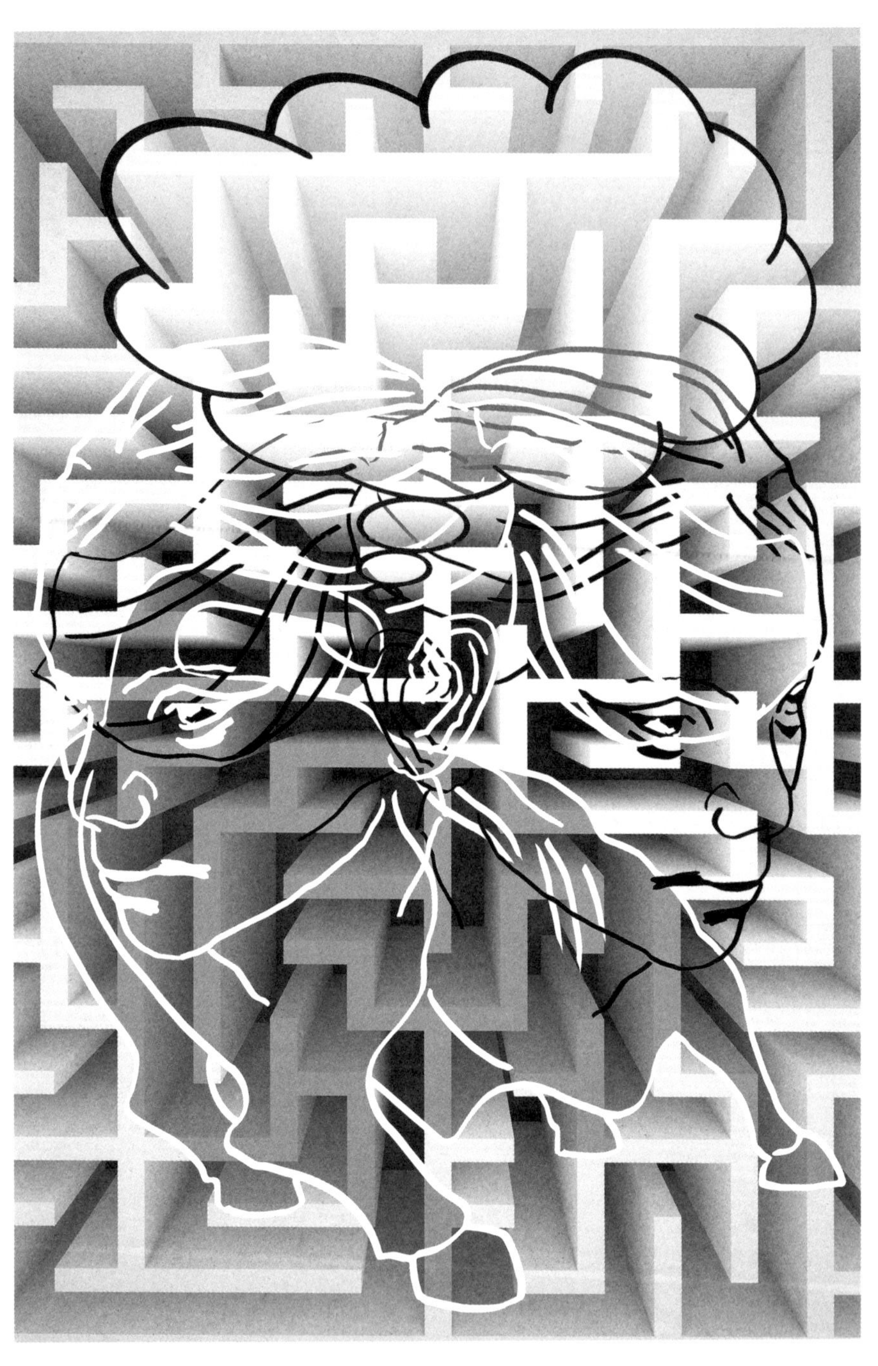

As in Every Mirror, There's Someone Who Knows and Waits
2021. 3D Lenticular print, 71 × 47 in.

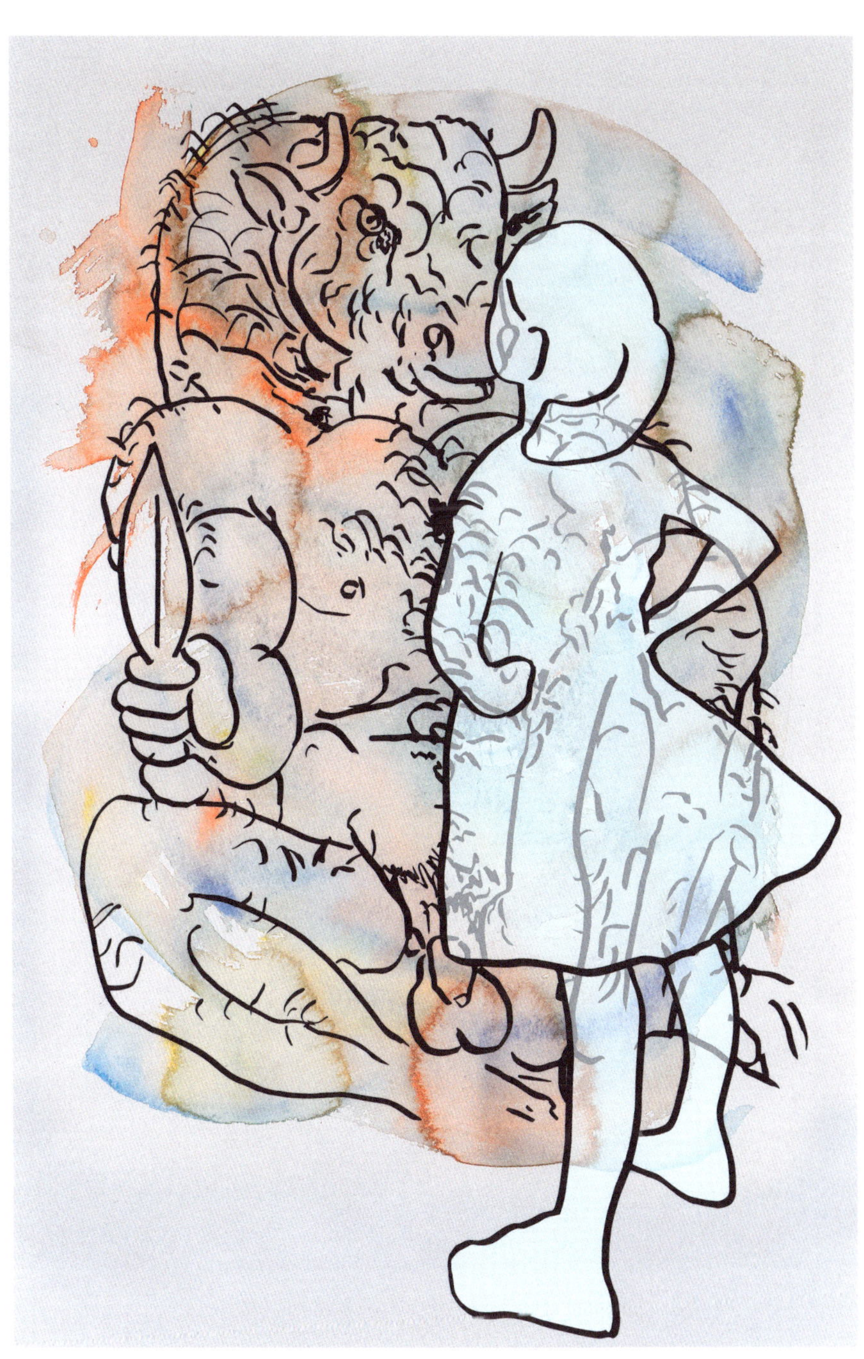

You Seem to Look Right Through Me
2021. 3D Lenticular print, 71 × 47 in.

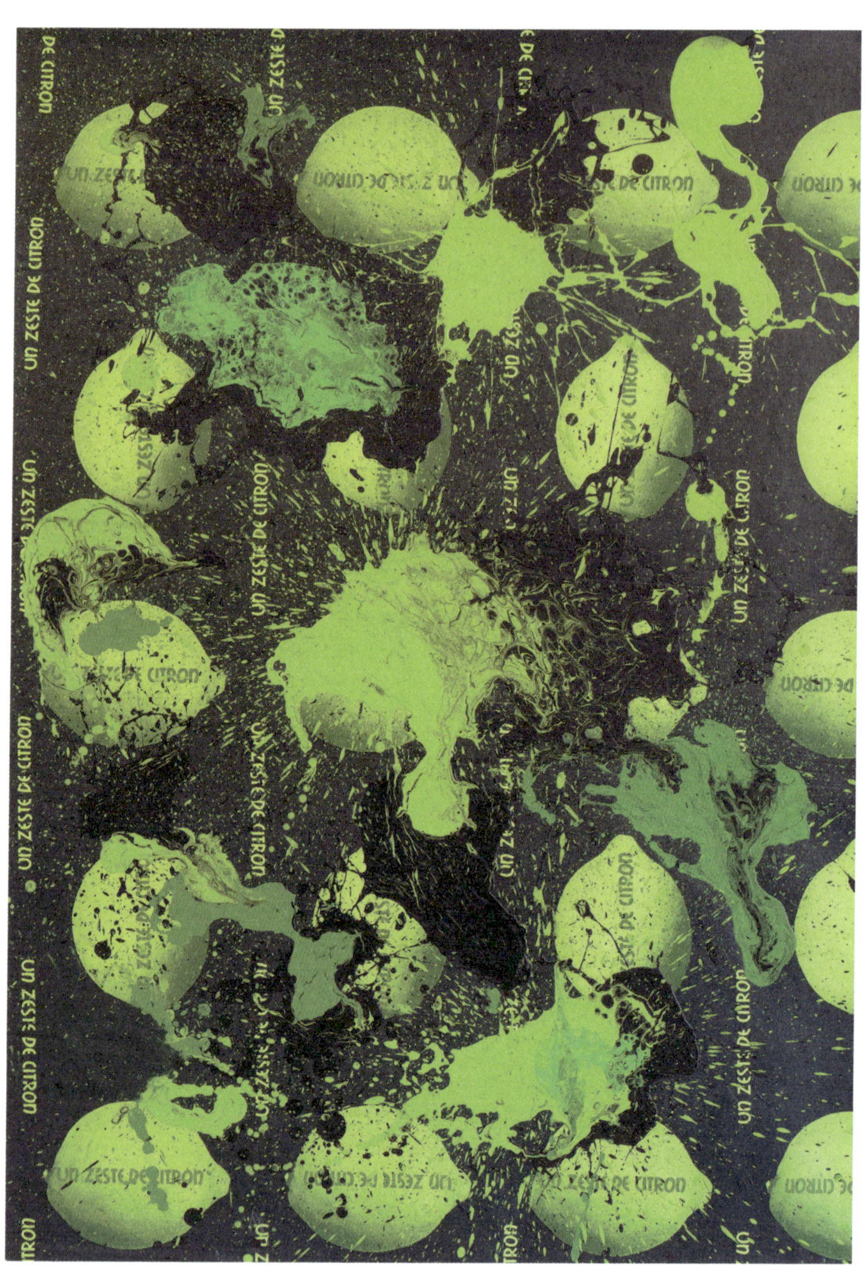

Lemon Incest
2022. Acrylic on oilcloth.
54 × 37 in.

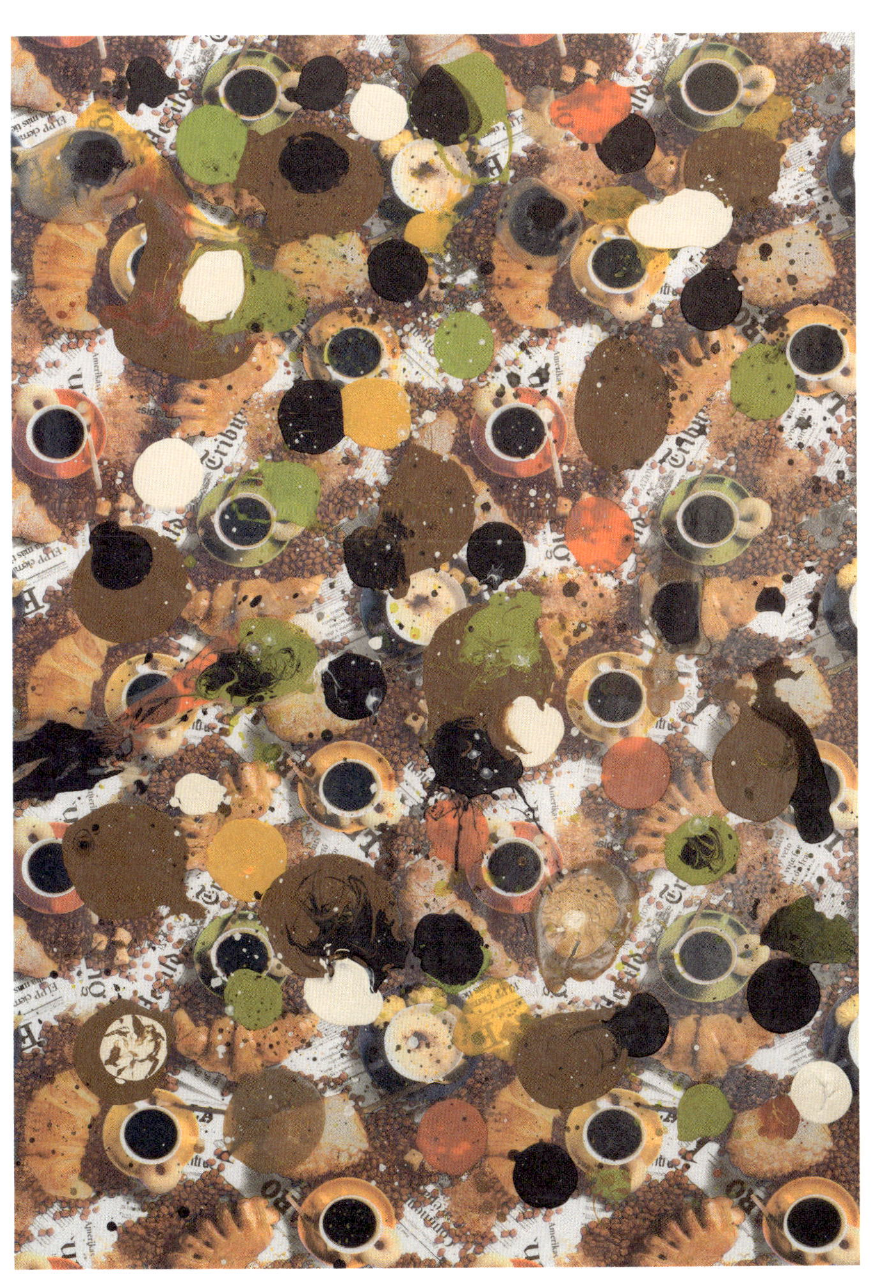

Couleur Café
2022. Acrylic on oilcloth.
55 × 40 in.

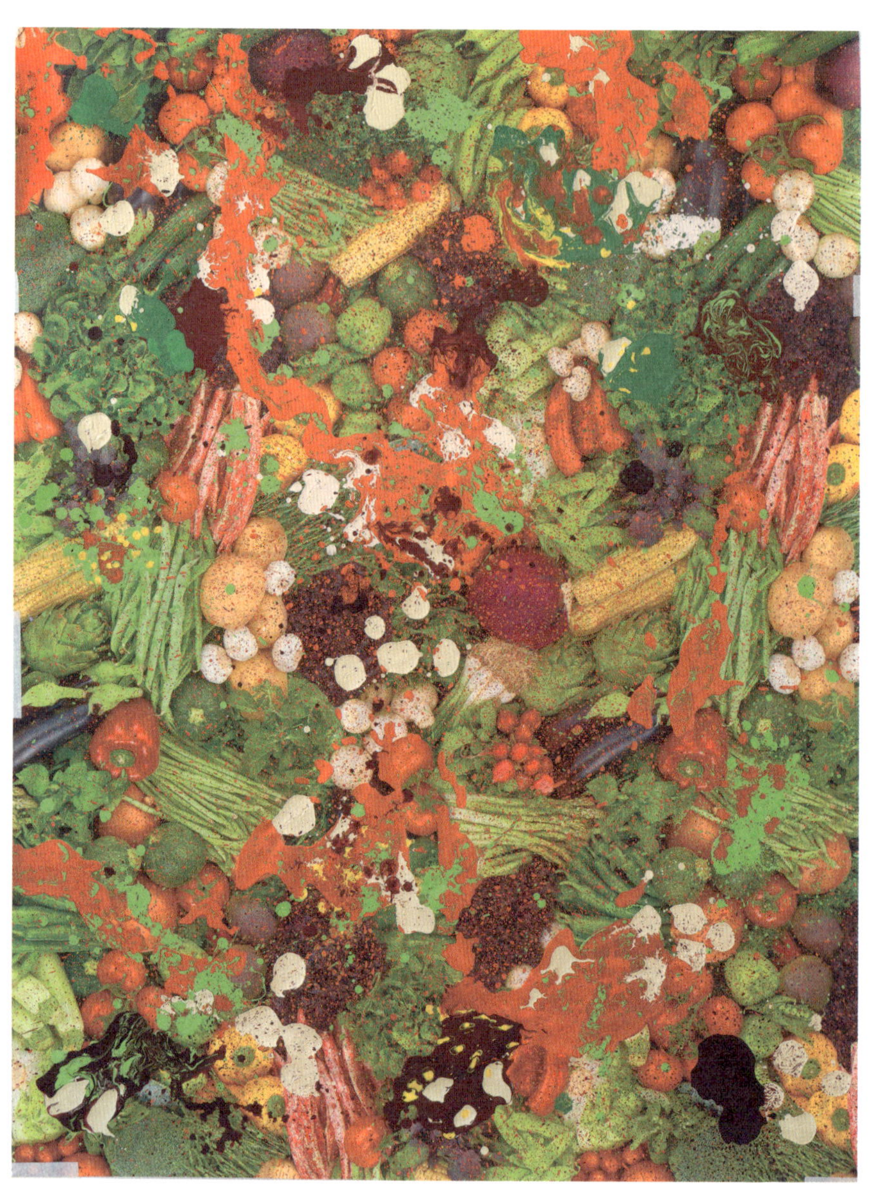

Aux Enfants de la Chance
2022. Acrylic on oilcloth.
54 × 45½ in.

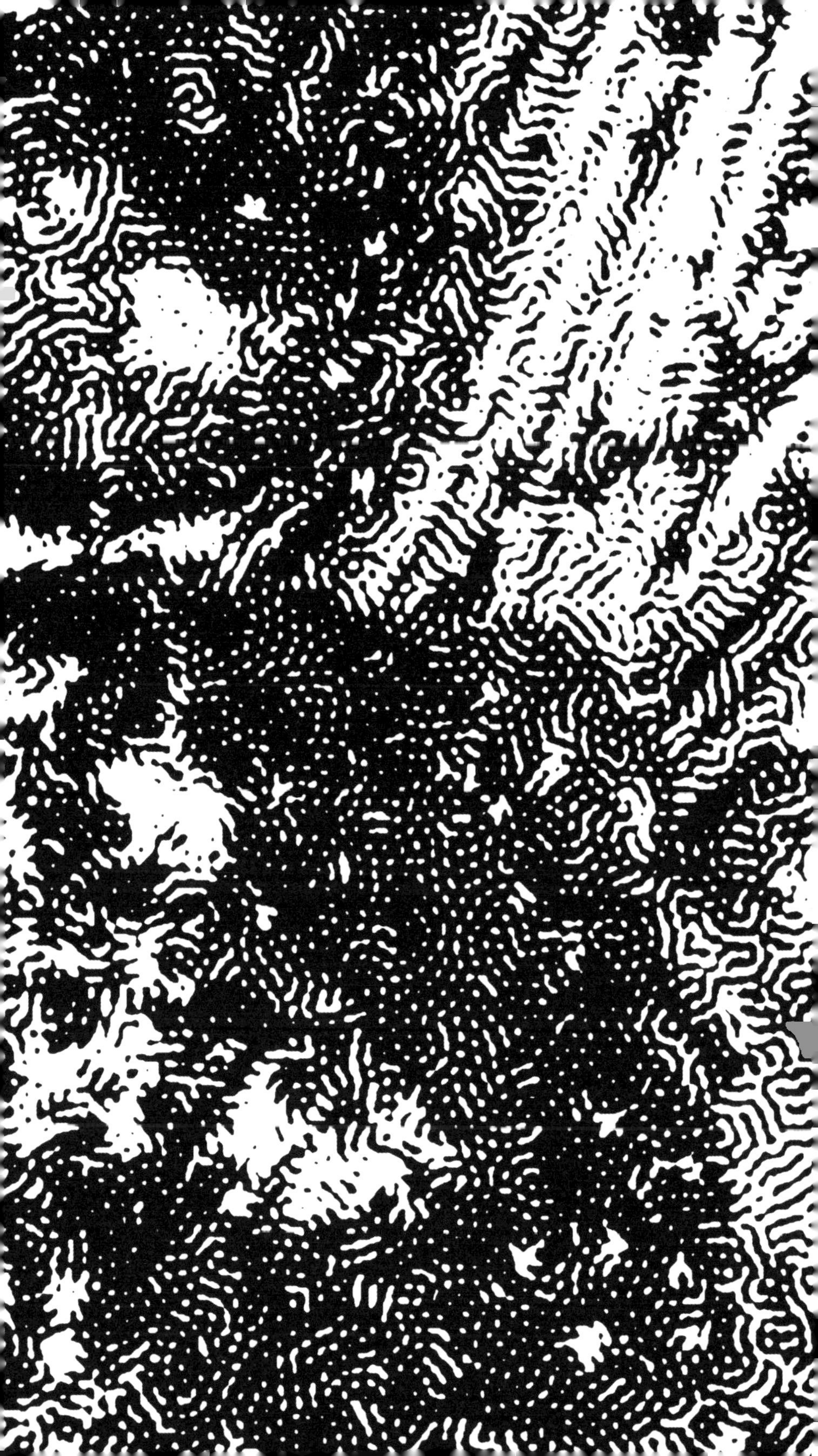

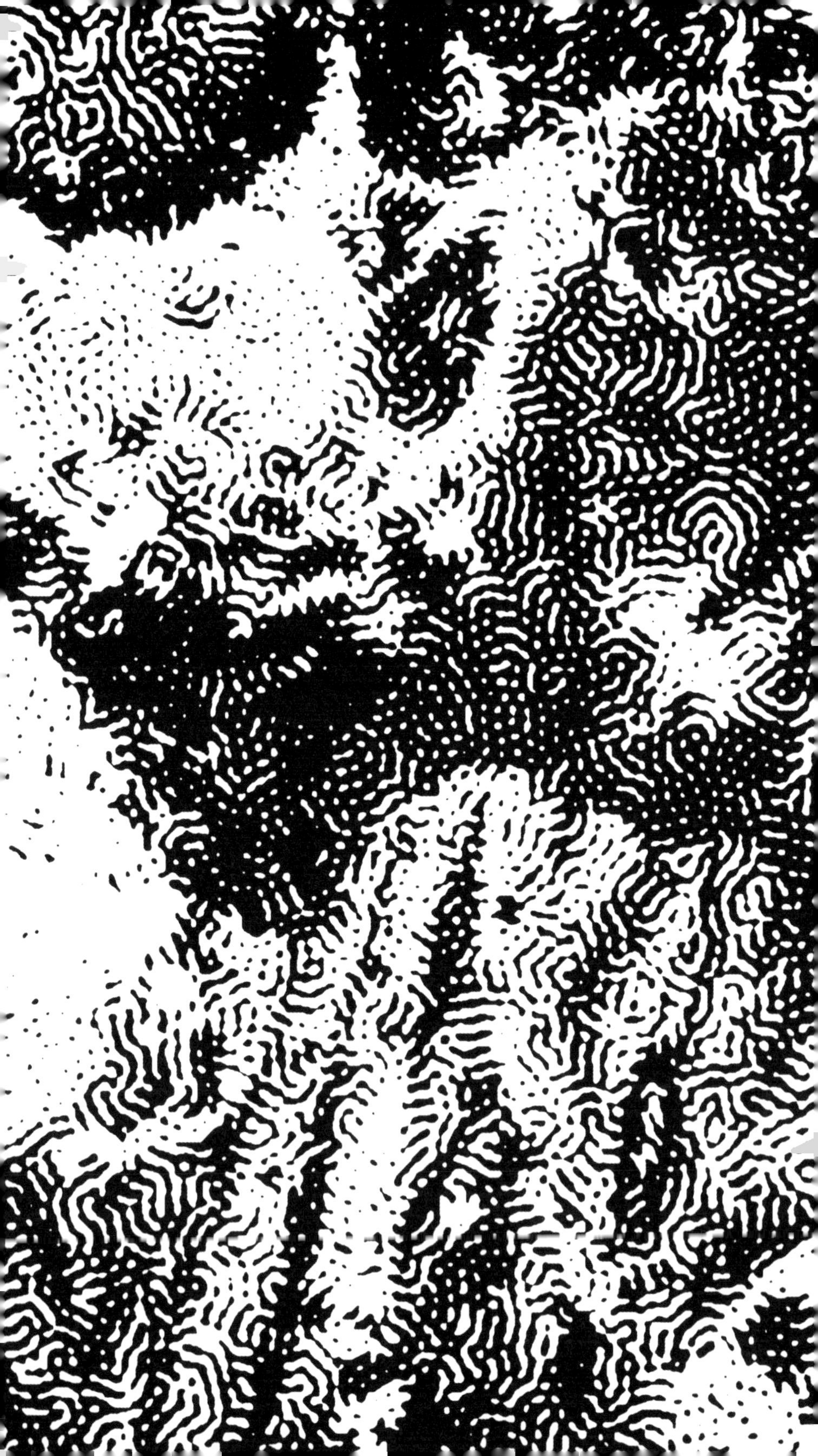

Image Credits

All works by Aura Rosenberg unless otherwise noted.
All images courtesy Aura Rosenberg except noted below.
pp11, 15, 19, 105, 106–107, 108–109, 114–115, 117, 118–119, 120–121: Photography by Argenis Apolinario. Courtesy Aura Rosenberg.
p13: Reprinted with permission from Northwestern University.
pp35, 125: Courtesy Kunst Halle Sankt Gallen and Aura Rosenberg.
p42: Collection of the Israel Museum. Gift of Fania and Gershom Scholem, Jerusalem; John Herring, Marlene and Paul Herring, Jo Carole and Ronald Lauder, New York. Wikimedia Commons, Public Domain.
p47: Photography by Atelier Selle & Kuntze. Wikimedia Commons, Public Domain.
p48: Wikimedia Commons, Public Domain.
pp50, 180: Courtesy Gasser and Grunert Gallery.
pp50, 212–213: Photography by Marjorie Brunet Plaza. Courtesy Efremidis Gallery.
p62: Wikimedia Commons, Public Domain.
pg 78: Photograph by Philip Capper. Flickr, Creative Commons License.
p81, 209: Photograph by Louise Lawler. Courtesy Aura Rosenberg.
p90: Photograph by Pierrette13. Wikimedia Commons, Creative Commons License.
p97: Public domain.
pp110–111, 112–113, 116: Photography by John Miller. Courtesy Aura Rosenberg.
p122: Photograph by Tom Powell Imaging. Courtesy Aura Rosenberg.
p126: Courtesy Roy Boyd Gallery.
pp129, 144–145: Photography by Werner Kaligofsky. Courtesy Muzeum Susch.
pp132–133: Courtesy Kunstmuseum Stuttgart.
p134: Photograph by Joe Clark. Courtesy Willhelm Hallen.
p143: Photography by Stefan Römer. Courtesy Martos Gallery.
pp154–157: Photography by Ernst Fischer.
p159: Photograph by Charles Benton. Courtesy Martos Gallery.
pp170–171: Courtesy Aura Rosenberg and Tyler Coburn.
p179: Photograph by Simone Gaensheimer. Courtesy Städtische Galerie im Lenbachhaus.
pp184–185, 194–195: Photographs by Jens Ziehe. Courtesy RL16 Gallery.
pp202–203: Photographs by Michael Underwood. Courtesy Meliksetian | Briggs Gallery.
p211: Photograph by Adam Reich. Courtesy Meredith Rosen Gallery.

Thank you

Aura Rosenberg
The Authors
Argenis Apolinario
Patricia and Jacob Asbæk
Tenzing Barshee
Julia Bernhard
Michael Briggs
Barbara Buchmaier
CCA Andratx
Amy Caulfield
Jozefina Chetko
Vivian Chui
Efremidis
Ernst Fischer
Gabriel Florenz
Kolja Glaser
Jackie Herbst
Scott Krafft
Louise Lawler
Brittany Maldonado
Jose Martos
Anna Meliksetian
John Miller
Markus Mueller
Pratt Institute
Florian Richter
Meredith Rosen
Carmen Rosenberg-Miller
Magnus Schaefer
Jonah Simonak
Audrey Tejada
Margaret Zwilling

Aura Rosenberg
What Is Psychedelic

Published by Mishkin Gallery and
Pioneer Works Press

Editor: Alaina Claire Feldman
Managing Editor: Micaela Durand
Assistant Editor: Alexandra Tell
Designer: Daniel Kent, Mei Lenehan
Copy Editor: Drew Zeiba

Distribution by
ARTBOOK D.A.P. USA
75 Broad Street, Suite 630
New York, NY 10004
Artbook.com

Printed and bound by Ofset Yapimevi
Paper: Munken Lynx Rough
Typeface: Signifier, Messina Sans,
Ruder Plakat

MISHKIN GALLERY

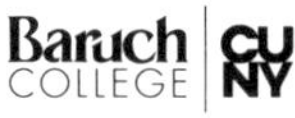

Mishkin Gallery
Baruch College
City University of New York
135 East 22nd Street
New York, NY 10010

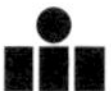

Pioneer Works Press
159 Pioneer Street
Brooklyn, NY 11231

ISBN 978-1-945711-17-6

Cataloging-in-publication data is on
file with Library of Congress

This publication has been realized on the occasion of the joint exhibition *What Is Psychedelic*, curated by Alaina Claire Feldman at Mishkin Gallery, March 10–June 9, 2023 and Pioneer Works, March 17–June 11, 2023.

The exhibition at Mishkin Gallery is supported by the Weissman School of Arts and Sciences at Baruch College (CUNY) and Friends of the Mishkin Gallery.

The exhibition at Pioneer Works is supported in part by public funds from the New York City Department of Cultural Affairs in partnership with the City Council, as well as the New York State Council on the Arts with the support of the Office of the Governor and the New York State Legislature.